Mountain Voices

Mountain Voices

Stories of Life and Adventure
in the White Mountains and Beyond

DOUG MAYER & REBECCA ORESKES

With a Foreword by Laura Waterman

Appalachian Mountain Club Books
Boston, Massachusetts

For our parents, John and Dale Mayer and Irwin and Susan Oreskes

AMC is a nonprofit organization, and sales of AMC Books fund our mission of protecting the Northeast outdoors. If you appreciate our efforts and would like to become a member or make a donation to AMC, visit outdoors.org, call 800-372-1758, or contact us at Appalachian Mountain Club, 5 Joy Street, Boston, MA 02108. outdoors.org/publications/books

A grant from The Frank M. Barnard Foundation, Inc., helped fund the production of this book. Distributed by The Globe Pequot Press, Guilford, Connecticut.

Front cover photographs by Jonathan Kannair/jonathankannair.com
Back cover photographs (left–right) courtesy of Celia Cox; courtesy of Julia Hodgdon;
    © Bradford Washburn Estate, courtesy of Decaneas Archive, Revere, MA;
    (top and bottom) by Jerry and Marcy Monkman/EcoPhotography.com
Cover and interior design by Alicia Zola and Athena Lakri

Library of Congress Cataloging-in-Publication Data
Mayer, Doug.
  Mountain voices : stories of life and adventure in the White Mountains and beyond / Doug Mayer and Rebecca Oreskes ; with a foreword by Laura Waterman.
     p. cm.
  ISBN 978-1-934028-80-3 (alk. paper)
  1. White Mountains (N.H. and Me.)--Biography. 2. White Mountains (N.H. and Me.)--Description and travel. 3. White Mountains (N.H. and Me.)--Social life and customs. I. Oreskes, Rebecca. II. Title.
  F41.52.M39 2012
  974.2'20922--dc23

                    2012019042

The paper used in this publication meets the minimum requirements of the American National Standard for Information Sciences-Permanence of Paper for Printed Library Materials, ANSI Z39.48-1984. ∞

Interior pages contain 30% post-consumer recycled fiber.
Cover contains 10% post-consumer recycled fiber.
Printed in the United States of America,
using vegetable-based inks.

7 6 5 4 3 2 1   12 13 14 15 16 17 18

MIX
Paper from
responsible sources
FSC
www.fsc.org   FSC® C005010

CONTENTS

FOREWORD

What's special is the connection between the present and the past.

—Ben English, Jr.

W HEN REBECCA AND DOUG asked me to write the foreword for
Mountain Voices, I remembered how honored my husband, Guy,
and I had felt to be interviewed for the "Mountain Voices" series when it
was originally published in the *Appalachia* journal. Now that the series has
grown and the interviews are being published together for the first time, I
feel both gratitude and humility at being asked to introduce a book that
includes men and women—so admired by Guy and me—who have devoted
their lives to the mountains that we all care about so deeply.

The seventeen individuals Rebecca and Doug talked to here give voice
to a collective memory that goes back to the early days of the twentieth
century. There are hundreds of years of knowledge, wisdom, and insight in
their stories. For each of these individuals the White Mountains have played
a crucial role, often over a lifetime. While their commitment to mountains
was central to their lives, and the stories of how they got there have con-
nections in common, their lives in the mountains are really quite diverse.
Each has loved the mountains, but they have expressed this love in various
ways: through writing about them and mapping them, through running
inns and guide services and making or selling hiking equipment, through
conservation efforts, through search and rescue or trail work, through education and stewardship. For each there was the strong desire to be in the
mountains themselves and to share the mountains with others. This dual
impetus has its roots in the past and forms an important part of our White
Mountain history.

I think back to the early 1800s and the Crawford family. They ran inns at both ends of the notch that today carries their name. At the upper end, the Gateway, Ethan and his father, Abel, cut a path to the summit of Mount Washington in 1819. Ethan began guiding his guests up the trail, now called Crawford Path, either on foot or on horseback. He built several camps in the woods so his clients could enjoy a night or two on the side of the mountain. By creating their hotel and guiding business, Ethan and his wife, Lucy, found a way to make a living in the mountains because they loved the mountains. Accompanying this love was a desire to make it possible for others to experience the beauty of these wild and windswept summits that had recently been named for the first five presidents of the United States.

By the mid-1850s two hotels were ready to receive overnight visitors on the summit of Mount Washington. People could hike up by one of the several footpaths, including those built by the Crawfords. The Mount Washington Carriage Road (today's auto road) opened in 1861. The Cog Railway was taking tourists up by rail by 1869. Both the Auto Road and the Cog Railway are White Mountain institutions today, carried on in much the same spirit as that of the Crawfords: a desire to make it possible for people to experience the grandeur and beauty of the mountains. Today, we experience as well a mountain range unique for its human history.

Doug Philbrook, who ran the Auto Road for more than twenty years, talks about caretaking "a major manmade tourist attraction" and improving it as "my deep pride." Ellen Teague—an indirect descendant of the Crawford family—took over running the Cog Railway after the death of her husband. She describes making a point of greeting the buses that brought the tourists who wanted to ride up Mount Washington on the Cog Railway. "I just wanted to know the people," she said.

In the heart of Pinkham Notch, between the Auto Road and the Cog Railway, sits the Appalachian Mountain Club's camp, offering meals and accommodations since 1920. For over thirty years this was run by Joe Dodge, known as the Mayor of Porky Gulch. Joe's name is invoked by almost everyone Rebecca and Doug interviewed for this book. Ellen Teague said, "I loved Joe Dodge. He loved Mount Washington. He loved the forestry, and he loved these people." Joe Dodge, like the Crawfords, has become a White Mountain legend.

What Joe Dodge, Doug Philbrook, Ellen Teague, and the other voices in the book have in common was a love of the mountains and a drive to share the mountains with others. As George Hamilton, director of New Hampshire's state parks, said, "I feel very proud of the fact that I've shared that love of mountains." George's greatest delight was "to teach and help others to learn to love the mountains."

For many in this book, that love came suddenly and while young. All were driven to find a way to support themselves while living in or near the mountains. The Limmer family settled in Intervale, New Hampshire, in 1950 because the mountains there reminded them of their home in Bavaria. They began making hiking boots—simply called Limmers, and worn by almost everyone who works in the woods. The family is now training its fourth generation. Bill Arnold, whose parents began spending summers in Randolph the year before he was born, returned to his parents' house, sidelined by ill health, after his freshman year in college. The only place he wanted to be was in the mountains. He has never left, finding employment with the Randolph Mountain Club, the U.S. Forest Service, the Appalachian Mountain Club, and finally as caretaker for the summer community's houses in Randolph. "I'm proud of just being able to live here, and I feel like I've contributed to the town," Bill said. "I've always felt that it's anyone's responsibility to somehow contribute to society."

What stands out among those interviewed here is that while some have gone away briefly—for World War II and the Korean War among other reasons—all came back, and stayed. That's what sets them apart: They stayed. Take Casey Hodgdon. About boyhood visits to his relatives in Groveton, Casey said, "I remember looking up at the Presidential Range…. It was always a great historical and spiritual feeling." Casey's first job was for Joe Dodge. Years later, when Brad and Barbara Washburn began survey work for their map of the Presidential Range, Casey, whose on-the-ground knowledge of the range was profound, joined them in doing much of the "legwork."

Hand in hand with finding employment that kept them in the mountains was their desire to share. As Tuckerman Ravine snow ranger Brad Ray said, "The best part of my job for me is helping people." His nicest moments are of people appreciating being in a unique place. "They've brought their children with them and are showing them what a great place it is.... I think that's the best thing for me, especially when you see people teaching their young ones."

For Rick Wilcox it is important to see people achieve their goals in the mountains. Mountain guide and owner of a successful equipment store in North Conway, Rick leads climbs around the world. "We set little goals for ourselves," he said "and we achieve them."

Many of the people Doug and Rebecca talked with were captivated by White Mountain history. Fran Belcher, the Appalachian Mountain Club's first executive director, had, as a young hutman in the 1930s, spent his days off exploring in the Zealand Valley. "You could see the signs of the fires that had scorched the area," he said. These fires were caused by sparks from the smokestacks of logging trains and had burned most of the Zealand Valley. In his explorations, Fran turned up everything from kettles and cutlery to roundhouses and parts of the trains themselves at the logging camps. Fran's book, *Logging Railroads of the White Mountains* (AMC Books, 1980), is a classic of White Mountain literature.

The excessive logging, whose aftereffects a young Fran Belcher witnessed, had pushed the government to pass the Weeks Act in 1911. This led to the establishment of the White Mountain National Forest. George Zink's thoughtful work for conservation, which resulted in Congress establishing the Sandwich Range as an official Wilderness in 1984, had its roots in this historical past.

By the 1960s, when the woods became crowded, campsites overflowing, Paul Doherty, of New Hampshire Fish and Game, came to understand the need for the "new ethic." His generation's old woods ways had to change to keep the ring of hacked-off stumps around shelters from spreading farther. Campers and backpackers were asked to give up the campfire, the very heart of every sojourn to the woods. They must learn to embrace the lightweight stove. They must learn as well to sleep on Ensolite instead of fir boughs, wash up away from streams, and pack out, not bury, their trash. As Paul Doherty foresaw, these changes ended a way of life in the backwoods, but they brought about a necessary revolution in backcountry living that led to the Leave No Trace practices of today. Guy and I read Paul's columns in *New England Outdoors*, where we had a column too. What we learned from Paul Doherty was how important it was to share our outdoor spaces with all recreationists. Paul felt there was room for snowmobilers and snowshoers. Just not together. Paul led us to see that there is room for everyone who loves being in the woods.

Dr. Harry McDade, who opened his practice in Littleton on January 1, 1959, and went on to become an expert in treating cold-weather injuries, said, "The mountains are a place for humility." Guy echoed that: "When you succeed in doing a technically difficult climb," he said, "or a climb in very severe weather, you feel grateful that you were able to have the opportunity to do that. You feel very humble in the sight of this very impressive thing." Humility, I believe, fosters respect for the land, for these beautiful places. Like Paul Doherty, we saw, with some concern, that more and more people were coming to the mountains. But we saw, as well, that they were learning to show care, and nowadays many hikers come wanting to give something back. It's called stewardship. It grows out of a sense of caring deeply enough about the land itself to want to pass this on to others. It's very encouraging for the future of the mountains.

The first personalities to receive major attention as figures associated with Northeastern mountains were Abel Crawford, his son Ethan, and their wives Hannah and Lucy. The first mountain trails to receive regular and frequent use were cut by the Crawfords. The first substantial wave of White Mountain tourists were guided up Mount Washington by this unique family. Abel and Ethan had moved into the notch from somewhere else and had made it their home. They were the first stewards, and perhaps, like snow ranger Brad Ray, they too could claim that their great pleasure came from watching parents teach their children about a beautiful, unique, and wild place. The White Mountains are filled with beautiful, unique, and wild places. They are there for all of us to find and enjoy, to love and care for.

Each voice here has much to teach us. Each speaks with wisdom and from a perspective that comes from bearing witness. These voices speak of change; each experienced change as they lived their lives of work, and play, too, in the mountains. Each paid close attention to what these changes meant for the mountains. Through their stories they give us their insights from a lifetime of caring deeply about a particular and much-loved place. What they have to tell us matters. It matters because we are the inheritors. If we are to make good future choices for our mountains, we need to understand what came before. By understanding our past we can be better stewards in the future to the mountain places that give meaning to our lives.

Let's turn now and listen to these mountain voices.

Laura Waterman
East Corinth, Vermont
March 2012

PREFACE

L IKE A NUMBER OF THE INDIVIDUALS PROFILED IN THIS BOOK, the two of us came to work in New Hampshire's White Mountains while still in our teens: Rebecca to work for the Appalachian Mountain Club (AMC) hut system, Doug as an intern for the Mount Washington Observatory. The mountain world is small enough that our paths inevitably crossed and we became friends. Having tasted the lure of the White Mountains we both decided to stay in the area. Going from seasonal to permanent jobs and settling in different towns, we continued to share many hikes and ski trips together, always with our beloved dogs. Over the years we've shared many discussions about the mountains, about how to preserve their wildness and how best to contribute to their care. Along the way we became writing partners as well as friends.

Twenty years ago, we were on a ski trip up to the height-of-land in Evans Notch, a remote section of the White Mountain National Forest along the border of New Hampshire and western Maine. The route to the height-of-land follows Highway 113, but the road is closed in winter, leaving a snow-covered path through thick woods with rising mountains on either side. Climbing steadily, we both anticipated the great run back and our conversation ranged far and wide. It kept coming back to the mountains, as it always did, and to the people who had made a lasting impact here. "Someone," we mused, "should capture the stories and voices of people who have been important to the White Mountains." The idea struck a chord. In the days to come, we found ourselves returning to the concept again and again. In time, we decided that the "someone" might as well be us.

We mulled over the mechanics of such an undertaking. Would these individuals, many of whom were quite private about their lives and accomplishments, be willing to share their stories? What names would be on our list? Who would publish these pieces?

Sandy Stott, then editor of *Appalachia*, AMC's mountaineering and conservation journal, saw that our idea was a natural fit with the journal's mission. He promptly embraced the concept—and we were on our way. Through Sandy's tenure, then Lucille Stott's time as editor, and now under Christine Woodside's leadership, the "Mountain Voices" series has grown into something far greater than either of us imagined that day in Evans Notch.

Our inaugural interview was with Fran Belcher, AMC's first executive director, in 1993. We were nervous and unsure of ourselves. But he was patient with his two novice interviewers, and the outcome provided fascinating insights into the development of AMC. We learned on the job to listen carefully, to follow up on the curious-sounding passing details, and to allow plenty of time for reflection on the part of the interviewee. We used a small, reasonably unobtrusive tape recorder so that our conversations would be as natural as possible—and quickly learned to keep the recorder running after we thought the interview was over. The best, most interesting comments often arrived as afterthoughts, over empty coffee mugs as we were saying our good-byes.

In many ways, the results of the interviews surprised us. What might have been a collection of charming reflections became something much more powerful—oral histories that included not just wisdom, but also opinions with no shortage of passion, whether about management of the White Mountain National Forest, changes in AMC, development of the mountains as tourist attractions, or any number of subjects. As we saw it, our job was to listen, learn, and record those views for future generations. We were challenged by some of the ideas we heard, but in trying to keep an open mind, we always walked away with a more in-depth understanding of the White Mountains and their human history. In every case, the passionate perspectives came as a result of a deep and abiding love for the mountains, and a desire to act in their care.

One of our early concerns was, "Will we have enough great material to share?" Today, we laugh out loud at that thought, as the transcript from each interview routinely ran over one hundred pages. Our challenge was quite the opposite of that first fear: Which great story do we hold back? How do we edit an article for space without losing the person's voice? What stays—and why? These have been some of our most difficult decisions. In the end, though, the wealth of great material forced us to focus on the content that mattered most—the stories that revealed much about the interviewee, the mountains, and the changes seen over a lifetime.

As the years went by, we began to realize that we had a remarkable collection of mountain stories—one that spans three generations and cuts across all aspects of the White Mountains. From the well-known to the not-so-very-well-known, our subjects have encompassed a wide range of vocations and contributions—from Cog Railway owner Ellen Teague, to former AMC trail crew member Ben English, Jr., to renowned international climber Rick Wilcox. Throughout the interviews we were reminded of the power that comes from having a commitment to a place and a dedication to public service, in all its many forms. Maybe most striking was the fierce passion that all of our subjects had for what they did in life. As Dr. Harry McDade told us, "'Dum vivimus vivamus: While we live, let us live.' Have a little fun as you go along."

Many of the people we've interviewed expressed to us their appreciation about being asked. It's not an exaggeration to say that the honor has been entirely ours. We've been privileged to sit down with some of the nicest, most interesting, and most thoughtful people one could imagine; to be inspired by what they've done; and to learn from every one of them. Many of these people were and remain "big names"—people who were already legends, whose names were uttered in quiet awe, when we first started working in the White Mountains as teenagers.

What affected us most over these last two decades of interviews were the common bonds we shared with each person we interviewed. Whether it was George Hamilton talking about his time working within the AMC hut system, Paul Doherty telling tales from his days as a New Hampshire Fish and Game conservation officer, or George Zink offering us a glimpse into his passion for the Sandwich Range Wilderness, whatever our backgrounds or day-to-day jobs, we all shared a love for the White Mountains, the people, the beauty, the wildness, and the many stories hidden amid the rugged topography.

Perhaps most of all, *Mountain Voices* is a celebration—over time and generations—of a shared White Mountain community.

ACKNOWLEDGEMENTS

Mountain Voices would not have been possible without the help of many people.

First and foremost, we gratefully acknowledge the support of the individuals profiled here. Each interview took many hours, and the months following were filled with emails and calls to check facts, search out aging photographs, and clarify details. Thank you for welcoming us into your homes, for the friendly and heartfelt conversation, and for taking time to reflect on your lives.

Special thanks to the *Appalachia* journal and its three thoughtful and encouraging editors over the past two decades: Sandy Stott, Lucille Stott, and Christine Woodside. Thank you for taking a risk on the series and for working with us to share the stories of these individuals, their reflections on the White Mountains, and the changes they've witnessed.

Appalachia plays an important role in the mountain community, both in New England and nationally. The oldest continuously published periodical of its kind, the journal contains a thoughtful and independent voice and is a vital contribution to important discussions of mountain ethics and stewardship. May it live on under talented editors for years to come.

Thanks to the hard-working staff at AMC Books: Publisher Heather Stephenson, Editor Kimberly Duncan-Mooney, and Production Manager Athena Lakri.

For assistance with particular interviews and updates, we'd like to acknowledge the help of Margie Teague Baker, the Belcher family, Betsy Washburn Cabot, Peter Crane, Faith Desjardins, Ginger Doherty, Becky Fullerton, Doug Gralenski, Julie Hodgdon, Anne T. Koop, Becky Parker,

Mike Pelchat, Hank Peterson, Andrea Philbrook, Nat Putnam, Fred Stott, and Sally Zink.

Our photographers, Jonathan Kannair and Ned Therrien, thoughtfully and skillfully captured the spirit of the individuals profiled in this series. We thank you both.

Thanks to Mary Gail Scott for our author photo.

Each interview was followed by many hours of transcription. Thanks to Patti Dugan-Henriksen for getting us started, and to Alice Darling Secretarial Services, Rosalie Prosser, Cindy Robertson, Sue Johnston, and Anna Van der Heide.

Thanks to Brad Ray for all of his support and for reading and commenting on many of the interviews.

For invaluable guidance and encouragement for so many years and on topics too numerous to name or count, including this series, we thank Guy and Laura Waterman.

We'd like to thank The Frank M. Barnard Foundation, Inc., for generously awarding AMC Books a grant that helped to fund the production of this book, enabling us to include many wonderful historical and professional photographs alongside the profiles.

Section One

Mountaineering

Brad and Barbara Washburn

Mountaineers, Mapmakers, Explorers

Brad and Barbara Washburn take a break during their 1940 Mount Bertha expedition in Alaska's Coast Range. (Photo © Bradford Washburn Estate, courtesy of Decaneas Archive, Revere, MA)

B**RAD AND BARBARA WASHBURN** remain two of America's most renowned explorers. With Barbara at his side and providing ever-present support, Brad pioneered the now-standard route up Denali (Mount McKinley); mapped the Grand Canyon, Denali, Mount Washington, and Everest; and captured some of the most beautiful mountain photographs ever taken. Barbara was the first woman to climb Denali. In addition to these accomplishments, Brad photographed the Presidential Range mountains in 1938, creating stunning black-and-white images of these well-traveled peaks. Together, Brad and Barbara charted the depths of New Hampshire's Squam Lake and mapped the Presidential Range during the 1980s, before Global Positioning Systems made such a task quite a bit easier.

In 1988, Brad and Barbara were honored with the Centennial Medal of the National Geographic Society. *Bradford Washburn Mountain Photography* (Mountaineers Books, 1999) was awarded the Banff Mountain Book Festival Grand Prize in 2000. Two books published in 2001, *The Accidental Adventurer,* Barbara's memoir of her historic climb of Denali, and *Exploring the Unknown,* Brad's diaries from his Alaska and Yukon Territory expeditions, offer personal glimpses into some of their remarkable accomplishments. *Washburn: Extraordinary Adventures of a Young Mountaineer* (AMC Books, 2004) collects Brad's amazing first-person stories of his exploits in the Alps, on Mount Washington, and on Mount Fairweather as a teen in the 1920s.

The parents of three children, they also led very busy personal and professional lives at home in Massachusetts. Brad was the founding director of the Museum of Science, Boston, and Barbara worked as a homemaker and as a teacher of remedial reading.

The White Mountains served as Brad and Barbara's home range in the years after they met and married. Given Brad's life as a mapmaker and founder of a science museum, it might be reasonable to assume that the Washburns viewed the mountains through the clinical lens of the scientist. But their appreciation for the windswept heights was deeper and more subjective than that. "Both Barbara and I agree about this," said Brad. "Your memories of these peaks are not about climbing. Mountains are friendship. Mountains are people."

We sat down with the Washburns in Brad's office at the Museum of Science in 2001.

In Their Own Words

BRAD: My cousin Sherman Hall took me up Mount Washington, via Tuckerman Ravine, in July or August 1921. That was my first White Mountain climb. The French Alps is where I really got started climbing, though. I made a trip to the Alps in 1926 with money my uncle had left my brother and me when he died. It helped pay for college expenses and also paid for guiding on our trips to Europe.

When I got back in 1926, having climbed Mont Blanc and the Matterhorn, I wanted to make some money. I began to add lecture income. I also wrote two articles, "A Boy on the Matterhorn" and "A Boy on Mont Blanc," for a magazine called *The Youth's Companion*. George Putnam read those articles, got ahold of me, and published them as *Among the Alps with Bradford*.

We also produced a little guide, *The Trails and Peaks of the Presidential Range of the White Mountains,* which came out in 1926. At the time there wasn't any guide to just the Presidential Range. The trouble with the AMC guide,[1] to this day, is that you have to buy something that covers everything, not just the Presidential Range. And, then, *Bradford on Mount Washington* came out in the fall of '27.

BARBARA: My first hike was with a friend who took me up to Mount Chocorua. It was long before I knew Brad. I did what any young girl does: Her boyfriend wants to climb somewhere, and you go along. And he ran. He wanted to go up fast, so by the time I got to the top of that mountain, I never wanted to see another mountain! When I finally did climb Mount McKinley, I got a call on the telephone one day. All I could hear was this loud, grumpy voice saying, "He must have carried you up!" I recognized the voice. He must have seen it in the paper.

Getting Together
BARBARA: How I met Brad is very interesting. He was already a fairly famous explorer. I had a lovely job working with graduate students at Harvard in the biology labs. One day the mailman came into my office

---

[1] AMC's *White Mountain Guide*, now in its 29th edition, has been published since 1907.

and wanted me to go over and have an interview with Brad, who had just been made director of the Museum of Science. He was looking for a good administrative secretary and had told the mailman, "When you're wandering around the buildings at Harvard, if you see a good likely candidate, let me know."

I said, "My God! I don't want to work in a stuffy old museum! And I *certainly* don't want to work for a crazy mountain climber!"

I wasn't impressed. I had no intention of taking the job. Brad gave me two weeks to think it over. He called me up every single day. At the end of about ten days, I said to my father, "If that guy is so persuasive that he calls me up every day, it might be kind of an interesting job. That museum might go places." So, I took the job.

We had no personal relationship at all until he proposed. In those days, you wouldn't think of going out with your boss. I was on my way to New York for a date. The janitor at the museum, who was on his way to do the projection for Brad's lecture in Hartford, suggested, "Why don't you come to Brad's lecture?" I said, "I can't do that. I'd die if he saw me. I'd be so embarrassed." But I went, and snuck into a corner of the back row. I wasn't going to even speak to him. Brad spotted me as soon as the lecture was over. He popped off of the platform and came running toward me. And I thought, *Well, at least he's not going to say, "What are you doing here?"*

BRAD: I said, "What the hell are you doing here?!"

BARBARA: But he said it in a tone of voice that made me think he was glad I was there. He asked me how I was getting to New York. I said I was taking the next train down. And he said, "Well, do you have a berth? I have a berth. I'll give you my lower berth."

Of course, today, we'd have gotten into the same berth, I think! I was very shy. I got into bed and the whole thing was kind of embarrassing, with your boss sleeping above you! Just as I was about to turn out the lights, this hand came down the side, literally down the wall, and I thought, *My God! What am I supposed to do? If I shake hands with him, he'll think I'm very bold. If I don't, he'll be mad at me.* So, I just gave it a little squeeze and said good night.

In the morning when we got up, he said, "I want you to come and have breakfast with me and Lowell Thomas."[2] I said, "Don't be silly! Lowell Thomas doesn't want to see me!" But I went.

BRAD: Six months later, Lowell Thomas told me, "I went home and told my wife you were engaged." Of course, neither of us had said anything. I asked him how he reached that conclusion. He said, "I saw it in both of your eyes."

BARBARA: When my boyfriend took me to the four o'clock train back home, there was Brad at the train. My boyfriend later became an admiral in the navy. He told me many years later, "I knew when I saw Washburn there that my goose was cooked!" That was in January. We got engaged in February. At that point, I had worked for him for eleven months. We had very few dates. I don't think he had even met my family. We'd had dinner together, and he sat in my living room and proposed. We've now been married more than sixty years.

Early Climbs

BRAD: There are an awful lot of people who didn't think I did any work at all. They all thought I had millions of dollars and could dash off to a mountain! We didn't have millions of bucks. I was getting three thousand a year running the Museum of Science, and I had three kids and a wife.

BARBARA: And I didn't have a washing machine. I was washing the diapers by hand!

BRAD: I had to lecture or write in order to keep above the turf and run the museum. I found out that was the way to make the extra money that was needed to make these treks.

The deal I made when I was asked to be director of the museum was that I would have at least one month a year in which I would make trips, because my lectures produced fifty percent of my income. Of course, it's true—I loved it. I wanted to do it.

---

[2] The well-known American broadcaster and writer.

The first trip we all got paid for was a flight over Mount McKinley in 1936, for *National Geographic*. They put up $1,000. We made the first photographic flights over McKinley. I got Pan American to do the flying for us for nothing. The money was used on film, processing, and travel to Alaska. I gave back a thirty-buck unused balance at the end of the job.

In comparison, we had a $150,000 budget for the flights over Mount Everest. *National Geographic* put up half the money, and the museum loaned us the other half. I had to raise the money to slowly pay the museum back. We came in $7,200 below budget on that project. I sent the chairman of the Geographic Society, Mel Paine, a letter with a check for $3,600.77. He said it was the first time he could recollect that any *National Geographic* expedition had gone through below budget, except for my flights over McKinley in 1936. He was "enclosing herewith the overpayment." It was a one-cent stamp, cut in half!

In 1937 and '38 we did a series of aerial flights over the Whites. It was just something to do. I used money that I got from lecturing to pay for it. It didn't cost much—$35 an hour to fly in those days. I flew with [well-known local pilot] Wiley Apte of North Conway in his airplane. You very rarely see snow like that nowadays, and I got some wonderful pictures.

BARBARA: You know, we never really had vacations, because every summer Brad had a project. And he has had one every summer since we've been married! We were never just going off and sitting on a beach and doing nothing. I think we'd have been bored! I wasn't just climbing mountains all those years. I also had my own little career. When our last kid was in high school, I just decided this is the time when you do your own thing. So I took a course and started teaching. I taught remedial reading for twenty years at Shady Hill School in Cambridge.

First Ascent of Mount Bertha

BRAD: The first ascent of Mount Bertha in Alaska's Coast Range gave Barbara a wonderful introduction to the challenge and beauty of a relatively small, unclimbed peak located not too far from civilization—only a hundred miles west of Juneau.

We had a neat group of young people with us: Tom Winship, captain of that year's Harvard ski team, and later distinguished editor of *The Boston*

Brad Washburn took this photograph of Mount Washington and the Southern Presidentials during his 1937 and 1938 aerial flights over the White Mountains.
(Photo from the Mount Washington Observatory Washburn Gallery, washburngallery.org)

Globe; Mal Miller, who has distinguished himself as a professor of glaciology; and Lowell Thomas's son, Lowell Junior, who later became lieutenant governor of Alaska.

BARBARA: Lowell was only sixteen. His father asked us to take him, because I think his father thought that Brad was taking me, so it couldn't be that hard. I really just followed along. I had never done anything like that before. We were just married, and this was sort of our honeymoon.

That was the first ascent of Mount Bertha. I'm strong, but I didn't know anything about handling a rope. Brad showed me as we went along. When we got partway up, he said, "Now you've got to tie this rope around you, and you've got to pendulum across this space." I could see that he didn't want to kill me in the first month of marriage, so I just did what I was told, and I kept going. That's how I got to the top.

But not all of us went with the first assault team. We stayed behind at about 8,000 feet for five days because of the weather. Every morning I would say a little prayer. When the weather got good, I wasn't sure I wanted to go to the top. I wasn't sure I could do it.

I really didn't feel very well, but I survived. I put some pilot crackers in my pocket to get me going on the summit day. When we got back down the mountains and were waiting for the boat to come in, I was still doing poorly. Brad said, "I think I better get her to the doctor in Juneau for a check." Well, the doctor came out of the office in front of all these people and he said, "Hell, Brad! There's nothing wrong with this girl. She's just pregnant!"

That night, we had a little farewell party with all of us. Tommy Winship looked at me and he said, "Barbara! You couldn't be pregnant! I was sleeping beside you all the time!"

BRAD: We not only summited Mount Bertha but also made the first crossing of the Brady Ice Field to reach the bottom of Bertha.

Everyone asks us who Mount Bertha was named for. Lengthy research finally yielded the unexpected fact that in the early 1900s Bertha, as a young prostitute in Skagway [Alaska], had given great happiness to the surveyors of the International Boundary Commission!

First Ascent of McKinley's West Buttress

BARBARA: When people make a fuss about me climbing Mount McKinley, inwardly I suppose I'm happy I did it and was the first woman to do it. But that wasn't my goal in life.

We did McKinley's North Peak too. I didn't set out to do it, but Brad said, "Everybody get up! It's a beautiful day! We're going up the North Peak!" So we all did it. It was cloudless and absolutely windless all day long.

You know, when a girl soloed it a few years ago, I got a telephone call. I was doing the breakfast dishes and wasn't thinking about Mount McKinley at all. The phone rang, and this guy said, "I'm a journalist from Anchorage, Alaska, and I want to ask you a question. A girl has just soloed McKinley. Do you have any comment?" And all I could think of was, "Oh, the poor thing! She missed all the fun!"

The fun for me was sitting around in the tent with the stove going and discussing some philosophical subject. For example, I was in an igloo on

McKinley for ten days when Brad was up at 18,000 feet. We were stuck in a storm. I was sitting around with two guys I didn't know—they weren't very attractive either—so, we did a lot of talking! I was discussing mixed marriages with a guy who was married to a black girl. I tell you, that set some sparks off, because the other guy with us was very conservative! That's my strongest memory. My job was to keep the peace!

Having a lady along also made the men a little more gentlemanly. One night the boys were sitting around the tent, up high, and they were beginning to swear. You know, I had a brother, and I didn't mind. But Ranger Grant Pearson didn't like them being at all crude in front of me. He banged on the table, and he said, "Boys! We have a lady in our midst. I will not have you talking that way in front of Barbara!" They almost died.

Mapping the Presidentials

BRAD: Back in the early 1980s, Allen Smith, who was then president of the Mount Washington Observatory, called me up. He had seen a relief map we had done of the Grand Canyon, and he wanted to make one of Mount Washington. I said, "There's no way you can make a decent relief map of that damn place without having a good map, because a relief map is based on a very good map." So I said, "Hell, let's start!"

BARBARA: Allen Smith helped us a lot, [along] with his wife and kids. We also had innumerable volunteers who helped us.

BRAD: We used to say that doing the map of the Presidentials was much harder to do than mapping Mount Everest because we had to walk all the trails and measure them with 100-foot tapes. On top of it all, the laser wouldn't show through the trees, and so we had to do it only in the fall when the leaves were gone. A lot of those trails, you see, were just like tunnels.

But Casey Hodgdon and I worked out a tricky system to mark them.[3] The rivers are all very accurately marked. And if the trail was anywhere near a river—and a lot of them are—we would go to a point where we could see

---

[3] Casey Hodgdon was a longtime U.S. Forest Service and Mount Washington Observatory employee, who is profiled on page 111.

Casey Hodgdon and Brad Washburn carry mapping equipment in the Presidential Range during the summer of 1983. (Photo courtesy of AMC Library & Archives)

a wiggle in the river so we knew where in the hell we were. Then we would measure 300 or maybe 600 feet with a long tape down the trail. And then Casey and I would take turns bushwhacking through to the river. It might be 50 feet, 250 feet, or 500 feet sometimes, all at right angles to the trail. We'd measure in like that, measure back, and we'd know where we were.

Once we were mapping the Rocky Branch Trail, way the hell off the trail in awful brush. I tripped and went flat on my face. I couldn't figure out what had hooked my foot. It was a wire. We left the tape there and walked along the wire a hundred yards, and here was a huge lumbering camp with a stove that had ten places to put the pots on it and a 36-inch saw lying there, all rusted. They'd had a railroad in there. It was fascinating.

On the map of the Presidential Range, there were about 200 miles of trails that all had to be taped. That's quite a lot of area with a 100-foot tape. It was a lot like starting in the dark in New York and measuring 200 miles in a tunnel, and then emerging in Boston. We had to use a compass, and we had to do a lot of drawing.

We got a tricky system you could use on Boott Spur, Glen Boulder Trail, or on Lion Head, anywhere where you could see opposite the trail. Barbara and I would take the tram up Wildcat [Mountain] and go along the ridge to where the trail breaks out of the timber. Then we would set up our theodolite and the laser machine. We'd made a site on the summit to give us the zero point, and that gave us a line, and angle, to every point we measured. Casey, Barbara, and I would have walked down that trail the week before, stopping at points along the trail where you could see across to Wildcat. We would take little pieces of aluminum—many of which are still on the trees; it's a hell of a job to take them off—and we nailed them to the tree. We'd letter them A, B, C, D, E, F, and so forth.

Casey would get to one of these points, and he'd have an orange target. We'd pick it up through the theodolite, which had an 80-power telescope. Casey had a signaling mirror that was blindingly bright. You could pick it up instantly. We literally peppered those trails with control points. Then we just had to map it in between those points. We used that system all over the place.

BARBARA: One day I had come up [Mount Washington] on the Cog Railway. I went out and stood out at Goofer Point. I was frozen stiff up there! Brad was down at a survey station at the base of the railway. We were trying to measure angles, and it went on and on and on. Then Guy Gosselin[4] called up and said, "Brad's going to meet you somewhere when you come down." And I said, "You tell him I'm getting a divorce tomorrow, and I'm not going to meet him!"

I didn't get a divorce—I didn't know how to! But I was mad. He kept saying, "Do it again, do it again. Move it this way and that way," in order to get the exact angle and laser distance. We never thought of quitting, although there was one time when I was writing down all the angles and doing the trigonometry, when I suddenly realized I could sabotage the whole project if I gave them the wrong number! There were a couple of times when I felt like doing that! But, I thought, *Oh, no! Wouldn't that be awful!*

BRAD: That night we were measuring the angle and laser distance from the observatory tower to the top of Mount Madison. We were measuring just that one angle and had to get it exactly right. Then we'd go back and measure other angles from the tower. These angles were very fussy, and they were done with great, great precision. We had no time schedule at all. We just

---

[4] Guy Gosselin was director of the Mount Washington Observatory from 1971 to 1996.

finished it when we finished it. And so, we finally did a very precise job. And it took us pretty close to ten years.

The reason that it took so long is because we were very, very fussy about the trails. Also, we couldn't take our vertical photographs at one time. To get the trails above treeline, we had to take pictures of the whole area after all the snow was gone, which means August. We returned late in the fall, before the snow arrived, but with all the leaves now off, so we could see the ground on which the contours had been made. Everest was mapped with one set of photos, the Grand Canyon was one set, but we had to have two completely separate sets of vertical photographs for the Presidentials map.

This was a very good project on which to have a lot of people helping you. It made it a more special project. We had scores of people involved in it: Alan Smith, Hersh Cross from Randolph, a profusion of friends, boys from Milton, foreign students visiting from Spain. People liked to help out because you were *doing something* when you got to the top, instead of just looking at the view. And I think they all liked it.

We got to see a lot of places. I think the place I've enjoyed most in the last few years is the Great Gulf. You meet almost nobody down in there, and to me Spaulding Lake is a marvelous spot. You know, Casey made an interesting comment I've never heard anybody make: Spaulding Lake is higher than the top of Mount Moriah!

Population Explosion

BRAD: To get philosophical, I think the biggest problem that we've got in the world today is overpopulation. Nobody has got the guts to face up to it. I think that the people on it will eventually destroy our world. [They're] going to destroy nature, at least. Men are going to destroy each other, because people don't want to realize what really is going on. It's so dreadful that they don't care. They want to say, "Let's keep on going and hope it won't happen."

That's what's happening with the White Mountains. It's just more and more and more people. It's going to get steadily worse, because we just keep ignoring the population situation.

I've watched this at Squam Lake. Everybody's moving in. Every time some wealthy person who owns twenty acres dies the kids divide it up, and all of a sudden, you've got four cottages where you had one. It's slowly and inevitably destroying the lake. The trails are getting chewed up. I think one

Brad Washburn uses a theodolite for his mapping project on the summit of Mount Washington, summer 1983. (Photo courtesy of AMC Library & Archives)

of the worst things that ever happened on those trails is allowing people to go there with rubber-cleated boots, because that's what takes the trails apart. Sneakers do not do that.

Back in 1925, I went across the Presidentials with Tom Rogers and David Crocker. We did the Webster Cliff Trail, went across the range to Mount Washington and the Northern Peaks, and down to Madison Hut. It took us three days. We had no reservations anywhere. We stayed at Lakes of the Clouds; we stayed at Madison. Now you have to reserve in December if you want to stay there in July! All I can say is, you've got to have some regulation, or in a relatively small number of years we're going to be in big trouble.

I have some good statistics on McKinley. Barbara and I were the first two people ever to meet anybody else trying to climb McKinley at the same time we were: Friday the thirteenth of June, 1947. We were coming down Karstens Ridge, and three University of Alaska boys were coming up. Last summer, there were 1,111 people trying to climb Mount McKinley.

Another thing that's causing all this trouble is our guidebooks, including the AMC guides. I've said that one of the things that have done a lot to destroy these places is the books that people like Ansel Adams and Elliot Porter and I, on McKinley, have written. People want to go there to see that wonderful country. And all of a sudden you realize that you're sort of committing suicide.

Savoring Past, Present, and Future

BRAD: A few years ago, we had four separate expeditions doing work on Mount Everest. Two of them were working on this GPS [Global Positioning System] stuff, taking measurements of snow depth on the top of Everest. The Chinese said there's only a meter of snow. I'm actually positive there's at least 15 feet and maybe more than that. And, we measured the movement of the ice in the Khumbu Icefall. It turns out, it's moving about 3 to 4 feet per day.

We did some very fancy surveying on Everest. We had to have a lot of little holes drilled into the limestone, on top of the mountain. We'd drill a hole, bang in an expansion bolt, then screw in the global satellite markers. We found that Everest is going steadily up.

The guys who worked on these projects said to me that it made it much more fun for them when they were climbing Everest to do something when they got there, instead of just getting to the top, turning around, and coming back down. Everybody likes to do something, rather than just climb to the top.

I enjoyed what I did on Everest very, very much, because I was dealing entirely with very bright, very competent young people. And they were doing what I really wished I could do myself. And I would like to have done it myself, but I couldn't. After all, I'm over ninety years old!

This year, we've been invited to fly to and land at the North Pole! And, in mid-July, we'll go back to Alaska to attend the fiftieth anniversary celebration of my first ascent of Mount McKinley by the West Buttress Route, to take place in Talkeetna on July 10. Since then, close to twenty thousand people have followed that route successfully to McKinley's summit.

Ninety percent of my memories of climbs are of the people who were on the trip. Guys like Casey Hodgdon. Certainly my most vivid and pleasant memories are of climbing with Barbara and Casey. Period.

Brad Washburn announced the result of his final Everest project—the new elevation of Mount Everest—at the 87th annual meeting of the American Alpine Club in the fall of 1999. He died at the age of ninety-six on January 10, 2007. At ninety-seven years old, Barbara Washburn remains upbeat, living in a retirement community outside of Boston.

Rick Wilcox

Expedition Leader, Mountain Guide, Rescuer

Rick Wilcox pauses while leading a trip to the southeast side of Kangchenjunga in Sikkim in 1997. (Photo courtesy of Celia Wilcox)

I N 1963, the first American expedition successfully climbed Mount Everest. In Boston, a sixteen-year-old boy heard about it, and insisted to his dad that they somehow find tickets to the historic lecture tour that followed. Sitting in the last seat of the last row, Rick Wilcox saw, for the first time, one of his major life projects laid out in front of him. Even at sixteen, he knew he wanted a life in the mountains, feeling that it was "programmed" in him to go someday.

Throughout the decades and nearly fifty expeditions that followed, Wilcox built a life around mountaineering. His climbing life is filled with remarkable accomplishments—research assistant for noted climber and high-altitude physiologist Charlie Houston; climbing guide at the inception of Eastern Mountain Sports' climbing school; participant in the second ascent of the storied Black Dike on Cannon Mountain in his home range of the White Mountains of New Hampshire; present at the birth of North Conway, New Hampshire, as a center for climbing; partner in the founding of the Mountain Rescue Service, one of the original volunteer technical rescue teams; owner of the outdoor gear store International Mountain Equipment; climber in most of the major mountain ranges of the world; and expedition leader of the 1991 New England Everest Expedition.

Such a list of accomplishments could easily lead to hubris. But an old-fashioned Yankee sensibility pervades Rick's thinking and his actions. In the face of enormous accomplishments and on the sides of treacherous peaks, it has kept him humble. "I've been in really tight situations where I had to pull out every resource I had, but I haven't had to make too many deals with God," he said. "How many trips have I not got to the summit of the mountain? A huge number. I don't get up every mountain. But I'm still here, I have all my fingers and toes and half my brains. I'm a very cautious climber and I have survived because of that."

We interviewed Rick in 2008, in his upstairs office at International Mountain Equipment, known as IME, in North Conway, New Hampshire. The walls are decorated with photographs of mountains around the world (many of which Rick took himself), pictures of family, and the framed permit to climb Mount Everest.

Having climbed all over the world, Wilcox continues to derive pleasure from his home in the heart of the White Mountains. "I live in the White Mountains because I love the White Mountains, and this is my base camp. I go out hiking every week. This is my home in the mountains, and then I go to the mountains."

In His Own Words

I was born down in Fall River, Massachusetts, in 1948. I wound up on the north shore of Boston in a town called Middleton, where I went to high school. Even in high school, I was attracted to hiking. My parents were back-packers in the White Mountains and they sent me to a boys' camp up here in East Madison called Camp Tohkomeupog. I went there and [later] was a counselor through college.

My first interest was in hiking the 4,000-footers, not an unusual goal for a young guy. I got the last couple done when I got my driver's license when I was sixteen. I jumped in my rat car, drove up here, and finished off Zealand and a couple of the other ones that I hadn't done. I had to go back and do Zealand because I hadn't done the 100-foot side trail to the real summit. I was a purist about that.

I always had this fascination with two things. One was big mountains of the world, like Mount Everest. I remember looking through all the books on the Himalaya. But, I was also very interested in rock climbing and ice climb-ing. At about age sixteen, I decided I wanted to be an AMC [Appalachian Mountain Club] hut boy. So, I went to Boston and joined the AMC. That was 1964.

I learned that the main focus of the AMC hut system wasn't on technical climbing. It was more on backpacking and this idea of carrying huge loads. I found out as a little guy that wasn't going to work for me. I never could carry big loads. Fortunately, on big mountains you don't have to carry big loads. That's a different thing. So, I changed gears. I got more into technical climbing.

I took the AMC beginner rock climbing programs in the Boston area. We did some winter backpacking and snowshoeing. They didn't do much ice climbing in those days. I ran into a guy named Bob Proudman.[5] He be-came my roommate in college at the University of Massachusetts for a while.

---

[5] Proudman later became the AMC trails director and now serves as director of conserva-tion operations for the Appalachian Trail Conservancy.

I did a lot of technical climbing with Bob. My first climbs away from the AMC were on Cannon White Horse and Cathedral with Bob and the AMC trail crew members.

Bona and Logan

In my junior year at college at the University of Massachusetts, Eastern Mountain Sports (EMS) opened a store in Amherst. It was their third store. I worked part-time in there, got to know those guys, and went on my first expedition between my junior and senior year to Alaska, to a peak called Mount Bona. I had a friend, Joe LaBelle, who was climbing the ten highest peaks in North America and Mount Bona is the ninth. The expedition was led by Tom Lyman, who was director of the EMS Climbing School at the time. I used a college loan to do that—which my parents would have freaked out about, but they didn't know, so that was OK!

Mount Bona is a 16,000-foot-high mountain in the Saint Elias Range. I had my first glacier experience, and it was kind of neat. Relative to the group, I did very well. I always hoped that altitude would not be an issue, because I heard that some people can go up and some can't. I was very pleased that I was above average.

In the summer of '70, after I graduated from college, I went to Mount Logan. Joe LaBelle came to me that spring, and he said, "Rick, you did OK on Mount Bona. You obviously know Arctic camping, you know glaciers and snow and ice, you know how to take care of yourself. Would you like to join us?" I said, "Sure, but what's the deal?" He said, "We're going to pay you for this job." I said, "Pay? I'm in!" So they paid me I think $800, which was huge in those days, to go to the Yukon, be based in Kluane Lake, just north of Whitehorse, fly around in airplanes, and climb mountains. We went up there in May and were there all summer 'til September.

I worked as the goon for the Arctic Institute for four months doing high-altitude physiology and research. I was the kid that ran around and dug holes! Charlie Houston was running the program.[6]

---

[6] Houston, a medical doctor, university professor, and former director of the Peace Corps in India, is one of the truly renowned names in American mountaineering. He was a member of the famed 1953 expedition to K2, and a pioneer in the field of high-altitude physiology.

Logan was the big project. We had a camp up at 17,000 feet. I lived there for fifty-eight days. It really went very well. And again, I had a great experience on Logan. Logan's the second highest peak in North America. It's 19,850 feet—250 less than McKinley. It's cold. It's arctic.

We did the fifteenth ascent of the main peak. And I got to know Charlie. He immediately adopted me as a son. I participated in some of the experiments and I learned a little bit about high-altitude physiology, but, again, living at 17,000 feet and climbing up to 20,000, I was above average in the group. I was able to maintain my physical fitness better and acclimatize better, meaning getting more oxygen and being able to perform better. My physical ability helped inspire me onto a high-altitude career that eventually took me to Everest.

I graduated from UMass Amherst [the University of Massachusetts] with a degree in forestry. The pieces of the puzzle all kind of fit. I could have wound up in [New Hampshire] Fish and Game or the [U.S.] Forest Service, but I went to Boston in the spring of 1971 and EMS offered me a full-time job. Through Tom Lyman, I was also doing some guiding with the EMS Climbing School.

The Draw of the Mountains

It's hard to explain why people are attracted to certain aspects of their life. But, whenever I looked at big mountains I had this feeling that it was programmed in me that when I had the opportunity to go to these mountains I would go, even if it just meant looking at them.

In 1963, the Americans climbed Everest, and I called my dad up and I said, "I have to go see the lecture in Boston." He said, "OK, we'll get some tickets." He wasn't very excited. It was at Symphony Hall because this was a huge deal, the first Americans on Everest. We got the last chairs in the last row, and I watched Jim Whittaker and Norman Dyhrenfurth do the lecture. I was sixteen years old.

One of the goals I set for myself fairly young was to try and photograph each of the 8,000-meter peaks. Maybe not climb them all. Sure, I would have loved to do that, but just to be in the area of each one and at least see it from a distance. I've done that.

I thought mountain climbing was tremendously rewarding, and I loved the adrenaline rush of rock climbing. And, I was good at it. I had failed miserably at team sports in high school. I was definitely a nerd. I tried out for football, got completely squashed. I was short, so I couldn't play basketball or track. They put me into the pole vault. That was pretty stupid. And I wasn't doing very well with the women.

In college, I joined the gymnastics team so I could rock-climb better. I was the tallest, biggest guy on the gymnastic team. I found my niche. My rock-climbing skills went way up as I got stronger and stronger in gymnastics. And only in my senior year did I drop off the team, finally, and it turned out to be the third best team in the United States that year. I was the worst member of the third best team in the country!

And that's kind of how I've always thought of myself as a climber. I was never a great rock climber, never a great ice climber, never a great big-mountain guy. But I was good at all of them. So I was the worst best all-around climber is the way I kind of thought of it. There are always better rock climbers, and there are always better ice climbers, but none of them could do all of that stuff and put it together, I thought, the way I did. So, I felt very well-rounded, which meant that I could go from Cathedral Ledge to Mount Everest and be comfortable in both places. That's sort of how my career formed.

IME and a Climbing School

In 1971, the guys who owned EMS came to me and said, "Would you like to run a store in North Conway, New Hampshire?" I had spent summers in the White Mountains, and my parents owned some land down in Eaton, which is where I built a house, and where I live now. It just worked out perfect. The first Eastern Mountain Sports store in North Conway—and the fourth in their chain—was right here, where IME is now. I was the store manager and eventually became the climbing school director. EMS moved across the street to the Eastern Slope Inn in '76.

I stayed at EMS three more years, 'til 1979, when they went public. The founders of EMS, who I had worked for, left, and the company that owns Franklin Mint bought it. I think it's been sold ten times since then.

I took over International Mountain Equipment that year. IME had been started by Paul Ross, Bill Aughton, and a guy named Frank Simon, who had the money.

Rick Wilcox, owner of International Mountain Equipment in North Conway, New Hampshire, shows sleeping bags to a customer, 2008. (Photo by Ned Therrien)

When I came in and bought IME, they were doing terrible. I thought, *I'll just start my own little company and everything will be cool, but maybe I'll go down and see what those guys at IME are doing.* You know, nobody needs another store in North Conway. So I went in and Bill just ran up to me with the keys, and he said, "We need you to run this company. We don't want to own it any more. Whatever it takes, we'll work it out." I put a mortgage on my house to pay some bills for like $90,000, to finance the inventory, and got it going. Five weeks later, I owned IME. I never looked back.

I always wanted to be involved in teaching climbing, running trips, and retail sales of the climbing gear. Those three things went hand in hand, so that was good. This is not an easy business, though. There're plenty of days when it's not a lot of fun, but it's worked out. I've always managed to pull [money] together to pay for trips and bills and whatever.

In 1986, the original EMS building came up for sale. It was cheap because it was completely screwed up. They had six tenants here and the building was in disarray. But I knew the building from the EMS days, and I'm a fairly crafty electrician, plumber, and carpenter. So I went to work fixing the building up and then we moved in in 1988. We've been here ever since. I don't have a savings account, I don't have a retirement account, I don't have anything like that. But I own the building, and some day this will be the nest egg.

We had the climbing school too, of course. Paul ran the school for a few years, but he eventually went back to England. I bought the school from him a few years after I bought the store. By the early '80s, I was pretty much running the school and the store. We had a lot of different people involved in the school over the years, like Mark Chauvin and Nick Yardley. Later, Maury McKinney and Brad White became my partners. Just recently, Maury's taken off and so Brad and I own the school now, fifty-fifty.

To the Himalaya

By 1979, I had not been to the Himalaya yet and knew that as I got into my thirties, it was time to get over there. High-altitude mountaineering is a young man's sport. In '85, after doing a lot of guiding in Peru, Argentina, the Alps, and Alaska, I got my first opportunity to go to the Himalaya. I was on a bare-bones expedition with some Polish guys. That turned out to be my most difficult climb and it went very well. We did the South Face of Cho Oyu—the sixth highest peak in the world. We were over there for three months, and I learned the ropes. That was absolutely the tightest budget in the world. Those Polish guys, they just run on no money at all.

Mark Richey and I did the third ascent of Ngozumpa Kang I, 7,940 meters, on this trip. This is the eighteenth highest peak in the world.

On this 1985 expedition, I began to think about Everest. I'm sitting there for three months looking at it every day and all the pieces of the puzzle started coming together. I was learning about how to run a Himalayan expedition, how you get a permit, how you put the team together, how you organize Sherpas, and what's your budget going to be.

The next year, Ned Gillette called me up. Ned was the extreme opposite of the Poles. He's a typical American. He said, "I got a permit for Makalu; are you interested?" I said, "Yes, absolutely. How much is it going to cost?" He said $15,000. We'd done Cho Oyu for $3,000. And I'm thinking, *Ten or fifteen thousand? Where am I ever going to get that from?* He said, "Don't worry, I've got plenty of money, I've got plenty of contacts. Give me $5,000 and we'll work it out." Unfortunately, he's gone now. He was murdered in Pakistan.[7]

So, Ned, John Bouchard, myself, and a guy named Chris Dube went to Makalu. We had a great trip. It was never just climbing with Ned. There's a whole story behind every one of these trips. But, I learned again that I was basically outperforming everybody else at high altitude. And on Cho Oyu, Mark Richey was a superb high-altitude climber. So I started thinking about Everest. Mark and I applied for the permit for Everest in '86 and we got a slot for '91. And it took all those five years to pull it together.

In the meantime, I went back to Nepal in '88 and led an Everest trek to Base Camp and climbed a small, 20,000-foot trekking peak called Island Peak. Then in 1990, I led an expedition with clients to a peak called Lang-tang, which had never been climbed by Americans.

Langtang would have been a great peak to climb with your buddies like Mark Richey or John Bouchard, but not with clients. They didn't do very well on it. Fortunately, we didn't kill any of them. It was way over the skill level of these people and we had an incident that wasn't too good. We fixed ropes up this 2,000-foot couloir and started up this knife-edge ridge. At the ridge I realized, *This is it. We're not going up.*

Well, in the afternoon, what happens to snow? It gets warm, especially in the Himalaya. So there was an avalanche coming down the couloir that hit the group and broke the rope that we were on. Six of us fell 2,500 feet down the couloir. Now, I had a lot of experience falling down the head-wall of Tuckerman Ravine. Like the headwall, this had a long runout, no big cliffs, no big rocks. Everybody survived the fall OK but boy, I'll tell you, that taught me about fixed ropes. We were using six-millimeter. I use all eight now. It was just a real good lesson.

The biggest lesson I learned about putting together a Himalayan expedition is you don't need to spend a lot of money to do it. Unfortunately, I think that Americans in general who have money don't understand that there are certain luxuries that you don't really need. When I was leading these expeditions, I had to know where every dollar was going; I had to

---

[7] Gillette, a world-renowned climber, was shot to death during a robbery attempt while on an expedition.

learn about budgeting. Budgeting is brutal, because you can just budget everything you can possibly think of and when you're done at the end of the day you're still off by ten percent. Every single trip I ever ran over there, I was always ten percent off. On a $150,000 trip, that's fifteen grand. Where are you going to get fifteen grand? They don't let you go home 'til you pay up.

I became good at liquidating equipment. I'd come home with a suitcase—no tents, no sleeping bags, no gear. But I always worked it out. I learned how to be creative and resourceful in the finances. That's also the key to good mountain climbing.

I've now been to the Himalaya twenty-five times. I don't run into the budget problems that I used to have. There are very few surprises, and every trip gives me one more thing that I learn about the Himalaya. I've got a terrific Sherpa staff. I've used the same guys ever since Makalu, and now their kids are working for me. I can get any permit for any mountain with a phone call. I know all the right people to bribe over there.

It's changed a lot over the last twenty-five years, obviously. Back in the '80s, the process of getting an 8,000-meter peak permit, particularly Everest, was very lengthy. It involved getting endorsed by the American Alpine Club and the Mountaineering Federation in Nepal. You had to guarantee certain things in writing. I had to guarantee I had $500,000 to do Everest. Now, I did it for $125,000, but if I told them that, I never would have got the permit because it was never done for that amount of money. I mean, the Americans in '63 spent a million in 2007 dollars on the climb!

Guiding on Everest

There're three kinds of expeditions now. There's the old school, which is what we did: me and Mark Richey and our six buddies get together, and the eight of us go over and climb the mountain. That still exists.

Then there's organized, for-profit. This is attractive to a person who's got money and who wants to climb Everest, but probably hasn't done a lot of climbing. For a fee of fifty grand, everything is done for you. You join a group of ten guys who you never met before. You pair up with one of them and you go climb the mountain with Sherpa support. I think that's completely idiotic to be on big mountains with people you don't know.

You need to know what the other guy's doing, what he's thinking, what his strengths are, what his weaknesses are.

Then the third kind of trip is full-blown guiding. You pay sixty to a hundred grand and you go and they hook you onto the rope and up you go. You don't even cook dinner.

I think they had forty or fifty expeditions on the mountain in May 2007. You've got huge traffic jams. You've got a lot of people, so instead of each team trying to do the climb independently, the Sherpas set a route and then they charge $2,200 apiece to use the ropes. So you pay your sixty grand, then you pay, pay, pay, pay.

The guiding business opened the door for people who had no clue how to get involved in a Himalayan expedition. They could just sign on. It opened the door for people who didn't go through the process that I went through of learning, learning, learning, and then actually doing it yourself. A lot of these people are only going over to the Himalaya once or twice in their lives. They're not committed to an area.

Up to '96, a solid guide might make $15,000 a year, and live in his car with a very modest lifestyle. If you were an Everest guide, you could make forty or fifty grand in two months. A huge amount of money came into the climbing community of guides that weren't used to making money. It was like a gold rush. It was just awesome. Then came the marketing. Guys like Scott Fischer were like, "Hey, give us the money, we'll get you to the top, doesn't matter if you're 300 pounds and you're out of shape."

Then in '96 they all got whacked. They lost fourteen guides and climbers. Scott Fischer and Rob Hall died, and they were losing customers left and right. It showed that you cannot go into these big mountains with a strange team and break all the rules.

The big rule that they broke was the turnaround rule. They had two competing companies going up the ridge, and at eleven o'clock, you should say, "OK, we've got to turn around and go down."

You've got all of these wealthy overachievers who were getting hauled to the summit. Sherpas that typically make $1,000 a year were now making ten thousand more than the average guy in Nepal. You show them ten grand and they'd haul someone to the summit. It worked. They hauled [a wealthy woman] up there during the '96 disaster. And when they had triage of who they're going to save, she was saved because she had the money.

It got into a money thing and a lot of greed. You can imagine. You pay a hundred grand to get up the mountains, and the team that's responsible turns around at noon and brings you down. You're sitting in the South Col, and another team goes up, breaks all the rules, gets to the top at three o'clock, turns around and they make it down. That's what was happening the year before. So the clients, they say, "What's wrong with our guides?" Actually, our guides are the smart guys.

After all these deaths, the guiding community reorganized. It was a good thing in the end, because people that guide today do it much more responsibly than they used to. They don't guarantee the summit anymore. They will turn people around who aren't going to make it by noon or one o'clock at the latest and they're much more cautious. It's still pretty big business, though.

Style and Paying Your Dues

There are some real differences in style issues, comparing what we did to guiding in the Himalaya today. I'm not knocking it. I'm a guide. But, you go up to Everest with some guides and you don't carry a pack, you don't put in the camps, you don't fix ropes, you don't even have to think about the money or the logistics. You pay a fee of $60,000 to $70,000, you get onto a bus, and you go for the ride.

That's the style issue. I'm just blessed that when we did it in '91 we had four climbing Sherpas. They helped us get through the Khumbu Ice-fall, they went up to Camp II, they carried a few loads up the South Col, and we went up alone and did the summit day alone. Because of that short window in May, which is sometimes just ten days, you've now got sixty people a day going up the ridge. They get three hundred people at the top on a good climbing season. When we did it, we were the only people on the mountain. There was nobody on the Hillary Step, just us. That could never happen again.

Style is the difference between flying the plane and riding in the back seat. I think there's good style and there's bad style and maybe a little bit in between. For example, when you go up to Huntington Ravine and you lead Pinnacle Gully, you're climbing in good style. When you're getting hauled up second and you're slipping and sliding and screaming and you don't even know how your knot is, that's a different style. Of course, you can come home to the cocktail party and say, "I just climbed Pinnacle Gully on Mount Washington." It isn't going to matter to your friends. But I think style in doing what you're doing is important.

In my case, I learned a little bit from the AMC and a lot from my fellow climbers. My main schooling was getting involved with people that knew what they were doing climbing big mountains, like the Polish and other Americans. Charlie Houston, for example. He taught me so much about high-altitude physiology. All these people were part of Rick's mountaineering education. I have a Ph.D. in mountain climbing. Nobody's born with this knowledge and everybody has to find a way to get it.

I always felt that if you wanted to be a climber—not a client but a climber —that you had to pay your dues. Imagine climbing a ladder with rungs in the ladder. You go from rung to rung to rung. First, you learn to backpack in the White Mountains, then you learn to rock-climb, then you learn to ice-climb, then you learn to winter camp. You'd learn all these skills, go take some avalanche courses, then go to Mount Rainer. You find out about crevasses. Then you go to South America, and you find out about bigger mountains, maybe get up to 23,000 feet on Aconcagua. Then you go up to McKinley and freeze your ass off.

And then, when you've done all of that—then you're ready. It was my twenty-fifth expedition that I was on when I led Everest. Now I've been on forty-eight expeditions. But my attitude was this: You took it a rung at a time. What is happening with guiding is that you're eliminating a huge amount of the rungs. People who have never been to Asia are going to Everest on their first trip. People who have never worn double plastic boots are going on big Arctic mountains on their first trip.

Let's say a client walks into my office and says, "I want to climb Everest." I say, "OK. Let's start with a mountaineering course here in the White Mountains. Maybe after that, we'll take you out to Mount Rainier. Then maybe we'll go down and climb a volcano in South America and then we'll go and do McKinley. And the guy's looking at you like, "Hey, I haven't got the rest of my life to do this. I'm sixty years old; I need to go climb a big mountain right now."

So, what do you do? You say, "OK. Let's go do Mount Rainier." They go to Rainier, they find out it's a ball buster, they do terrible, they get altitude sick, and they find out that mountaineering isn't always music playing in the background with beautiful views and the weather being great and standing on top with the flag. How many trips have I not got to the summit of the mountain? A huge number. I don't get up every mountain. But I'm still here, I have all my fingers and toes and half my brains. I'm a very cautious climber and I have survived because of that.

Here's one example. A woman came into the shop who was about thirty-five years old and overweight. She says, "I went on a bus trip to the Alps. I saw the Matterhorn and I want to climb it." I said, "OK, I want you to go up to Pinkham Notch and I want you to hike to Tuckerman Ravine. Then, come back and tell me how long it took." The first time she went up, she didn't make it. She tried two or three times. When she finally made it, it took her five hours.

I said, "OK, come back when you can do it in an hour and a half." I really thought she'd never come back. And when she came back, she was fifty pounds lighter. She said, "This is important to me."

I wound up rock-climbing in Huntington Ravine with her so she would learn about what the Matterhorn's like. We took her out to Mount Rainier, we took her to the Grand Tetons. We took her over to Switzerland, she climbed the Matterhorn, and she came back and she sat down and she said, "Rick, I'm the happiest person in the world." I mean she was as happy as I was when I climbed Mount Everest.

I said, "What's next?" She said, "I'm all done climbing." I said, "What are you going to do?" She said, "I'm going to have a baby!" For her, that was a chunk of three or four years of her life dedicated to a project, obtaining a goal, and then moving on to the next thing in her life. I just never forgot that. That was so cool that somebody could do that. Basically, that's what we all do in life. We set little goals for ourselves and we achieve them. And when we share that—that's part of the business for me that's fantastic because I share in those successes.

Climbing Everest

During those earlier trips to Cho Oyu, and Makalu, I realized that, yes, I did have the physiological ability to go up to these extreme high altitudes. And my friend Mark Richey could too. So we decided to apply for the Everest permit. We got the endorsement from the American Alpine Club, we got some money, we got the paperwork going.

Things looked good for '91. Immediately, people were approaching me who were way under-qualified, wanting to join the team. We decided that we wanted to climb with people we knew and had climbed with before who had prior Himalaya experience. We were very strict about this. An expedition like this also means months away from home. We were away on Everest for almost four months. We left in March and we came back in June. It's a huge commitment.

We got all of our ducks in a row and sort of lied about the money. You know, we just made it happen. Then I got the piece of paper—that I framed. It says, "Dear Mr. Wilcox, Congratulations. You have received permission." This is in '89. So I called up my fifteen buddies, and I said, "We're in, we're going, this is going to happen!" Seven of them dropped out. In the end, we had fifteen people on the permit but only eight of us actually left the United States.

The team commitment was key. We had a great team: Mark Richey, Barry Rugo, Mark Chauvin, Yves LaForest, Dick St. Onge, Mike Sinclair, Gary Scott, and me. Fortunately, of the eight guys that went, they were all experienced high-altitude climbers. They all had climbed with me.

We just had one guy with his own agenda. He got into a [mindset of], "I'm going to do it without bottled oxygen and I'm going to try Everest from base in one day after the expedition is over." He was kind of into this one-day thing. And he wasn't doing the teamwork thing. We called him Apollo. But you know, we're all mountain climbers, we had the balance of the egos.

We took off in March of '91. It was my fourth trip with the Sherpas that I worked with. Things went like clockwork in Katmandu. We got out of there in a week, which is excellent. It was paperwork, paperwork, radio permits, this, that, this, that.

We got up to Lukla and started the trek in. We got to Base Camp in mid-March, and started to work on the Khumbu Icefall. There were a couple of other teams there. We joined forces with them and their Sherpa staffs to get a route through the icefall. Everybody worked together. Things went really well. Gary was the only one who really started to slip back. Here's a guy you thought would be carrying the biggest load, and Mark Chauvin and Mark Richey ran him right into the ground. Those were our two guys who were out front. They're really strong.

Here's a funny story about those differences. We were at Camp II, and we had a big cache of gear at Camp I that we were moving up. Camp II is a better camp, so we were living at Camp II, which is at about 22,000 feet. We'd go down during the day, pick up a load, and bring it back up. I was overall expedition leader, but Mark Richey was climbing leader. He said, "Rick, we want you to bring up Gary's load. He only brought it up about an hour above Camp I. It's a huge pack." Gary had gone off to the nearest town to rest, Namche Bazar, which is three or four days down the valley. And I'm thinking to myself, *Oh my God, it's probably sixty pounds. I don't know if this is a good idea or not.*

So, four or five of us hiked down and there was the pack on the side of the trail where he'd left it. I looked at this pack and I walked over to it and—it was full of nothing. It was just foam pads or something. But I looked like an ant carrying this giant load. I put this pack on and said, "I think I can handle this guys. I'll see you back at Camp II," and carried it up.

Trouble on Everest

All of us started to get into place, and toward the end of the expedition, when we made our final push to the summit, we went up twice to the South Col. The first time we went up, it was Mark Chauvin, Barry Rugo, me, and Mark Richey. And Chauvin put everything he had into that trip up to the South Col, pretty much like always. But, this time, he wasn't pacing himself quite as well. We went down for ten days and rested because the wind was blowing. Then we went back up.

Seven of us went back up in early May, to Camp II. On the thirteenth, the wind died and we went up from there. Within an hour, Chauvin turned around at Camp II and said, "I can't do this." I felt he was ready to go but his body was worn out. We cried.

There were five of us who continued on past Camp III to Camp IV. We were going up two camps in one day, that's how strong we were. I mean, it sounds egotistical, but we did two days from Camp II to Camp IV in one. I only let the guys use oxygen at the high camp, at Camp IV.

So, five of us started up: Mark, Barry, Yves, myself, and Gary Scott. Gary started falling behind. We had a turnaround rule. If you weren't in camp at two o'clock, you turned around and you went back to the last camp. It's almost like a summit-day rule.

We got into Camp IV about four that afternoon. It was a twelve-hour climb, and we were pooped, but we had gathered up all of the extra oxygen tanks that were left at the South Col, and hooked them up with little plumbing hoses. We had a little oxygen in the tent, so that was good. We found quite a bit of oxygen, actually. We were up there eight days altogether. We used it for sleeping. It was great.

We assumed Gary had turned back to Camp III. At midnight, we did a bed check on the radios. He wasn't in Camp III and he wasn't in Camp II and he wasn't in Camp IV. So, the night of the thirteenth into the fourteenth, Yves, Barry, [and I] went out looking for him. This is after climbing twelve hours that day. We found him on the Geneva Spur, below the South Col, sitting on a rock. He'd been out there twenty-three hours. We brought him into camp.

Here's the guy who's going to do the whole climb without oxygen and we're all blowing him into the weeds without oxygen. To make a long story short we got him into camp, and he sucked down a bottle of oxygen. That rejuvenated him. We said, "Tomorrow morning, you're going down." And he did.

We slept through the day on the fourteenth, and at midnight on the fifteenth of May, the four of us were off to the summit. It was just a great day. There was no wind. It was clear; it was cold. We got to the south summit at seven in the morning, after seven hours. A lot of people get there at noon or one o'clock. It's two hours from there to the very top. You do a knife-edge ridge, the Hillary Step, and then a low-angle snow slope to the top. Yves and Mark were on top at eight-thirty in the morning, I was on top at nine forty-five, and Barry at ten. It was great.

I realized I was going to make the summit about one minute before I got there. I had a lot on my mind on the way up. What's going to go wrong? Am I going to run out of oxygen? Is the wind going to come up, is the weather going to change, is something going to go wrong, is one of the guys going to get in trouble and we're going to have to help him? Even though we said we wouldn't, we would. We had thirteen hours each of oxygen. So we had to be on top by 10 A.M., three hours down and back to the South Col by one. That was the plan.

The night of climbing was the hardest part, because it was really cold and we weren't climbing together. We were kind of spread out. We weren't roped. We never roped for the whole climb. We had agreed that if somebody got hurt we'd leave him behind. It makes sense on these extreme climbs. We're not hired guides, where your goal is to minimize losses. Why lose two guys when you lose one? We had some pretty serious chats about that. We said if the person isn't going to make it—if something has gone wrong to the point where if we try and help them we're going to become victims too—then we're going to have to leave him behind.

The summit isn't worth losing your buddy. But, it isn't worth losing more than you need to lose, either. That's a tough subject. A lot of people die side-by-side with their buddies. It happens over and over and over. And it happens in guiding. Guides don't leave clients to die. That was what that whole '96 thing on Everest was about. Rob Hall would not leave his client. He could have come down, sure, but he died with him. We weren't going to lose more than we needed to lose.

Fortunately, everything went smoothly. It was a beautiful day. We were on top from 10 A.M. to 11 A.M. We turned off our bottles and sat up there and just had a great hour.

Barry had some trouble getting down—he ran out of oxygen. He and Yves were pulling away from me as the day went on. I think he turned up his oxygen to catch up—it's like stepping on the gas of your car. Of course, that meant he was not going to have as many hours of oxygen. Barry dropped back and climbed to the summit with me. So when we started down from the summit, he immediately started falling behind me.

I stayed with him to the south summit, which is the real danger zone. You're down-climbing the Hillary Step with no rope. This is the real thing. We started down after the Hillary Step and Barry said, "Go. Don't wait for me, go."

I got down to the South Col at 1 P.M. He got down at five that night. We could see him the whole time coming down. He was out of oxygen. That was the difference.

I was surprised that we'd actually made it to the summit. On Makalu, we were so close but didn't make it. And that was after a three-month commitment. I knew that there were no guarantees. But when I was on the summit, I thought, *My life is going to change now. I can put this project behind me.* That's the happiness side of your brain. The other side of your brain was saying, *Most people get killed on the way down. It ain't over yet. We're not down to Base*

Camp, or to my bed in Eaton, New Hampshire. When you look at Mallory and Irvine and the history of Everest, you realize that an awful lot of people were near the top or made the top and didn't make it down. There are numerous dead people who you see on the way up, all of whom had died on the way down.

I had three emotions. There's the happiness that you've done your life's project. There's the relief that [with] every step I take from now I'm going home, to my family, to what I miss in Eaton—to sit by the pond and look at the pine trees. And then there's the stress of [wondering], *Can I do this without screwing up at the last second?* You're done with all the years of work, done all the hard work to get to the top. I felt very strong on the way down. I made it down to the South Col in three hours.

Decision-Making in the Mountains

I think you process Mount Everest the way you process a hike on Mount Washington in the winter. You get to the Lion's Head, you stop and look around, and if there's no wind and it's clear and it's noon, then you keep going. If it's three in the afternoon, you can't see a hundred yards, and the wind's blowing, well, you process that information. A lot of times, you try to second-guess yourself. *Should I have kept going? Could I have done it?* That's a bad thing, I think. You have to accept your decisions and live with them. I did the right thing on Makalu by turning back in the high winds. I thought I would be just another dead guy up there if I kept going.

There's a tremendous amount of on-the-spot decision making involved in processing that information. I'll give you an example of something that happened to me that was interesting. I started to cross the knife-edge ridge on Everest. It was scarier than I thought it would be. I was all set for the Hillary Step, which was 40 feet of rock climbing, no net, and 10,000 feet on both sides. I was ready for that. I'd been studying that for years. Nobody told me that the knife edge would be really pointed and really scary with huge drops on either side. It was about 100 yards long. I got into it and I went, "Holy—" you know. I'm thinking to myself, *Boy, I didn't plan on this.* I thought I knew every footstep of the summit day. Well, I didn't.

Accidents are never one event. They're usually a combination of things that happen beforehand. So, here's the scenario. I'm going across and I'm scared, so what do I do? Turn up the oxygen. You've got a little valve, and you think, *This'll give me a little go power. I'll get across the knife edge sooner and I'll turn it down.* So, I turned it up. I started moving and my goggles immediately fogged up.

The reason they fogged up was there was a teeny crack in the goggles and there was just enough extra heat coming off my body with the oxygen turned up, so they fogged right up. Now I can't see. So what do I do? Take my goggles off. If you take your goggles off at 28,000 feet on Mount Everest, you're going to be blind in twenty minutes. Then we're into this scenario: Are we going to help Rick, who's blind, or leave him behind? I put the goggles up and sure, I could see but I knew that my eyes would be damaged very quickly and I couldn't keep going like that. So what do you do? Turn down the oxygen. Less oxygen, less body heat, and then the goggles returned to normal.

The accident [report] would have read, "Rick tripped and fell off the ridge." But, he didn't trip and fall off. He turned up his oxygen, he couldn't see, he took off his goggles, he went snow-blind, then he fell off the ridge. You see? That's how it happens.

Not a Hero

Climbing Everest changed my life because I'm much more secure in my position in the mountaineering world. It was like one of those prerequisites to get checked off. Now, I don't feel like I have to perform any more for other people. Everything I could do from now on I'd do for me.

I've been able to go to places in the Himalaya that people don't go to. If I told you I went to the Langtang or the Garhwal or the Lo Monthang, you'd say, "Oh that's nice, but have you been to Mount Everest?" Everybody knows Mount Everest. Climbing Everest gave me the feeling that no longer did I have to worry about being a proficient high-altitude mountain climber. I am a proficient high-altitude mountain climber.

It gave me a financial boost too. I've always lived on the edge, financially, and the money that I've made lecturing about Mount Everest has put [my] kids through college and put food on my table. That's a part of the big picture. I'm not bashful to say that it was a blessing to summit Everest. I wonder how it would have gone if I had made it to the south summit and turned around like so many people have to, and come back just another guy who tried to climb Mount Everest. Maybe a few years later, I'd get it together to try again, but I was forty-three years old. I didn't want to be fifty-six or -eight when I was trying Everest. It was time to do it. I came back very relieved to enter into another world—the financial world of getting caught up on mortgages, credit cards with $20,000 on them, and a business that was floundering.

I went through the hero thing. I couldn't go buy groceries without people stopping me and saying, "Wow, you're the guy that climbed Mount Everest." That was all wonderful, but at the end of the day it doesn't change who you are, I hope. I'm not some kind of Superman. I'm a guy who did what I wanted to do and dedicated the commitment to it to make it happen.

Mountain People

You want to talk about money? Our checking account was overdrawn this morning. I don't have any other place I can get money except for this store. I've got kids in college calling me up saying, "I need another grand." OK, we go and we find it. I mean, I'm just a middle-class guy struggling through the business world and doing what I enjoy. I've met people that are in a different financial world than we are. But they're not happy. They're not as happy as we are. I think that the mountain people that I deal with, people that have dedicated their lives to what they really love, who live in the mountains, they don't make the money you could make in the city, but they're happier people. I see this in all these countries.

You talk about Pakistan, Tibet, and the Himalaya, and probably Afghanistan. When I've been up in the mountains dealing with porters and Sherpas and other local people, they are just like us. They want to work for a living; they want a day's pay. They don't care about politics, they don't care what religion you are. They just want to go into the mountains and get a day's pay. They live there and they love it and they're friendly and loyal and honest and they don't steal from you.

Getting Lost in the White Mountains

I never thought I could get lost in the White Mountains, but I did. I was guiding a winter range traverse. We had gone up Mount Madison to the Madison Hut, and we camped in the trees just below the hut. The weather wasn't very good.

Rick Wilcox sits on the cliff of Cathedral Ledge in Echo Lake State Park, overlooking the Saco River Valley, New Hampshire, in 2008. (Photo by Ned Therrien)

I took the group up to Star Lake and we were futzing around up there. I said, "It's time to go back to the camp," and I started across the Parapet Trail—that takes you over to the Osgood Trail and bypasses Madison—by accident! I'm just hiking along, and all of a sudden, the clouds came apart and what was supposed to be there was the Madison Hut—and it wasn't. There was this mountain over on the left and there was this ridge that went down here and nothing in my brain computed what I saw. It was like you had dropped me in the middle of the most remote mountain range in the world, and I just froze.

I had folks saying, "Great, Rick, where are we going now? Where's the hut?" And I'm like, "I don't know." I didn't know if I was going north, south, east, or west. So I turned around, and I said, "If I go back, I can get back to Star Lake and start over again." And I did. I went back, rearranged myself—there was a sign with an arrow, Hut This Way—and we figured it out.

How many people does that happen to, and then they just keep going? "Oh, we'll figure it out." You know, fortunately I made the right decision. Finally, they started asking me, "Rick, what was that all about? How come we went on that trail and we turned around and came back?" I said, "I made a wrong turn. I was lost." What was scary about it wasn't, "Oh darn, I'm on the wrong trail—it's back there, it's over to your right." It was like, "Where am I?" Fortunately, I haven't had that feeling too many times in the White Mountains.

My greatest fear in the mountains is being rescued by Mountain Rescue Service.[8] What I tell them is don't rush, because I carry a cyanide pill and they're not going to take me alive! No way.

Why the White Mountains?

The White Mountains have got everything.

Of course, I was raised in New England. I've enjoyed living here because, for me, the White Mountains have more dramatic seasons than anywhere. If you want to freeze to death, you go to Alaska; if you want to be hot, you go to the desert; you want good skiing, you go to Utah. But we have it all right here, with the exception of high-altitude peaks. We have Mount Washington. It's just as arctic a peak as Mount McKinley. We have skiing—in ski areas and in the woods. We have Tuckerman Ravine. We have the best, most accessible ice climbing in the whole country. We have excellent Conway granite for rock climbers. We have a trail system where you can hike your brains out.

I just think it has an awful lot to offer. But, in order to make a living here, you have to be very resourceful. I do at least four jobs. I run the store, I run the climbing school, I run my trips overseas, I do a lot of lecturing and occasionally a video or something, to make a few extra bucks. I'm also

---

[8] Wilcox is a co-founder of the Mountain Rescue Service.

a very independent person. I snowplow the road into my house. I can be a plumber, electrician, or carpenter. I cut my own firewood. I sort of like being less dependent on technology, other people, computers, stuff like that.

The Future

I'm slow to change. I'm not one of these guys, "Oh, change is great." I mean, I went through a nasty divorce; I've got a great wife now, and I never would have her today if it weren't for the nasty divorce, so sometimes the change is good.

I'm turning sixty in February and I get outdoors a lot. I still plan to do that for the next ten years, as long as I can, or lead guided trips to Africa and Asia. Yeah, I just did a trip to Nepal and every July we do a trip and safari to Kilimanjaro. I'm getting outdoors enough and certainly still roaming around the White Mountains and still finding places in the White Mountains that I've never been to before.

I have an option with Mammut to buy the store and the retail business—someday, maybe! And then I could be the landlord, own the building, and collect the rent. I might stay involved as a consultant. I don't know. This is sort of new water for me. I haven't thought much about retirement. I didn't plan very well for it. I don't have any trust funds or anything building up. I did make a college fund a few years ago for my kids, and it was all lost in the stock market. So I'm not very excited about that. Real estate's been good to me; my home in Eaton's gone up in value, and this store. Those are my only two real investments. And the business pays the bills every year and sort of breaks even. There's profit and nonprofit business. We're trying for profit.

I'm most proud of being a happy person who believes in honesty and who likes to go to work every day.

In addition to continuing to run International Mountain Equipment in North Conway, New Hampshire, Rick Wilcox is still climbing and hiking in the White Mountains and throughout the world. Along with his wife, Celia, Rick led his thirtieth trip to the Everest region of Nepal in 2012, his sixtieth expedition overall. You can find out more about Rick's guided trips at ime-usa.com.

Harry McDade

The Cold-Weather Doctor

Harry McDade is shown here in 1975, photographed by George Bellerose. (Photo courtesy of AMC Library & Archives)

B ORN IN 1924, Dr. Harry McDade of Littleton, New Hampshire, won renown as a surgeon and expert on cold-weather injuries, a mountaineer and climber, a pilot and amateur radio operator, and a botanist and ornithologist. His profession and passions took him around the world to climbs in Alaska, Mexico, Peru, Nepal, and Switzerland. Some of his greatest accomplishments, however, were here at home, where many residents of the North Country, as well as people from "away," owe life and limb to Harry McDade's talent as a physician.

Climbing with noted New England mountaineer Ad Carter on Alaska's Mount Foraker in 1963, McDade developed a lifelong love of the far north. Later expeditions included a 1973 trip with fellow adventurers Bill Nichols and Paul Doherty (see page 213), navigating a twin-engine Aztec 300 miles north of the Arctic Circle to photograph the wildlife and to fish for Arctic char.

We talked with McDade in July of 1994. At his Littleton office, we could not help but notice the citations and photographs that chronicled his life. His love for the mountains and their inhabitants was obvious not only in his stories, but in the particularly warm way in which he pointed out one of his favorite pictures, showing the Boyle family, residents and woodsmen of Lincoln, New Hampshire, each with a deer, "and Hannah Boyle, who walked to Lincoln through Carrigain Notch, shot a deer, and carried it out on her shoulder."

McDade's wife of twenty-two years, Connie, said that they met through their work but "turned out to be kindred spirits who shared the same love of the natural world." Together they raised two children, Donna and Ted.

In His Own Words

I grew up in Pennsylvania and first came up to the White Mountains as a child. Years later, when it came time to practice medicine, I really thought I wanted a rural practice, and first I landed in Lincoln, New Hampshire.

My old classmate, Ralph Parker, was practicing in Franconia. So, I picked up the phone and said, "Ralph, you need anyone up there?" It just so happened that Ralph had a place for me up in the mountains.

Everything seemed to crystallize, and I actually started full-time in Lincoln in March of 1949. I was there for about three years, and then I had to leave for the Korean War. When I got back, I spent five and a half years in a residency in surgery at Mary Hitchcock [Hospital] in Hanover. Following that, I was planning to go back to Plymouth Hospital, until Dr. Frank Dudley—a really good skier I knew from the mountains—said he needed someone up in Littleton. I said, "All right, that's even a little farther north!" I came back to Littleton and started here on January 1, 1959.

Mountains and Medicine

My interest in climbing and search and rescue really began when I was in the navy. I was stationed in Alameda, California, where I flew VR2s. We'd bring air evacs back through Oakland Naval Hospital. Those were long, lumping runs to Pearl Harbor—thirteen hours into the wind, twelve hours coming back, with four great big engines groaning away. When I was at Alameda on the weekends, I was always in the Sierra. I started climbing with the Sierra Club in Yosemite, with guys like Steve Roper.[9] We did some of those nice climbs on beautiful granite.

In 1959, when I got back to New Hampshire, it was the year when those two guys died on Cannon Mountain ridge. They had to bring up [climbers] Bill Putnam and John Perry and all that crew to help out. I volunteered to help, and I met everybody that way, including Roger Damon and Danny Brodien. For years, we were the three people who got called because we were the only ones close by.

In those days, the 1950s and '60s, most of the accidents were on Cannon Mountain. But there were lots of times people would get in trouble in the Presidentials, particularly in the winter. One time we spent three days when the wind was 130 MPH with 30-degree temperatures, trying to get to Edmands Col. We tried Caps Ridge [Trail], we tried pushing straight across, and then finally one of those troughs came through and we made a dash from the top of the mountain. We got the people off there and a chopper took them off the col. Lots of times I'd get a call at three in the morning saying someone's dead and he's still up there.

One time, I was in surgery, taking a cancer out of a guy's lip. I had his mouth all apart. Bill Norton of Franconia Notch State Park called and said,

---

[9] Roper went on to become one of the best-known climbers in the western United States, and was a noted writer and editor.

"Somebody's trapped up on the arches right by Echo Lake, on the Lakeview climb. And they don't have any climbing gear!" These guys had read about climbing, and they went up to Cannon on a clear day. Then, all of a sudden, it started misting rain. They were in street shoes, with no climbing gear, and they were literally hanging there in midair.

With the impetus of Bill Putnam, we got a lot of the forestry people and the guys on Cannon Mountain Ski Patrol, so they could come up second on a rope. We had to go up into all the duff that hangs there; that stuff's floating, and there's nothing to drive any protection into. So, we had a spider web of ropes. We went all the way back into the pucker brush and tied in, then we had to pendulum all the way over to the climbers. Then—the climbers wouldn't let go! But, anyhow, we had another rope. We got 'em on there and hauled 'em up, one at a time.

Of course, I fixed up the guy with cancer first. First things first!

Each rescue has its own unique tale. You see the end results, and you see all the things that go into these accidents—the cascade of events that causes them.

I envision a mountaineer as somebody who's really at home in the mountains, as someone who's sensitive to the environment. Today, we have produced a generation of what I call "rock gymnasts"—people who would possibly be better off on some of these artificial climbing walls, rather than subjecting themselves to the vagaries of nature. There is a lot of objective danger in climbing—anything from icefall to avalanches, bad pitons, rock that comes out due to frost action, lightning strikes. If you're going to climb, you've got to face some of those dangers—there's no question about that. It's not like lying on the sofa watching a ballgame. The mountains are a place for humbleness, but today we see so much arrogance.

I did a fair amount of climbing with Ad Carter. We climbed in the Alaska Range, in Europe and the Andes, where we did some first ascents. We were getting to high altitudes—20,000 feet and above. I was supposed to be the doc on the expedition, so I figured I'd better know something about mountain medicine.

Later, back in the Whites, we used to work our butts off getting somebody down in a litter. Then everybody else would go home, and I would go take a shower, get in the scrub suit, and fix them! I learned by having the need to learn—by having it all dumped on me. And I learned from colleagues; colleagues in Alaska and, of course, from Dr. Murray Hamlett.[10] I'd get and make calls from and to all over to discuss a case or ask questions. I've even had calls from the Himalaya.

Off on His Own—The Pemi

I often hiked solo because I had nobody to climb with. Those were some of my favorite hikes. I'd get a break from work, I'd skip a bandage in the hospital, get a break in the weather, and go. Lots of times, I'd go to the Pemigewasset—climbing, and botanizing everything that was around the climb—and I'd be in there a couple of weeks at a time. I learned the Pemi inside out from the old-timers who knew it.

Then they had a good trail into Carrigain Pond, and if you went into the old twenty-one landings and went up over the landings, there was a two-sled road. I bet you can still see the blazes.

I talked to old Quint Boyle, who used to be the scaler there.[11] You know where you go through the falls there, then you go up and the river sort of bends and then goes up and gets out of the ledges, but there's a great big white pine there? Abe Boyle left that. These people were very sensitive to the terrain.

When you're going up toward Camp 18, there's a little brook you cross— Crystal Brook. It's so cold it almost makes your teeth hurt. Billy the Bear's son, Don Boyle, one of the logging bosses, used to put his pack down there and look at that and say, "Isn't that beautiful?" And these were the guys who were doing the logging!

Most times in the Pemi, I wouldn't see anyone except guys like Monk McCloud, who was a real character. If you wanted to know where something was in the Pemi, you'd ask Monk. He was one of the Lincoln people who got into difficulties when he was in basic training for World War II. They were out in the West and digging foxholes when they got outmaneuvered. Well, Monk dove into his foxhole, with about three rattlesnakes. He got himself all chewed up, and had all sorts of toxic reactions. I guess he damn near died. He was never quite right afterward, as they said. I think

---

[10]   A well-known expert on hypothermia and cold-weather injuries.
[11]   A scaler measures logs on a timber harvesting job.

Monk was always Monk—but he didn't argue with them. He got a retirement and went off and lived in the woods.

Another time, during a break in my residency at Hanover, I went into Zealand Valley when there used to be a camp at Stillwater. The Boyles had a camp there, which they'd built from boards left over from the original Parker Young logging camp. It would sleep six comfortably. The camp was always stocked, and you reached underneath the floor to get the key. I went in there and stayed overnight with my Newfoundland, Bosun. Then it began to snow.

Today, the trail goes around the little peninsula, but in those days you went straight through Camp 18, across the river, and up a very steep bank. There used to be a cable trolley there, which you could use to yank yourself across. The camp was 8 miles in, on this little peninsula where Stillwater Junction comes around, then makes a turn, and Anderson and Carrigain brooks come in.

I was planning to go through to Lincoln. Well, at that time the woods were regrown just enough after being logged that they didn't keep much snow off the railroad track. The footing along the tracks wasn't very good, so I tried to walk down the river. But then I was afraid I was going to lose the dog into the ice. Bosun was a big dog, at least 150 pounds or so, and he was carrying his pack. We didn't make very fast progress and I only got out as far as Camp 7—Franconia Brook Shelter at that time. Well, the guys in Lincoln knew I was up there, and they got worried. They got the town plow, and plowed it out all the way up to Camp 4 bridge. Then they got a toboggan brigade together. I got down to where Birch Allen Brook comes in and heard these guys talking! Poor Bosun was exhausted by that time. He got on that toboggan, put his feet right on the curve and groaned, "Aaahhh!" He didn't move. It wasn't really a rescue, but it sure was a big help.

Sometimes, my trips into the Pemi would be interrupted. One time, I was at the little camp at Stillwater. I had gone in there for one of my couple-of-week stints in June—I've always loved June, because that's when birds are nesting and all the good plants are in flower. Anyway, I went in with Don Boyle, and at three in the morning Don's son came in and told me that somebody was hemorrhaging and they needed me at the hospital. I left Bosun with Don, grabbed my pack, and got down to Lincoln. They drove

Harry McDade mans his ham radio station at his home in Littleton, New Hampshire, 1995. (Photo by Jonathan Kannair, jonathankannair.com)

me to the hospital, I put my pack in the scrub room, took a shower, got some black coffee, shaved, saw the guy, and did a gastrectomy on him.

I was stuck for two or three weeks in post-op care with him. It was one of those nightmare hemorrhages. He had visited his brother up to Three Rivers, Quebec, and they said, "You want to clean them ulcers up, you take some hydrogen peroxide." So, this fellow drank a couple bottles of hydrogen peroxide. It turned his stomach into a bloody wet cave. We used thirty units of blood on him before we were done with him.

The [U.S.] Forest Service burned that Stillwater camp down when they turned the Pemi into a wilderness. We had managed to keep the camp hidden until the snow machines came along, and then some of the younger people at Lincoln were too lazy to go in and brush up the snowshoe tracks. Those tracks led the Forest Service right to the camp. They had spent thirty years looking for that place!

Birds and Change

Of course, the mountains are a lot more to me than just rescues and frost-bite. I do enjoy the botany and ornithology. I guess my family was always interested in birds. Nobody ever said, "Look at the birdie," they'd say, "Look at the northern yellowthroat." I grew up like that. Ornithology was always a major interest in my life. I've been banding birds for the Fish and Wildlife Service for thirty-some-odd years. I also do blood specimens on the birds, looking for blood-borne parasites. That's a spring ritual of sorts. I used to band upstairs in my office in Lincoln, and then come down for office hours. I'm putting together thirty-seven years of data.

I've seen many changes in the White Mountains, most of them population driven. In the old days, when you'd see somebody parked near the trail, you'd think, *Maybe we'll go someplace else today.*

Recently, I was shocked to see something like seven cars at the Greeley Pond Trail. That turned me off. So, I went down to the East Pond Trail. There was nobody at the trailhead, but there was all this broken glass from where someone had broken into cars and stolen the radios. That really turns me off. East Pond was always a lovely spot with a little pine brook. I used to sneak in there sometimes for a quick overnight, just to get away and be in the woods, catch a trout, have him for breakfast, and be on my way. You can't do that anymore.

When I was in Lincoln I used to go up in the Lincoln Woods, where there was a little microenvironment that was very interesting. I did a lot of banding work up in there, and the place had a lot of botany I was interested in. I'd spend a couple of weeks at a time in there. You'd never see anybody, except maybe Monk McCloud or some of the old natives who practically lived off the land. In those days, you could put your pack down and it would be there when you came back. Now, you don't dare turn your back. I'm really saddened by this.

You used to be able to go, grab your sleeping bag and ground sheet, and head someplace. There was almost always a shelter you could get into, so you didn't have to lug a tent. Now, you ought to have a tent if you're going to a shelter, because the odds are the shelter's going to be full. And for people with limited means, for young people who don't have a lot of bucks, it costs more in equipment than it ought to to enjoy an overnight.

It was also nice when you didn't have to lug around an air mattress or a whole hunk of Ensolite—when you could cut a couple of boughs and throw them down, and you really didn't hurt anything by doing that. You weren't deforesting the area, since there wasn't anybody else to deforest it! The boughs went butt down and bow up, so you'd have spring in them. It really smelled good! Obviously, you can't have that anymore.

I hate to see the Forest Service restrict use, but in some areas you have to do that. I'd hate to have somebody tell me I couldn't go in the woods. Maybe the answer is that Smokey Bear ought to be able to curl up a lip and show a tooth every once in a while. I think maybe we really ought to have some teeth in the rules, and have knowledgeable people who understand that you're not dealing with Davy Crockett and Daniel Boone but some city slicker who's coming up and doesn't understand what he's trying to do. It's an educational thing, but there are times you make him stop and clean up.

Despite all this, what makes the White Mountains special, first of all, is that there are still reasonable tracts of wild country. The Whites lend themselves to some of the larger animals and critters that require a fairly large territory to range in. You can see a bear, you can see moose. It used to be that you could see a lynx, and today you can still find a wildcat. Some places, you can still see a pine martin if you're lucky. In the old days it was exciting when you'd see moose track; now we see moose all the time. Seeing the moose come back is exciting. I like to see 'em. Even if I gotta drive slow in the fog.

The future of the White Mountains is going to be affected by people. For example, the *Potentilla robbinsiana* on the trail on top of Lafayette Ridge: Fred Steele[12] and I found a few plants that we recorded, but I've been back several times and have not seen 'em since. Then there's the water supply, with people pooping all over the place up there. Nowadays, I wouldn't think about a long trip without having available water. Those are the sorts of difficulties the Whites are going to face.

And then, of course, just like the Pemi right now, you get just a couple of people who are careless and you end up with a couple of bears around that make your life a little bit uncomfortable. It isn't the bears' fault. We're

---

[12] Frederic L. Steele, noted alpine botanist and author of *At Timberline: A Nature Guide to the Mountains of the Northeast* (AMC Books, 1994).

in their terrain, and we should act accordingly. But, we have people who for most of their lives are so far removed from the mountains that they're not sensitive to these things.

Keeping On

As for my own future, I have a fairly heavy operating schedule. I enjoy what I do—but I hate the environment I have to do it in: third-party carriers, the government second-guessing you. They're wasting medicine, period. I fix people. I'm practicing. As long as it stays intellectually honest, I can put up with it.

I'll also keep flying. I've got to get into the high north again. I'd like to get out sometime to Coral Harbor, on Southampton Island in Hudson Bay. There's a very large walrus colony up there. Sometime, I might crank the Aztec up and go do that. I'd also like to get back to Alaska and get out by Kantishna.

If you ask me what I'm most proud of, I'd say it's just, because a few of us lived close by, that we could get to someone who was in trouble in the mountains—before they could get hypothermic. We probably saved a life or two. So, I think maybe I've gotten a little reward seeing someone walk away a little less injured than they would have been.

We're up here because we love it. "*Dum vivimus vivamus*: While we live, let us live." Have a little fun as you go along.

Harry McDade took his last big flying trip in 1990, to Alaska on a fishing expedition with his wife, Connie. He received many professional and personal honors in his lifetime, including the 1995 New England Surgical Society's Nathan Smith Award. Harry died on October 13, 1997, at age seventy-three.

Section Two

Conservation and Wildland Ethics

Guy and Laura Waterman

Pioneers of Wilderness Ethics

Guy and Laura Waterman take a short break in the pea patch at "Barra," their home-stead in East Corinth, Vermont, in 1994. (Photo by Jonathan Kannair, jonathankannair.com)

F OR MANY PEOPLE IN NEW ENGLAND AND BEYOND, discussions of wilderness cannot take place without mentioning the writings of Guy and Laura Waterman. Their books *Backwoods Ethics* (1979) and *Wilderness Ethics* (1993) forced many among us to consider exactly what wilderness means in today's world of technology and growth. While such considerations have not always provided comfort, they have always been illuminating.

Accomplished writers, climbers, and homesteaders on twenty-seven acres in Vermont, Guy and Laura Waterman lived more lives than many of us combined. Some of Guy's exploits included working as a Washington, D.C., speechwriter for two United States senators who each later became president and for Dwight Eisenhower after he left office. He was also a professional jazz piano player, and a corporate speechwriter for General Electric. Laura worked for several New York publishing houses before becoming the first editor at *Backpacker* magazine. Having given up their lives in "mainstream" America in 1973 for their remote homestead, they lived there without running water or electricity for nearly thirty years.

When not tending their land, the Watermans spent more than thirty years hiking and climbing in the White Mountains, with several first ascents to their credit. With their first book, *Backwoods Ethics,* they became leaders in the low-impact backpacking movement, later called Leave No Trace. Authorities on the history of Northeastern climbing and hiking, they became outspoken voices for protecting our wild places and experiences from the crush of human technology.

We spoke with Laura and Guy in 1998, at their Vermont homestead, and found that their lives may be best reflected in Laura's words: "It's important for people to be responsible to themselves for themselves, make their own decisions and live by them. If something needs to be changed, see that and then change it. Be adaptable, but have values."

In Their Own Words

LAURA: My first encounter with the White Mountains was when I came as a counselor with Cragged Mountain Camp in 1958 and '59. We stayed at Carter Notch Hut, and I thought it was one of the greatest things that had ever happened to me. We swam in the lake, and the hut boys took us out to the boulders. I started hanging around with one of the hut boys. It was a weekend romance. We climbed Wildcat and Carter Dome—a pretty standard camp trip, and then that was the end of it. I didn't dream of coming back. Women couldn't work in the huts in those days, so I did other things.

GUY: My parents took me up [Mount] Chocorua and Mount Washington in 1945. My father was an outdoorsperson, but his main focus was the Maine woods and canoeing the lakes up in northern Maine. He was mildly interested in climbing, so occasionally he'd get me up Chocorua or Mount Washington. I used to spend a long time in the woods with him. When I was a kid, I used to play in the woods all the time.

Later, I went through a long period where I was a night person—the years where I was a nightclub piano player and then in politics—and not interested in the outdoors. Then, slowly I realized that really wasn't where my fundamental interests lay, and I got back to playing in the woods again. I started coming back in 1963. Beginning in '64 I used to come up with my sons every summer.

The actual turning point that made me realize I wanted to be out of Washington, D.C., and in the outdoors was when I read a book called *The Climb Up to Hell,* which is the account of all the deaths on the Eiger. From then on, I started hiking wherever I could find places to hike, and then I started climbing. I met Laura climbing in the Shawangunks in the Hudson Valley. I was an instructor that particular weekend. We began to climb together a lot. We climbed in the Gunks all the time and went up to the Adirondacks in the winter. We also started hiking together. At the Shawangunks, I asked Laura to marry me.

LAURA: And I said, "Yes."

GUY: A lot of people ask us why we gave up our jobs in New York—mine as a speechwriter for General Electric and Laura's as an editor with Backpacker magazine—to homestead in Vermont, to live without electricity or running water. Well, during that eighteen-year period when I was focused on other things, I had realized that I didn't want to spend the rest of my life working in New York City, working for a big company. I had always liked the idea of living a much simpler life in the woods, away from all the pressures of society that didn't appeal to me. But Laura and I always figured that to live successfully so, you'd exchange one kind of drudgery for another—you'd have to work all the time just to grow your food.

The event that tipped the scales for us was when I went climbing one weekend with a very good friend of ours, Brad Snyder. We were in Mount Washington's Huntington Ravine, and he had just been reading a book by Helen and Scott Nearing, *Living the Good Life*. He said, "You ought to read this book." We spent that weekend, when we weren't climbing, talking about what you could usefully do in life. So Laura and I both read *Living the Good Life*. A number of things the Nearings said made us realize that it was possible not to have to work all the time to keep your head above water if you were living like this. They had organized their lives in such a way that they had plenty of time for music and writing, and to do the creative things they liked to do as well as the homesteading.

So, while there are a lot of things we do differently from the Nearings, we really feel very grateful to them for pointing the way. We always honor the day on which Brad Snyder told us about the book as the start and the germination of what we call the anniversary of the "Idea of Barra."[13]

LAURA: The transition of moving here was really pretty easy. It was everything we'd wanted it to be. It was right for us. However, a lot of people were very skeptical about our being able to live this way. Guy's coworkers at General Electric thought he'd be back in six months.

GUY: And I think they all wanted me to be back. They didn't want to know that it could work, that you could leave corporate America. For a lot of people to move up here in winter, with no electricity and no plumbing and so forth, would really be a hardship. But for us—we had been going winter camping every weekend. Now we had the luxury of an outhouse!

We really fell in love with the White Mountains. It's in my nature not to want to dabble.... I mean, some people sort of take the approach of *I've seen these mountains, now I'd like to see some others*. Some people go [out] West every summer. But Laura and I decided early—in part for financial reasons,

---

[13] "Barra," the Watermans' homestead, was named for the Scottish island of Barra.

Laura saws firewood during sugaring season, 1998. (Photo by Ned Therrien)

which made it impossible for us to go out West—that we wanted to get to know one area in great depth, rather than dabble in different ranges. The White Mountains were one area that I had been growing very attached to from those summers with my sons. We had come up some in winter too. We had some exciting times in winter up here! Once we moved here, I was really glad to renew the close association with the White Mountains.

LAURA: Every trip we've taken in the White Mountains has been great. I mean, literally every trip. There are some, of course, that stand out!

GUY: Our life here is very seasonal, one that allows time for hiking and climbing. January through the end of February or the first week in March is available for us to go winter climbing, and we use that time to our avail. We'll go out climbing as much as we can and then come back and get things dry. Then there's a month of sugaring. Next, there's about a two-week interval between sugaring and getting the garden started—we used to go to the Gunks for many years during that period. Then we're tied down by the gardening between the end of April and the first part of June. After that we'll do some climbing and hiking in the summer months, and then, as soon as we harvest the freezables, we'll get in a week trip. Later, we have other vegetables to get in and the firewood to finish. But when that's done, by around Thanksgiving, we have a certain amount of time for hiking. We're not hiking so much these days, but at one point I estimated that we were in the mountains on fifty percent of the winter days, and we were sleeping in the mountains one night out of three.

My love of hiking and climbing led me to the Appalachian Mountain Club. In the late 1970s I was very active in the AMC. One of the issues then was the hiring of women. It was also when decisions were being made to expand the use of helicopters and two-way radios in the huts.

My son Johnny, who was especially interested in climbing, first drew my attention to some of these issues [during this period] when he told me he didn't want to be an AMC member anymore. I mean, he explicitly did not want to be associated with AMC anymore, wanted to drop his membership. When that happened I wrote a long letter addressed, I think, to Fran Belcher[14]—I have it in the files still—saying that my son John doesn't want to be a member of the club anymore, and this should give us reason to wonder, *What's going on here?* Here's a guy who loves the mountains, wants to devote his life to the mountains and climbing, and he doesn't want to be a member of AMC. He doesn't just not want to be a member himself; he doesn't want me to send in the money to keep him a member. Doesn't this raise questions for us? Johnny's concerns were about the civilizing of the mountains, about bringing too much in the way of radios, helicopters, that kind of thing, to the mountains. I think the kind of things that still bother people a lot bothered Johnny a lot...and they still bother me.

LAURA: We really feel it's important not just to complain about how the mountains are managed but to give something back ourselves. Mainly because we were a little unhappy with the work that the AMC trail crew had done building scree walls in 1977, we began doing trail work on the Franconia Ridge in 1980. We felt that building walls was a very drastic measure, that possibly other means should've been tried first, like some kind of education to get across the point of staying on trail and not walking on the plants.

---

[14] AMC's first executive director; see page 149 for his story.

GUY: We worked on the Franconia Ridge for fifteen seasons, and we learned an awful lot about what could be done with physical obstacles to induce people to stay on trail or to keep them off of the vegetation. We learned that the scree walls had a function and that we could live with them. We also quickly learned that scree walls alone would not do the job. We saw that people were still going off trail in many places; that it needed something besides scree walls. Good, well-placed cairns are essential to keeping people on the trail and off of the fragile vegetation.

LAURA: We also learned that educational signs are very important, but what we don't have in the White Mountains that has been key in the Green Mountains and the Adirondacks is an on-site presence—a person up there to talk to hikers.[15] All of these experiences hiking and climbing, and my original job with *Backpacker* magazine, led us to writing about the mountains. When we first started homesteading, Bill Kemsley from *Backpacker* realized that we were going to be spending the summer outdoors building our house, and he said "You have to eat, right? I'd like you to test and write about freeze-dried food." So, we ordered freeze-dried food from all the various companies, and we ate it to do taste comparisons. I think I've blotted the taste of freeze-dried food out of my memory!

GUY: From those columns we started writing occasional pieces. Our philosophy has always been anybody who wants to come is welcome, and we really enjoy seeing people experience mountains, but we don't need to drum up trade! And so we addressed our column only to people already going to the mountains.

LAURA: We had a great deal of fun with that. We wrote about places all over New England. We were really careful not to attract people, and we never wrote about what we considered the secret places.

---

[15] Together, AMC and the White Mountain National Forest launched such a program in 2000.

GUY: We got one very important thing out of writing for a magazine called *New England Outdoors*. Their objective was to unify the backcountry users, so we had to write for an audience that included hunters and fishers. It taught us tolerance. It taught us that we are all in the outdoors together and that instead of picking fights with each other, we should try to see what the common ground is.

LAURA: Our columns led to our books *Backwoods Ethics, Wilderness Ethics, Yankee Rock and Ice,* and *Forest and Crag. Backwoods Ethics* didn't get much promotion, and the numbers of circulation weren't large. But it continued to sell a little bit, for year after year after year. The National Park Service, for instance, picked it up and carried it in all their stores, even out West. And while we felt a lot of people didn't see it—we would've loved to see it promoted—we felt the right people were reading it. We felt it was having an impact on policy in the White Mountains and elsewhere. In a way, the fact that *Backwoods Ethics* wasn't immediately on the bestseller list didn't bother us because we had already latched on to the idea of doing *Forest and Crag*, a history of climbing and hiking in the Northeast.

GUY: *Forest and Crag* turned into a ten-year project—something we'd never expected. It was very joyous and extremely frustrating. It was positive but difficult, with a lot of hard and discouraging moments. We won't go into the hard moments!

One of the high points of writing *Forest and Crag* was getting to meet Thelma Bonney. The Boston AMC had a rock-climbing contingent during the 1930s which was mostly upper-crust Boston. During our research, we'd go and visit them. We'd be going to Belmont [Massachusetts] and these manicured lawns and shrubs placed in just the right places and these very handsome homes, and very nice people—Boston patricians—and they'd all say, "You have to meet Thelma, Thelma Q. Bonney!" So we got her address and got in touch with her. She lived in a trailer park in Peabody, where the next trailers were ten feet away on each side. As it turned out, she [had] worked in the mills in Lowell, and somehow she got in touch with the AMC and wanted to go climbing. She had climbed with all these people from the upper crust, and she was just a wonderful person. It was quite clear from talking with everybody else that everybody loved Thelma. When we said we'd seen Thelma or were going to see Thelma, these people living in these beautiful houses in Belmont would say, "Oh, please give her our best!"

LAURA: One thing that kept *Forest and Crag* going was that we were far enough into it that we felt we had almost an obligation to the people who had invested time with us to keep going.

GUY: Our other book, *Wilderness Ethics,* became a discussion of, *What do we really want in the backcountry?* We ask people to think. We say throughout the book, we don't care if you agree with us on specific issues as long as you're thinking about these things. We don't want people casually saying to increase the use of radios in the backcountry without realizing that it has a cost.

A very important issue that we tried to raise in *Wilderness Ethics* is the relationship between communication and wildness. So often people's thoughts about communication are poorly thought out—as if there's nothing wrong with increased communication. If you can get into the backcountry faster, why not? If you can contact people who are in trouble in the backcountry, why not? We tried to get people to think. We wrote in *Wilderness Ethics* that an attribute of wildness is that you're not in communication with the outside world—that this is a very important experience. So, when we think about what we see for the future, I think one key area that nobody knows the answer to as to what'll happen, but it's really something we ought to think about, is the technology for communication. It's just racing along: cellular phones and very, very light radios and the developments in accessibility; the lighter and lighter helicopters and now the various devices for soaring, the hang gliders—all of this stuff now for people who go technical-climbing, reach the top of a peak, and then soar back toward the road. A lot of them say, "Why not?" People are using mountain bikes to get to locations that were once very hard to get to: "Why not?"

People have to stop and think: *What kind of backcountry do we want?* Do we want just a gymnasium where we can go do all these things fast and get out fast, or is it the essential quality to the backcountry that it takes awhile to get there, and it takes awhile to get back out? Isn't that an important part of it? People say, "Well, if you've got it, use it." Not necessarily! I mean, we've

Guy Waterman wears his signature Scottish balmoral hat, circa 1990. (Photo courtesy of Laura Waterman)

got the technology to build roads through all the wilderness areas, and we don't do that. We obviously make a decision. We have some technology that we will not use. And I would hope that [with] the technology unfolding in communication and aircraft accessibility, that we'll have the restraint that if we want to preserve a particular kind of backcountry, we cannot use those things. That's the thing that really concerns us about the future: Will we have the restraint to not necessarily use all this technology?

Somebody said we have an open mind, but it isn't empty. In *Wilderness Ethics* we present a point of view. We all want to preserve the backcountry as an area different from the "frontcountry," if you will. If we only stop and think about it, we all really do want to preserve the spirit of wildness out there, and we're all not going to come to very different conclusions if we really think hard about it. So we do feel people would agree with us a lot if they'd only think about it! We don't want the issues to be dependent on Laura and Guy Waterman going around and saying, "This is what you do." We want people to sit down, maybe having been inspired by our book, and think through the issues themselves. I would say we've been really pleased with *Wilderness Ethics* because we've had a lot of indications that many people are thinking hard about the issues. The Appalachian Trail Conference and the Green Mountain Club both have had not just one but a succession of discussions at different levels in the clubs. The Appalachian Trail Conference sent the book to every member of their board of governors and asked them to read it and be prepared to discuss it at the next meeting. So people are trying to think, *How do these issues affect how we run the Appalachian Trail, how we run the Long Trail?* And we could not feel any better.

LAURA: I'm sure there is a connection between our appeal for a wilderness ethic and the lifestyle we lead. We believe a land ethic begins at home, and we're concentrating on our own twenty-seven acres. It's important for people to be responsible to themselves for themselves, make their own decisions and live by them. If something needs to be changed, see that and then change it. Be adaptable, but have values. And I think that's what we felt when we moved up here. In the backcountry too, people should have a vision of what they want the backcountry to be and then move forward with that, adapt it to the circumstances. And feel a sense of responsibility—here we feel responsible for the land, and we want to do as well by our twenty-seven acres as we can. The managers in the mountains and the hikers should feel that when they walk into the forest, they want to be as responsible in their actions as they can be. I think you get so much more out of what you're doing, in your life or in your trip to the mountains, if you feel that way about it.

We feel this responsibility to all wild places, but there is something special about the White Mountains. I just remember back to when I was a senior in high school and going up to Carter Notch. I'd never seen anything like that in my life. The hugeness of the boulders and the random jumbleness to it, with high mountains on either side—but it was all organized in the way that nature is. It went straight to my heart. If you spend years and years in [the White Mountains], you can find out their secrets and their beauties.

GUY: Two things make the White Mountains particularly special to me. I think one is that any place that any individual hikes a lot becomes special to that individual, so in a sense the White Mountains are special to us in a way that any mountain range can be special to the people closest to that range. It doesn't mean they're unique, but they're unique for us.

But then I think also there is this incredible wind in the White Mountains. It's just in a class by itself. People who've been to many different ranges all tell us that they've never encountered anything like it, and it's just routine up there, especially in winter. It's just so impressive! Day after day. Sixty to eighty mile an hour winds! And, of course, sometimes much worse.

LAURA: And you get used to it!

GUY: And to make that world your own and to feel comfortable in that world is just such an exciting thing. When you have experience in dealing with those conditions a lot, you can go up there, and you can be in that wind and weather, hour after hour, in terribly demanding terrain. But just barely!

I don't think of myself as ever going out there to conquer a mountain. It seems to me the mountains, when they want to, always show who's boss. When you succeed in doing a technically difficult climb or a climb in very severe weather, you feel grateful that you were able to have the opportunity to do that. You feel very humble in the sight of this very impressive thing.

George Mallory said, "Have we conquered the mountain? None but ourselves. Have we conquered enemies? There's none but ourselves. And so, we've conquered our own frailties." I think that applies to how we feel about the mountains, that there should be a tremendous respect for the land and for the beautiful places.

LAURA: Of course we've seen some changes over the years. Today we certainly see greater numbers of people using the White Mountains. Everyone would agree to that, I think.

GUY: Especially numbers of people in winter. People seem to be looking for challenges in the outdoors. And the outdoor-equipment industry has rushed in to say, "Oh! We have all these things which will do this and do that for you." They promote the idea that it's the equipment that makes it possible for you to do the climb. And a lot of these people up there think it is. They'll have all the latest packs and all the gadgets and all the latest fabrics. When I was winter caretaking at the Gray Knob cabin on Mount

Adams, a bunch of guests were talking, deploring the price of one-piece Gore-Tex suits and how it's hard to afford them. Then one of them said, "But of course, if you're going to be up here much, you have to have it." And I'm sitting there in my scratchy wool mitts, shirt, and my Air Force flight pants, and those guys don't get up there as much as I do.

LAURA: I think there are also positive changes; people are showing more care and concern for the mountains, especially in the alpine areas.

GUY: More and more, people have the message to stay on the trail.

LAURA: And they're spreading the word. There is just a huge number of hikers out there who feel they want to give something back to the mountains, and they're doing it through trail work. There could be more! There could be more!

I'm guardedly optimistic about the future. Almost all our friends we've met in the White Mountains. And, you know, those are lifelong friendships, and somehow it's very, very important to us, the friendships that we've formed. They're people who care about the White Mountains. We're very hopeful. I mean, everyone feels such a sense of commitment and stewardship to the mountains' future that it's being carried on.

GUY: Somebody said an optimist thinks this is the best of all possible worlds, and a pessimist fears that's true. My feelings about the future depend on the mood I'm in. I think a lot of times I could really be quite pessimistic. There's so much technology, and there are so many people who just don't see anything wrong with using it. But then, on the other hand, sometimes I realize a lot of people are all working hard to preserve these good values. One thing I think is very encouraging is we see so many young people coming along and they have some very good values. Maybe it's a fundamental thing, that people have good values and realize that the mountains ought to be a certain kind of place.

LAURA: For our own future we are very happy tending our twenty-seven acres. Guy can get to the mountains more easily than me and my knees. But that doesn't mean we're walking away from the mountains by any matter or means. In fact, I go rock climbing when I have the opportunity. Going hiking less has opened up a new road for me. I'm writing short fiction now, and I can tell you it's just about as exhilarating to have a story accepted for publication as it is to reach the summit of Mount Adams on a blowy day in winter. That, and working in our gardens, our wood lot. Oh, "it's a good life if you don't weaken," that's what that amazing, hard-driving Don Whillans said, the British climber. It always makes me laugh. And Guy still bushwhacks up stream valleys.

GUY: Yeah, I still can bushwhack, but I'd rather have Laura without mountains than mountains without Laura. What really pleases us is to spend the days that we have right here working on our land and trying to make this land a better place.

In addition to pursuing his lifelong love of baseball through the Society for American Baseball Research, Guy Waterman collaborated with Laura on a collection of mountaineering stories called A Fine Kind of Madness: Mountain Adventures True and Tall, *which was published in 2000. On February 6, 2000, Guy Waterman hiked up Franconia Ridge in the White Mountains and intentionally froze to death. He was sixty-six years old.*

Laura Waterman continues to hike and climb. Her memoir, Losing the Garden, *about her homesteading life with Guy and his long-planned suicide, was published in 2005. She's currently working on a novel about the 1881–1884 Greely Arctic expedition. Shortly after Guy's death, Laura joined with several friends in founding the Waterman Fund. The fund's mission is to support education and stewardship to preserve the alpine areas of the Northeast. To learn more about the fund visit watermanfund.org.*

George Zink

Mentor, Scholar, and Wilderness Lover

At the Wonalancet Out Door Club celebration of the Sandwich Range Wilderness designation, George and Sally Zink are presented with T-shirts, July 1984. (Photo courtesy of Sally Zink)

W E INTERVIEWED GEORGE ZINK IN 2006, when at age eighty-eight, he remained very much an agitator. He told us, "I have the feeling that Hamlet expressed: 'The world is out of joint. O cursed spite, that I was ever born to set it right!' I'm always saying, 'That needs fixing. What can I do to fix it?'"

Agitation is for naught, however, without persistence—and Zink had plenty of that too. Those two forces, at play over decades, made Zink a leading advocate for a variety of thoughtful stewardship policies in the White Mountains.

His tireless efforts are best known for leading to congressional designation of the Sandwich Range Wilderness in 1984. Known as the "Father of the Sandwich Range Wilderness," Zink politely demurred about the title, preferring to share it with others who contributed to the designation.

It was not uncommon for Zink, who was remarkably well read, to intersperse metaphors from literature with examples from science, woven together with a historical anecdote. Through it all, one sensed the importance of community engagement to Zink, and an omnipresent enthusiasm. "I think it important for an individual to become involved— to find something that is meaningful to him and do it," he said.

To the great surprise of George Zink alone, he was recognized by the U.S. Forest Service for his influence on many wilderness managers, young people, and volunteers when he was honored with the Forest Service Eastern Region's Individual Champion of Wilderness Award in 2000.

But wilderness advocacy was only one part of his varied life. A teacher for more than forty years, George helped to shape and influence countless lives. Trained to teach English, he found himself instead in a chemistry classroom. "English came easily, so I didn't always empathize with the students' needs. But in chemistry, with which I'd struggled as a student and never done very well, I could empathize."

We talked with George at the home he, his wife, Sally, and their four children built. The house was filled with books and testaments to George's love of mountains and his lifetime of being involved.

In His Own Words

My background is rather ordinary. Neither of my parents had gone to college. My father hadn't graduated from high school. But, they had a great love of learning. Of course, that made a great difference in my life. I grew up in Ballard Vale, a rural community that is a section of Andover, Massachusetts, about five miles from the town center. It was in the country but not isolated. I was the second son. I have a brother four years older and a brother two years younger. No girls, darn it!

We had a large vegetable garden. My mother canned vegetables and fruits to last through the winter. We raised chickens, ducks, pigs, and pigeons. My father raised pansy plants, which my younger brother and I marketed throughout the community, hauling the plants on our cart.

I was a loner. When I came home from school, I'd spend the whole afternoon out in the woods. There were miles of woods around then. So, I was an outdoor person from the earliest days. My father and I learned all the visible constellations, and borrowed the high school's telescope to observe the moon and planets. I caught frogs and snakes that were housed in deep barrels, had an herbarium and a collection of butterflies and bugs. I loved to go out "hunting" with my bow and arrows. Just a regular country boy, I'd say.

I was a mediocre student, and I was unsuccessful in high school sports. I was small in high school, only about 5-foot, 5-inches and weighed about 112 pounds. The only competitive sports were basketball and football, and a short, light person isn't going to be very good at either one. I was a master of nothing. But I always got involved and did my best.

Climbing with Fred

There was one man who was a strong influence on my early life, the Reverend Frederick B. Noss. Fred had a great interest in mountain climbing. He loved to be out-of-doors and he loved to hike. He was the minister of the church that sponsored the Scout troop that I was in, and my family was very active in Boy Scouts. My brothers and I all became Eagle Scouts.

The first mountain I ever climbed was Monadnock, because we could get there easily from Andover. With Fred Noss, we usually hiked in the Sandwich Range. It's the southernmost of the Whites, and the shortest drive from Andover.

Hiking was not a popular thing then, in the mid-1930s. But after a few visits, I really fell in love with the Sandwich Range. I never remember seeing other hikers. We almost always climbed by ourselves.

In those days, you didn't go to EMS [Eastern Mountain Sports] for hiking equipment—you built everything yourself. I built a pack rack myself, in about 1936. It had a tumpline. There were no little flaps or pockets to open to get out a map or a hat. You'd carry everything in one duffle bag. I didn't have to use the shoulder straps—I'd carry it simply with the tumpline, with all the weight on my forehead. Of course, that's what the Indians did. We'd fasten the duffle bag to the pack rack with a diamond hitch. At that time, we considered it the epitome of comfort and convenience!

On one of our first trips, we climbed Mount Chocorua. It was December 31. The temperature was below zero. In the morning, we'd often have bacon and eggs. The eggs would be frozen, so we'd crack the shell and pick the shell off, put the frozen ball in the fry pan and it would slowly settle down, melt, and become an egg! Marvelous.

On another occasion, my elder brother, a friend, and I made a two-week hiking trip. We started in Franconia Notch near the Flume, then [hiked to] Franconia Ridge, eastward to Crawford Notch, up Dry River, then northward over the Presidential Range. Next, over Pine Mountain to Gorham, where we bought supplies before traversing further. Across the Androscoggin [River], through the entire Mahoosuc Range to Old Speck. In Mahoosuc Notch, we found caves filled with ice. This was in September! We never met other hikers on that whole trip. I took several later trips in the Mahoosucs, one time with my father. It was, we felt, more primitive than the wildlands within the [White Mountain] National Forest.

Changes and Overcoming Challenges

I grew up in a family of all boys, close to nature, and a real individualist. However, I had a lot of drive.

My brother was at the University of North Carolina, so I went there for my undergraduate work. My brother told me that each fall at Chapel Hill, they had a 2-mile cross-country race called the Cake Race. The person who wins that race becomes a "big man" in the college community. So, what did little George do? I started running a year before I went to Chapel Hill. I won the Cake Race my freshman year and set a new course record. I was so exhausted for a week that my stomach was tight. I couldn't eat properly. I overdid it. It's been my nature, and that has been my life. That's the way I am.

One of the biggest changes in my life occurred when I was a senior in college. I began to sense that something was wrong. I was sweating, with pain in my side. I had an infection of the kidney. I had to withdraw from college and return home. At Lawrence General Hospital, they removed a kidney. They found a big cyst on it. I was in the hospital for a long while, recovering. Following the operation, the surgeon urged me to give up any thought of competitive wrestling, a sport that had become important to me. It was a severe blow, and I didn't immediately decide to take the advice.

Meanwhile, a regular visitor to my hospital bed was Fred Noss. After my release from the hospital, a mutual interest in literature led to the suggestion that we do some reading together. He suggested that we begin reading *Paradise Lost*. We would read individually, and meet once a week to discuss what we had read. For the first time in my life, I began to understand how important a teacher can be to a young person. I now realize that year was a turning point in my life; my days of competitive wrestling were over. I had discovered teaching.

When I went back to Chapel Hill the next year, I enrolled in education courses. I had a double major, really, in English and in chemistry. I had a strong Elizabethan Renaissance point of view of everything. I believed in being the complete man—not just literature, not just hiking, not just cross-country, not just wrestling.

At Chapel Hill, I was strongly influenced by the Quakers. During World War II, during the time of the draft, I registered as a conscientious objector. Due to the fact that I had only one kidney, I was put in category 4F, which meant I would not be drafted. By the time of World War II, the government had come to the conclusion that conscientious objectors could contribute to the country in a nonmilitary way. Following graduation, there was one year of graduate study in English at the University of North Carolina before becoming a teacher.

A Lifetime of Teaching

My entire life has not been devoted to wilderness advocacy, or the White Mountain National Forest. Primarily, my life has been that of a teacher. My first teaching [job] was as an English teacher at Brooks School, an all-boys,

George Zink sits outside his home in Tamworth, New Hampshire, in 2007.
(Photo by Ned Therrien)

independent school in North Andover, Massachusetts. It was wartime. After several weeks there, the headmaster said, "George, I can't find a chemistry teacher. Would you be willing to teach a course in chemistry?" How could I say no? I had a degree in chemistry as well as one in English. After a couple years teaching both subjects, I found that I was a better chemistry teacher than I was an English teacher. English came easily, so I didn't always empathize with the students' needs. But in chemistry, with which I'd struggled as a student and never done very well, I could empathize.

Every summer I studied at some university. In the summer of '43, I went to Harvard and took a course with an exceptional linguist named I.A. Richards. Richards was internationally known. He had written several books, one that has been very influential to a lot of people. It sure influenced me. It's entitled *The Meaning of Meaning.*[16] In working with Richards, I learned

---

[16] *The Meaning of Meaning: A Study of the Influence of Language upon Thought and of the Science of Symbolism* was co-authored by I.A. Richards and C.K. Ogden and published by Harcourt in 1923; it was reissued in 1995 by Routledge/Thoemmes Press, London.

the significance of words in our daily lives. It's meant a great deal to me. I've come to an understanding of how language works. During several following summers, I studied at the University of New Hampshire, Cornell, and Tufts.

In '52, we moved to Groton School, in Groton, Massachusetts. I was hired as a chemistry teacher. Teaching at an independent school is very demanding. I ran a dormitory, had dining room duties and study hall responsibilities, coached teams, led bird walks and mountain hikes. It was sixty- to eighty-hour weeks. There were compensations: financial security; three years of sabbatical leaves for study; lengthy vacations each summer, at Christmas, and in early spring; generous housing for Sally and our four children; financial support that enabled our children to attend boarding schools.

In later years, I became interested in teaching advanced chemistry— Advanced Placement courses at Groton and at St. Paul's School in Concord, New Hampshire, during the first few years of their advanced studies program.

In '81, we retired and I finished forty years of teaching.

Coming to Wonalancet

We realized by 1964 that we were spending our lives at Groton, and we didn't own a home. We could have all our meals at the dining hall if we wanted to, and we felt that our kids hadn't learned how to work. We were quite dependent upon the school.

Sally and I decided to purchase some land somewhere and have a house where we could go for vacations. Where would we go? Well, I knew the Sandwich and Tamworth [New Hampshire] region, so we started looking for land there.

We were driving with a real estate person along Route 113 in Tamworth when Sally said to the real estate man, "We don't need to get a house, because all we need is land. George, the children, and I can build a house!" He jammed on the brakes as he said, "Well, there's a piece of land here which is for sale." That was in the spring of 1964.

We built this place ourselves. We did all the woodwork, the plumbing, everything. We've got photographs of our children shingling the roof and putting up the rafters. The whole family was involved. A daughter and I built the garage one summer. She was nineteen.

We bought here because of the mountains. One of the first things we did was to hike. We all loved the out-of-doors. We joined the Wonalancet Out

Door Club (WODC), in the mid-sixties. Within a year or two, I became the trails chairman. In later years, I filled at one time or another every office. Eventually, I became president for several terms.

Toward an Earth Community

I think it important for an individual to become involved—to find something that is meaningful to him and do it. If your children would like to climb, what about helping clear some trails, build a bridge, or paint signs? And of course what happens when you do that is you meet other people who are involved. I have a "Hamlet complex." I have the feeling that Hamlet expressed: "The world is out of joint. O cursed spite, that I was ever born to set it right!" I'm always saying, "That needs fixing. What can I do to fix it?"

I have been conscious for years that Americans are too self-centered, too driven by the acquisition of material things. In this sense, our values are out of joint. In addition, we are anthropocentric. We think only in terms of mankind. In the U.S., we think wholly in terms of the U.S. What I'm concerned about at the moment is, *Are we going to turn this country from being an empire to being an interrelated country, interconnected with the whole community of Earth?* Not man-centered, anthropocentric, but ecocentric, intimately interconnected with all life forms as well as the material and energy resources such as water, air, soil, the sun, and, in fact, the entire universe. We are related to all life forms and the resources upon which all life forms are dependent.

Several things have influenced me strongly. I majored in English, so I'm interested in all forms of communication. Then, for forty years I taught sciences, so I'm interested in the ways in which mankind has learned to understand the nature of the world in which he lives. A scientist is also optimistic and welcomes change.

I have worked long enough to know that scientists are always working to discover something they don't understand fully. They also realize that no matter how much they study, no matter how much they learn, they will not reach a complete understanding. Every time a discovery is made, it uncovers more questions than it answers.

I have no belief in what I would call absolutism or absolute truth. I don't use the word "truth"; I use the word "understanding." We have an understanding today, but it isn't truth. Tomorrow we're going to discover something that we don't know today, which will change our understanding. When we see a mushroom on the ground, we say, "Oh, there's a mushroom." Well, what we see exposed above ground level is the fruiting body—the flower, not the whole organism. The main body is underground, the mycelia. Some are nourishing the nearby maple tree.

Wilderness

In the 1970s, the [U.S.] Forest Service was forced by Congress to involve the public in its planning. In the early days, the Forest Service managed the forest without citizen consultation. Previously, the public was allowed no input.

The National Wilderness Preservation Act was passed by Congress and signed by the president in '64. The act required all federal agencies that managed federal land—not just the Forest Service—to look at their land and identify roadless areas that had wilderness potential. They were required to do so every ten years. As a result, in the mid-1970s, the Forest Service nationwide initiated what they named Roadless Area Review and Inventory I, or RARE I. At the end of the lengthy process, they found millions of acres of potential wilderness, but not a single acre east of the Mississippi River. The Forest Service's definition of potential wilderness only permitted consideration of land that had never been modified in any way by earlier settlement. If there were signs of old roads, stone walls, or previous land occupancy, the land was ineligible for consideration.

Congress was so upset by this restricted definition that it quickly passed the Eastern Wilderness Areas Act of 1975. Under the '75 act, wilderness designation could preserve areas that had signs of use by man: roads, timber cuts, foundations, and so on. Areas such as the Sandwich Range could be designated. The big selling point was that it was important to have wilderness within a person's capacity to reach it. Not many people in New England were going to get a chance to experience wilderness if it were restricted to areas at great distances.

The National Forest Management Act was passed in about '74.[17] That act determined that the public must be involved in planning. That was just

---

[17] The National Forest Management Act was passed in 1976 in response to a number of lawsuits over forest management, as an amendment to the Forest and Rangeland Renewable Resources Planning Act of 1974.

about the time I became president of WODC. The Forest Service was going to develop a forest plan. It was going to occur in several stages. They sent out a questionnaire. We responded at that time. A lot of other mountain clubs never cared for forest planning, but WODC was deeply involved in every stage of it, so I was able to play a substantial role from the very start.

I became determined to work at developing a proposal for designation of a Sandwich Range Wilderness. The Sandwich Range was an area that I knew well. I was beginning to have a political life. I was conscious of the fact that we could create enough interest in the Sandwich Range to designate it as wilderness.

The Forest Service wasn't opposed to a Sandwich Range Wilderness; they just didn't want part of it to the west because of Waterville Valley's interest in expanding cross-country skiing. They didn't want it farther east because of an existing snowmobile trail. And they didn't want it farther south because they wanted a road giving access to Flat Mountain Pond. But there was agreement that there should be a Sandwich Range Wilderness!

WODC's political involvement was all part of a plan. It was a very opportune time for the Wonalancet Out Door Club. There were four or five people who were willing to work. The three principal leaders were me, Ralph Weymouth, and Ted Sidley. We were all activists willing to talk or lead a discussion on the topic. Ralph and I talked at many venues throughout the North Country for several years.

Of the then one hundred WODC members, only three were opposed to wilderness designation. All the others were enthusiastic supporters. When the Society for the Protection of New Hampshire Forests appointed a Wilderness Committee, five of the seven were WODC members. The club voted financial support to send a representative to give witness at a congressional committee meeting in Washington.

It wasn't just me. At a club celebration following designation, Sally and I were presented with T-shirts reading "Mother of the Sandwich Range Wilderness" and "Father of the Sandwich Range Wilderness." But the reality is that wilderness designation was achieved through the labors of many people—members from a half-dozen other groups and literally hundreds who wrote letters and gave necessary support.

The Actual Greatest Achievement

There was a friend living here in Wonalancet who spoke to me one time following passage of the 1984 New Hampshire Wilderness Act. He said to me, "George, I don't know whether you realize it, but you have just completed the most important achievement in your life. Achieving designation of the range was your greatest contribution." I think he was simply misinformed.

Teachers are fortunate in being remembered by former students. I cherish a stack of letters, many of them recalling events long past. They've not forgotten, nor have I. Accepting the risk that what follows may reveal a private communication, I give this example. About ten years ago, I received a book in the mail—a university-level biochemistry text written by a former student of mine for students of cell biology. I opened it, and what did I find? "To George Zink, with longtime admiration and thanks.... St. Paul's School Advanced Studies Program." Inside, the author acknowledged several people, including me, "who inspired my love of scientific inquiry."

There was also a letter that accompanied the book that read, in part, "I don't think we have spoken for over thirty years, so this letter may come as rather a surprise. I am sending you a copy of a textbook that I have just published. The philosophy of the book and its forthcoming sequel is that questions are more important than answers. I want you to know that I learned this concept from you when I was in your advanced chemistry class at St. Paul's. I remember particularly fondly your encomiums to Linus Pauling and your exhortation, 'Are you confused? Good!' It was this class that stimulated me to become a scientist, and I am embarrassed that I have never previously told you so."

So, if I were to evaluate my life, I think teaching and working with young people has been more significant to me than wilderness designation.

George Zink remained active in local land protection projects and issues until shortly before his death. Said his wife, Sally, "He thought he could change the world." He died on July 21, 2009, at age ninety-one.

Section Three

Life on the Trails

George Hamilton

More than a Hutman

George Hamilton relaxes for a moment at Zealand Falls Hut in 1994.
(Photo courtesy of Helen Hamilton)

ORN IN 1924 IN PHILADELPHIA, George Hamilton grew up in
Marblehead, Massachusetts. He was introduced to hiking and climbing while at a summer camp in the mid-1930s. When he returned home
from World War II, a friend introduced him to Joe Dodge—longtime
manager of the Appalachian Mountain Club's high huts system—who
promised Hamilton $10 per week and "all you can eat." It sounded like an
improvement over army chow, so George accepted.

From that starting point, Hamilton went on to a career in the mountains that few could ever match. Appalachian Mountain Club (AMC) hut
crew member, Fish and Game conservation officer, AMC huts manager,
director of New Hampshire Parks and Recreation, and chairman of New
Hampshire's Land Conservation Investment Program—George Hamilton
saw the Whites from many different perspectives over more than fifty years.
In addition to his life in the mountains George went on to another career in
banking and remained an avid student of history throughout his life.

Said Hamilton, "Foremost in all my activities were the White Mountains, one way or another.... I feel very proud of the fact that I've shared that
love of the mountains. Joe Dodge used to say that his greatest delight was in
teaching and helping other people to learn to love the mountains the way he
did, and I couldn't put it any better than that."

We spoke with George at his home in Bow, New Hampshire, in 1995.

In His Own Words

I started hiking in the Presidential Range in 1938, but soon the war inter-
vened. In 1942, at age eighteen, I joined the U.S. Army Air Forces. I was discharged on Washington's Birthday, 1946. Not long after I got home, my old
friend Dick Trefry told me that he was going back to Pinkham Notch to work.
I went with him and met Joe Dodge for the first time in late March 1946. Joe
promised a job washing pots and pans, mixed in with some backpacking!

I would wash pots and pans at breakfast and supper for a sometimes-
irascible chef, Tex Benton, the "Powder River Kid"—an appellation he
enjoyed. In between kitchen work, I had to pack supplies into Tuckerman
Shelter, manned by Vandy Porter and Gus Peterlie. The shelter was a CCC
[Civilian Conservation Corps] concoction, an attractive log cabin destined
for an inglorious end due to a fire a decade later. One aspect of the building

I remember unkindly was the noxious odor emanating from the chemical toilets—that could bring tears to your eyes!

In the Huts

My first hut was Madison, where I served as assistant hutmaster in 1946. Brookie Dodge, son of Joe Dodge, was only sixteen years old, but he was hutmaster because he knew how the huts operated. Chuck Rowan and I were the neophytes. I thoroughly enjoyed my summer at Madison, the challenge of climbing the 3.6 miles to the hut from Boothman's barn in Randolph where our pack house was located, carrying as much as we could respectfully handle, cooking for up to sixty people, responding to a variety of emergencies, learning the vagaries of mountain weather and the camaraderie amongst the crew, emanating from dealing with mutual problems!

I returned to full-time studies that fall at Springfield College, after an absence of four years. I decided to make up for lost time by taking two summer schools. At the end of the following summer, in 1947, I called up Joe Dodge. He said I should get to Greenleaf [Hut] as rapidly as possible, because the hutmaster had left, involuntarily, and the other two crew members were ailing.

As soon as I got up to Greenleaf, I found out that Pete Walker and Dick Hayes were both incapacitated—one with a bad ankle, the other with "walking pneumonia." As a result, I had to pack almost daily for close to three weeks. But after working at Madison, Greenleaf was considerably easier in terms of packing and running the hut. I remember lugging 100 pounds to Madison in three hours and ten minutes, while at Greenleaf I carried 102 pounds in two hours and eight minutes!

I went to Madison Hut in '48, after summer school, to help Professor Stuart "Slim" Harris and his wife, Cal, run the hut. My job was to do the packing. Cal was a great cook, and I remember especially eating a lot of mountain-cranberry pies!

I graduated Springfield College in June 1949 and then reported for work as hutmaster of Lakes of the Clouds. I was fit as a goddamn fiddle; but wouldn't you know it, I hadn't been at Lakes a week when I slipped on a loose rock with about 120 pounds on my back around the old corral just below the summit of Mount Washington. Jesus H. Christ, I hit the ground hard and came close to being knocked out. After sitting there and practicing my Marblehead and GI vocabulary, I managed to drag my packboard against a pile of rocks. I was lucky not to be injured from that, but around two o'clock the next morning I awoke with a sharp pain in my groin. I knew it was appendicitis. The Lakes crew had a pair of binoculars, because we always used to count [approaching hikers] to decide how much water to put in the soup before supper. So I told the rest of the crew, "Keep an eye on me and make sure I don't collapse." I made it to the summit in about twenty minutes. Annie Dodge took me down to the hospital in North Conway so Dr. Harold Shedd could snake my appendix out. In 1959, word had not yet reached the North Country in the medical community that it speeded recovery if patients were put on their feet as quickly as possible. I was finally allowed to stand up after eight days in bed! I wasn't supposed to pack, so I ended up cooking daily for several weeks, which I found so taxing I ended up with mononucleosis!

In 1949 to 1950 I studied toward a master's of education, and although I didn't finish it then, I did finally nail it down, a degree I found helpful to have in later job searches. After that, and a stint as a lifeguard the summer after I was recovering from mononucleosis, I took a crack at retail merchandising. I worked as a management trainee with the W.T. Grant Company in Milford, Massachusetts, and Hartford, Connecticut. After several months I decided I really was an outdoor guy and that retail stores were not my bag! I called up Joe Dodge and said, "Look, I have no idea what the hell I'm going to do, but I am going to leave this job and need some time to get my head straightened out. Have you got any jobs available?" Joe said, "I've got just the job for you! We are going to run Dolly Copp Campground for the Forest Service this summer, as their budget has been cut back drastically." I said, "Jesus H. Christ, Joe, I don't know anything about running a campground." And, giving me a lesson in leadership, he said, "I don't either! We'll learn together!"

We learned by trial and error and it was a great summer. I liked it so much I returned the following summer. Fortunately I had a great crew, with guys like Bill Hastings, Al Catheron, Chris Van Curan, Jack Middleton, and the like, making my job easier.

Turning to Conservation

It was the summer that I was running Dolly Copp that I met Conservation Officer Paul Doherty.[18] He would stop in to see us and talk with us, and we all liked him. Paul was always a fountain of information. One day he and I were just sitting somewhere talking, and he said, "George, what're you gonna do after this?" I said, "I don't know; I really got to start thinking about it." Paul said, "Have you ever thought about becoming a conservation officer?"

So I did think about it, and the next summer, I applied. Paul helped me prepare for the exams. Over the next year we used to hike together. He'd help me with the trees I didn't know and similar sorts of things.

I had to wait a year to hear about the results of the interview. So I worked as the hutmaster at Pinkham in the fall of '51 and the winter and spring of '52, and I ran Dolly Copp that next summer as well. I finally heard from Fish and Game, and I got the job as a conservation officer. I was a C.O. from 1952 to 1955.

There were a lot of characters at Pinkham in those days, but one of the most colorful guys we had and one of my all-time favorites in my whole life was woods cook Freddy Armstrong. Joe hired Freddy out of the Brown Paper Company in Berlin [New Hampshire]. Freddy almost had a conniption when he found out I was gonna be a game warden.

Freddy loved young people, and everybody loved Fred. He introduced me to a lot of the last of the old woodsmen. Here's a guy with a very limited education, but he knew more about the woods, and he'd tell me about the old logging days up in Canada and Maine—that's where he'd spent most of his life.

He took me aside the day before I left to become a C.O. and said, "You know, I kid a lot about this, but there's places up there where they shoot wardens." I said, "I'm not too worried about it." Freddy said, "I know you're not, but I am! Goddamn it, Hamilton, you take care of yourself."

Freddy and Joe Dodge had a blowup about something, and Fred went off to the Brown Company again, to their camp, where they took their VIPs during the hunting season, and they got Fred up to cook for just a short period. He got up one morning—of course, he smoked like hell, and he

---

[18] See page 213 for Paul's story.

was way overweight—and the first thing he did was have a cigarette. He was going to go over to the cook shack, and dropped dead. That was very emotional for me.

Anyway, I started out in Wolfeboro as a conservation officer trainee, and then in June I was assigned to Colebrook, where I spent the summer. After that stint I got assigned to Conway. My work varied with the seasons. In the winter, I did something that most of those old-timers hadn't done: I went in to Kennett High School, once a week all through the winter, and I talked about different things. I found out that most of those kids who were brought up looking at those mountains had never been up there.

When I was working, I'd look for trap lines, check trappers, do a lot of snowshoeing. I used to love to go up to Passaconaway Valley because a couple of trappers lived at the very end of the road, just before where the Passaconaway Campground is today. Cliff and Mrs. Pratt had been there since 1920. They were a wonderful couple. They're long gone.

Fires and Rescues

Part of a C.O.'s job was fighting forest fires with the Forest Service. We had a lot of fires in the 1950s. I fought in the Ossipee fire, and up on Mount Washington, on Boott Spur. We fought a fire up on Mount Success in the Mahoosucs. In fact, we went down the ledges on ropes. It was the first time in my life I ever had to worry about a rope burning!

There were a lot of search and rescues too. Some of the rescues were very traumatic; for example, the 1959 Cannon Cliff tragedy. I had to organize the rescue. In those days, we didn't have the technical climbers around that you have now. I had an AMC list, and I had to call around. Most of the climbers were from Massachusetts. I remember that Robert and Miriam Underhill[19] were always interested. They were my mentors—Miriam especially. And so I called up Miriam on Randolph Hill, and I stopped up in Randolph on the way over. Dawn was just coming as we came around the curve where you

---

[19] The Underhills were well-known mountaineers with a number of first ascents in Europe and the United States. In 1932, Miriam was part of the first all-women's ascent of the Matterhorn. Robert is known for introducing modern alpine climbing techniques to the United States.

can see Franconia Notch. I looked up, and the clouds were about 200 feet over our heads, screaming up from the south. I said, "Miriam, we've got a problem." Anytime you see the clouds coming up through the notch from the south, you got a problem.

It was rainy and cold and just above freezing—absolutely miserable. We all got drenched. I had to stay underneath the cliff all day. Rocks were falling continuously, and we came close to having a couple of bad falls. It was just to the left of the Old Man [of the Mountain], and [the climbers] got over in there and couldn't go up or down. By today's standards, it would not be that difficult. But these kids, well, they were nineteen or twenty years old. One's dad was in the construction business. Their climbing rope was about one-inch manila. For pitons they had reinforcement rods, and they had a carpenter's hammer. One of these kids was able to talk to the lead climber on the first rope. The climber told them to hang on, but the kid died literally right before their eyes. The other guy never said anything. I guess he was comatose, and he died as well. Hypothermia is so insidious. It was a very sobering experience.

AMC Calls Again

I guess I had only been with Fish and Game a short time, about two and a half years at that point, when some people from the AMC approached me in early '55. They said, "Joe Dodge is going to retire, and Bob Temple's left, and, you know, we think we'd like to see you go up there and learn the ropes and become huts manager at some point." I enjoyed Fish and Game, so I wasn't too enthused!

I said, "I don't think I'm cut out for it. You know, Joe's a good mechanic, and I'm just a half-assed mechanic." They said, "Oh, you can always get somebody to work for you to do that. We need a manager. The hut system is growing." I thought about it for a while, and they came and talked to me about it again in the spring. Finally I said, "Well, somebody's got to do it, and it would be an interesting opportunity."

I really felt badly about leaving Fish and Game after such a short time, but I did. There wasn't a definite timetable for Joe's retirement. As it turned out, it was a little over three years. At the end of '58, Joe retired, and January 1, 1959, I became the huts manager.

George Hamilton stands proudly on the Cannon Mountain Rim Trail, 1994.
(Photo by Jonathan Kannair, jonathankannair.com)

Pinkham and the huts were growing. I knew I needed two key people to help me. I needed a tremendous secretary, and I needed a tremendous right-hand person. I feel comfortable in dealing with people and managing problems, and I always felt that the mark of a manager is the ability to hire somebody smarter than you are so they can work for you. I was able to get Bruce Sloat, which was the smartest thing I ever did, along with hiring Emmy Lou McLeod as my secretary.

Bruce and I worked with the Hut Committee and we put together a game plan of a lot of capital projects, and we got them done. For example, we were getting more and more complaints about the long distance between Zealand Falls Hut and Lakes of the Clouds [Hut]. Families didn't like it. You know, people just can't walk the way they used to. And even if you're an experienced hiker, that's a hell of a hike. So, that's when the club started talking about Mizpah, and we had a committee look at it. Brad Swan, who was the chairman of the Hut Committee, and I went up and looked at that site. We knew there were going to be water problems, sewer problems, and so on, but it sure dovetailed nicely between Zealand and Lakes.

Justice Douglas

One of the most interesting things that happened during my days at Pinkham was in '59. I got a letter one day, and my secretary, Emmy Lou McLeod, said, "George, have you been in trouble with the law lately?" I said, "I can't think of anything. Why?" She said, "You've got a letter here from the Supreme Court!" I looked at it, and goddamn it if it wasn't the Supreme Court of the United States! It was from [Supreme Court Justice] William O. Douglas. He wasn't sure what he wanted to do, but he wanted to do something with the huts. He was writing this book, *North to Katahdin*, and wanted a little help.

I wrote Justice Douglas back and said, "Let me know what your time frame is, and as a quick little trip, we could do the high country and go to Madison and Lakes, in, say, three days." So we did.

I can remember we started our hike at the Ravine House in Randolph. We hiked the King Ravine Trail. I had read about this guy and knew that he had hiked all over the world, and I deduced that he wasn't a real technical climber, but he was an avid hiker. I didn't realize at the time that he only had one lung! If I had known that, I might've picked a little easier trail!

We didn't start until about 1 P.M. We made our way through the Elevated, around all those huge boulders in the floor of the ravine. We didn't see a damn soul all afternoon. We were talking and getting to know each other.

Justice Douglas always wore a western Stetson. We got to the King Ravine headwall, which is really pretty steep. The paint blazes were fading, as usual, and we could hardly tell if there were any cairns there. So, we got about halfway up that goddamn headwall, when I heard this gasp, and the old judge had fallen back between these two big boulders. Thank God, he had fallen against a nice white birch, and below there was about a 20-foot drop. I said, "Jeez, don't scare me like that. If anything happens to you, I'm gonna head for Montreal and keep on going!" And he laughed. The only thing that bugged him was that his Stetson had come off and fallen in that hole. He said, "George, could you get that hat for me?" It was somewhere on that headwall that he said, "You not only have twenty-five years on me, but I only have one lung." I said, "No kidding!" And I went and got his Stetson. He told me that story—one hell of a story—about how a horse rolled on him out West and he was rescued by the Forest Service.

George Hamilton uses a snowmobile during a 1961 trip on Chamberlain Lake in the Allagash. (Photo courtesy of Helen Hamilton)

So we got up to the edge of the Gateway at the top of the headwall, and by that time the clouds were just about at the Gateway and we could look down to Madison Hut, and they were just putting the lights on. It was great. In the *National Geographic* story [Douglas wrote], he talks about the first time he saw Madison Hut. He was hungry and tired, but Madison became his favorite hut.

We went across the range the next day to Lakes [of the Clouds Hut], and it was a cold night. We slept in what they called the overflow bunk room. I can remember the next morning I said, "Well, Judge, how'd you sleep?" He said, "I slept cold!"

The third and final day we went down over Boott Spur. On that trip I can remember saying, "Judge, you know, you've done quite a few stories for *National Geographic*. The hut system here would make a hell of a story." He said, "You know, George, it would. That's a good idea. As a matter of fact, I'll call M.B.G." I found out later he meant Melville Bell Grosvenor, the president of the National Geographic Society!

Bill Douglas ended up writing me about the article idea and said, "George, I've seen M.B.G and he wants to talk about this." It turns out that

Paul Doherty and I were going to be in New York at the New Hampshire booth of an outdoors show the same day the judge was giving a talk at this big, fancy Fish and Game dinner that's put on once a year in New York. So we decided to meet up there and then head to Washington.

Justice Douglas invited us to his place and we had a tremendous meal. The three of us killed a bottle of slivovitz that the Yugoslav ambassador had given him. In the middle of the night, the old judge drove us home. He said, "I'm gonna pick you boys up at eight o'clock in the morning, and we're going to the Yale Club for breakfast." And he did. I said, "Jesus H. Christ! I don't think I could stand this Washington pace. I gotta get back home!"

Anyway, the article about the huts came out. I tend to think that the influence of that article was overblown by a lot of people. We had a surge of interest and job applications that we could directly attribute to the article, but that was about it. It was the bigger trends that were far more important. Americans were really turning to the out-of-doors then, and the hut system was expanding. The early sixties were the start of an enormous wave in hiking and camping.

From AMC to the State of New Hampshire

By that time, Bruce Sloat and I were getting our long list of projects whittled down. Mizpah was the culmination of it all. It took us two years to build that hut, more or less. That was a real challenge. We enjoyed it, and it worked out well. I was beginning to feel, though, that I'd like to see what's over the hill.

I left the AMC and worked for a while with Mary Louise Hancock, New Hampshire's director of state planning, and one year as special assistant for planning on Governor Walter Peterson's staff.

Eventually, Russell B. Tobey, the director of Parks and Recreation, re-tired, and I was offered the job. I started there in '71. It just seemed a natural [fit] for me. I felt right at home, since I was familiar with the state parks system for many years. We dealt with a lot of financial issues, always trying to do more with less. But we were able to expand the state parks system. We fixed up Fort Constitution at the mouth of the Piscataqua River, and we also did some very important restoration work at Odiorne Point State Park. That was very satisfying, since it coupled my outdoors experience with my longtime interest in history.

If I had to pick one thing I'm the most proud of, I guess it would be chairing New Hampshire's Land Conservation Program in the 1980s. It was a big effort, just under $50 million. There was the Trust for New Hampshire Lands, the private side, and the Land Conservation Program, the public side. I chaired the public side.

The LCP was a tremendous operation. We were all volunteers. We have left a legacy of more than a hundred thousand acres either in fee or less-than-fee acquisition through conservation easements. The reason I feel so good about it is that we have provided lands for a variety of recreation—access to public waters, all different types of trails and beaches—and we've protected unique natural areas.

Balancing the Future

I wonder about the future of the White Mountains. We now have so many interest groups all trying to have their say about what we do, and we have this tremendous divergence of views: the over-protectionists (put a fence around the forest and don't let anybody in) and just the opposite (develop, develop, develop). The state and the federal government need to seek balance!

I have satisfied my ambition in the post-World War II world to have jobs I enjoyed with variety in scope. Foremost in all my activities were the White Mountains, one way or another. I have to say, despite growing up around the ocean and boats, I'm basically a mountain guy. I feel very proud of the fact that I've shared that love of the mountains. Joe Dodge used to say that his greatest delight was in teaching and helping other people to learn to love the mountains the way he did, and I couldn't put it any better than that.

Throughout his life George Hamilton remained an avid reader and student of Civil War and World War II history. He continued this passion until his death on January 26, 2012. He was eighty-eight.

Ben English, Jr.

A Trails Connection between Past and Present

Ben English, Jr., examines an ax used by today's Appalachian Mountain Club trail crew in an equipment shed at AMC's Hutton Lodge in Pinkham Notch in 2009. (Photo by Ned Therrien)

A LOW-KEY AND UNASSUMING FIGURE, Ben English, Jr., is not widely known outside of a small circle of mountain friends. His contributions to the White Mountains, though, have reached many thousands of people over many generations. They span his days working on trails, his support of the Appalachian Mountain Club (AMC) professional White Mountain trail crew, his work coediting two books, *Our Mountain Trips: Part I, 1899 to 1908* and *Our Mountain Trips: Part II, 1909 to 1926* (Bondcliff Books, 2005), and his photography—his railroad photographs appear in the book *Trackside Around New Hampshire With Ben English, Jr., 1950–1970* (Morning Sun Books, 2009). A third-generation AMC member, Ben joined the club when he was twelve. He served on five of the committees that edited and revised AMC's revered *White Mountain Guide* (the 1969, 1972, 1976, 1979, and 1983 editions).

Husband to Judy, father of two children, and a retired schoolteacher, Ben says, "I don't mind being not known." The mountains have been part of Ben's life since childhood, reading his grandparents' journals detailing their adventures in the White Mountains, bird-watching with his grandmother, staying in the huts with his parents, and later working as a member of the AMC trail crew. He continues to be involved with the trail crew. He visits them in the woods, shares stories, and invites them to his house. He says, "Trail crew has probably shaped or created a whole life for me. I still hang around with them, and they come here and visit. It's very meaningful."

In a world where so many of us multitask and pay only casual attention, Ben listens, observes, and pays close attention, especially to our mountain world. "On January 1, 1960, I started one of those five-year diaries," he says. "I write four lines a day, and I've done it faithfully ever since. I've missed about ten days in fifty years."

We spoke with Ben English in 2009 at the cozy, simple home his parents built in Jackson, New Hampshire. The view from his dining room ranges from Carter Dome, to the northern Presidentials, to Mount Monroe, the Gulf of Slides, and Mount Isolation. He loves the view, but he loves being out in the mountains with the trail crew even more.

In His Own Words

My mother and father met here in Jackson [New Hampshire], in the mid-thirties. Both their colleges happened to have ski weekends at Moody's, now Whitney's Inn [at the base of Black Mountain in Jackson]. My mother's car got stuck in the snow and the boys went over to help. That's how they met.

After World War II, we started coming up to Christmas Farm Inn in Jackson as a family, for vacations and on weekends. Around '50, my parents decided we were spending a lot of money at the inn. It was great, but they figured we should look around for a chunk of land. So, they came in here with a real estate agent. There were two acres here for sale. My father and mother came in December '51 on snowshoes and looked at Mount Washington and said, "That's it! We'd like to buy this." The original part of the house was a 30-by-15 [foot] woodshed that had been across the road from us, down in Topsfield, Massachusetts. My father and another guy numbered all the timbers, and they put it on a truck and brought it up here in the summer of '52. Now we had a camp.

I went to Topsfield High School for two years. I didn't study worth a diddly, but I got A's. My parents knew I was coasting. They said, "Boy, you're going to have to go to school somewhere else. We're going to have to pay to educate you." So, I went to Mount Hermon School for two years. I wasn't smart enough to get into Bates or Bowdoin or UNH or all those places, so I went to Nasson College down in Springvale, Maine. It was a great place.

Signing Up for AMC Trail Crew

In August of '55, my parents and I were at Madison Hut. Back in those days, the guests helped with dishes after the meal. We'd wash and wipe and put the dishes away, even though I'm sure we didn't put them in the right places, but the hut crew appreciated the help.

Well, I am a pretty quiet guy. I'm a low-profile person. So I went out in the kitchen and probably put away three or four dishes. There was a tall, skinny guy who was clearly not part of the hut crew. He and the hut crew were talking, and I tuned into words like "tent," "cooking over fire," "ax," "trails," and "sleeping out." And those words, they rang a big bell with me. So, after they got done talking, I went over to this guy; I looked up at him. I said, "I like the sound of what I heard." He told me that they were talking about the AMC trail crew. He said, "If you're interested, write in and get an application," which I did. His name was David Hayes. Stretch Hayes. He was the AMC trail master in 1955.

So, I filled out the application that fall, and later in the winter I got a letter from Joel Nichols who lived in West Newbury, Massachusetts. I still have the letter. It said, "My name is Joel Nichols. You don't know me from Adam. I'm going to be your boss this summer. Don't let that scare you. I put my pants on one leg at a time just like everybody else. Some people say I resemble the Old Man of the Mountain so I'm also known as the Great Stone Face." His profile and his chin stuck out. He's a cool guy. That was in March of '56. I was sixteen years old. I was on the trail crew the summers of '56, '57, and part of '58.

Hutton Lodge

Those were the days when AMC had a house in Whitefield, New Hampshire, right in the village up on the hill. The house was Hutton Lodge, named for Jack Hutton. He was on trail crew and trail master in the late '30s. He was a highly respected trail master—and not just trail stuff, either. He was just all-around respected. Then he went in the Marines, and got killed on Iwo Jima. So they named the house Hutton Lodge.

When the AMC trail crew started in 1919, they looked at Whitefield for a base, because it's to the north of three notches. You can run down to Franconia or Crawford [notches], just go over to Gorham and come down to Pinkham, and go a little further east and come down south to Evans. You can also get over to Kinsman Notch.

For the first decade, the crew used the trains to get around. The Profile & Franconia Notch Railroad ran up to the Profile House from Bethlehem Junction. The Maine Central [Railroad] came down from Crawford. There were plenty of passenger trains. You know, Portland to Saint J [St. Johnsbury, Vermont]. Pinkham was a little more difficult to get to, but they'd take a train to Gorham from Whitefield.

AMC Trail Crew in the 1950s

We went into the woods on Saturday morning, came out Thursday afternoon; we were in Whitefield Thursday night, Friday, Friday night and back into the woods on Saturday morning. There were nine people on the crew back then. There were eleven my second year, and I think there were eleven in '58. The AMC hired a woman from Littleton to come in and cook for us. Mrs. Chamberlain was one wicked cook. Geez, was she good! We'd work a half a day on Thursday, then run down the trail, get out of the woods, get in the Jeep and drive back to Whitefield. She always had steaming biscuits waiting for us, whether it was three o'clock or five o'clock. They were slathered with real butter. We'd eat probably four or five big biscuits as soon as we'd get in the door. Then, we'd take a shower. We'd put on clean T-shirts and clean pants. Mrs. Chamberlain always had a big supper for us. We had a dining room, and we ate at a table with the trail master at the head. The upper-years were along the sides and the first-years were way down at the end.

After supper, we'd take our laundry over to the Whitefield Steam Laundry. Then some of us would go out. There was Chase Barn Playhouse right there in Whitefield. We'd get dressed up. We'd put a jacket on. There were girls there, the usherettes. Some of us would go to the movies. There were drive-in theaters in Littleton and Twin Mountain. And of course, we always had to grease our boots and sharpen our axes. On Friday, we'd do chores, get the laundry, and get food all lined up for the next week.

We had three vehicles: a '47 Jeep (a real Jeep—the window flopped down on the hood), a '51 Willys pickup truck with wooden bows in the back with canvas over it, and a '49 Chevy wagon. We'd take these vehicles down two or three times a summer to Ken Jordan who ran the Gulf station in town. He'd say, "What do you boys do with these vehicles?! I get them all fixed up for you and you come in here five or six days later, the exhaust systems have been torn out and the brakes are all worn!"

We didn't abuse them, though, but we did use them. In '56, we had to go into Desolation Shelter with a big load. The Signal Ridge Trail was a whole heck of a lot better than it is now. We said, "Why are we going to walk 7 miles dragging all this crap on our back? We've got this versatile Jeep!" We thought we'd drive up there and see how far we could go. I didn't think we could get all the way to Desolation Shelter, but I thought we ought to be able to knock off a couple of miles. And so we did, but it was a little hairy. We got as far as the junction of Carrigain Notch Trail and Signal Ridge Tail and the Carrigain Brook crossing [a distance of 1.7 miles]. We couldn't get across, so we unloaded all the stuff and tied it onto our packboards. It probably took us longer to drive to that junction than it would have if we had packed.

Moses

Everyone on trail crew had woods names. Mine was Moses. I started trail crew late my first year. My parents drove me up to Whitefield. Alan McLean was there and he said, "I'm a first-year also. Everybody else is in the woods. We're late." There was a note from trail master Joel Nichols. It said, "There is food in the refrigerator; make yourself at home, go upstairs, find a bunk, and I'll see you tomorrow morning." That's all it was.

So the next morning Joel showed up and he showed us—sort of—how to put food and things in boxes. And he said, "Get in the Jeep. We're going to go to the Mahoosucs." I had no idea what he was talking about. The Success Pond Road at that time was just a one-track road. It was for logging trucks and there were pull-offs every now and then. No bridges. No culverts. You had to ford every bit of water. We used the Jeep or the '51 Willys truck. We drove up that road in low gear for an ungodly long time [a distance of 8.1 miles]. We were headed to Carlo Col Shelter.

We got out at the Carlo Col Trail and Joel showed us a packboard and gave us a clothesline to tie the boxes on. I remember seeing Joel lash two boxes quickly to his packboard, put it on his back, and then he was gone. And here Alan and I are, numb, naïve, green, and thinking, *Geez, how did he do that?* Well, we figured it out, and we got our boxes on, and Alan went off a little ahead of me.

My legs are short, so I cannot walk as fast. I mean, I think I'm going fast, but I'm not. Well, anyway, I was behind. Now, it's only 2.4 miles up to Carlo Col Shelter. I didn't see Alan and I didn't see Joel, but I figured, I'd packed before. I wasn't scared or anything. I just went along and figured I'll get there eventually. I had all day. It was probably 9 A.M. Well, by the time I got up there, it was probably 2 P.M. Alan was already there. And Joel said, "Where have you been?" He said it politely. I mean, he didn't make me feel like a mole or a worm or anything, but he did emphasize, "Where have you been?" I said, "I don't know. I was just coming along." I felt all right. Nothing hurt. I was tired. And he said, "Moses spent forty days in the wilderness, didn't he? You're Moses." So I was Moses.

I think I know the reason I was so slow. I noticed that Joel had two boxes. He had his personal box, which included his sleeping bag and wool shirt and toothbrush, and he probably had the pot kit, which is very light. And Alan

Appalachian Mountain Club trail crew members carry their full loads: (left to right) Ben English, Warren Lightfoot, Stephen Waite, and Tom Lisco, getting ready to leave Zealand Falls Hut for Guyot Shelter in 1957. (Photo courtesy of Ben English, Jr.)

had his personal box and a box of food. We all had our axes and clippers. But old English here, he had his personal box, probably a food box, and he also had a case of oranges.

[Later Nichols gave an explanation for the oranges.] Nichols said, "I'm going to find out about this English guy and see if he can work and earn his way." I just figured everybody takes a case of oranges or something. So we get up there, and how many are there, twenty-five or thirty oranges in a case, and there were the three of us for two days. I think we ate a lot of oranges, and we might have heaved a lot of them into the woods too. I spoke to him about that oh, three or four years ago in Vermont, and he just smiled.

Life on Trail Crew

We started the season with patrolling—clearing out winter brush, trees, and branches with an ax. Patrolling was great. We covered a lot of miles. We saw a lot of country like the Mahoosucs. After the patrolling was done, we standardized, which means cutting brush and branches so the trail was 6 feet wide and 8 feet high, so you could go through it without a pack hitting branches.

A lot of folks think that standardizing is dull and boring and all, but I didn't find it to be that. It was like mowing the lawn. You know, mowing the lawn may be dull, but it isn't to me because I like to walk, and I can also see what I've accomplished. After standardizing a section, I'd turn around and look and think, *Wow, nice corridor!*

Well, the AMC had, we estimated, 365 miles of trail to maintain in the White Mountains. We patrolled everything, every year. Our goal was to standardize one-third of that, 100 miles, each summer.

We also built and maintained the shelters. That was fun. And we were responsible for signs. There were seven hundred AMC trail signs. And on patrol, we'd make note, just like they do now, of any signs that were missing or broken. If there was a bridge or a shelter that needed to be rebuilt, we did it. Usually a bridge was just two logs, two stringers.

In '57, the trail crew built Ethan Pond Shelter. Bob Scott and I—it was my second year, he must have been a third-year—we were sent in with a mess of food and axes, and I guess we had a tent. We were told to cut all the trees we could find, and peel them and stack them in a week. So we did. We cut, limbed them, and we peeled bark off enough trees to build that shelter.

We had pitch in our sleeping bag, on our sleeping bag, in us. My glasses had pitch on them, in them. You even tasted pitch. I'm not complaining. Even then, I don't think we complained. It was just a result of being in there. You couldn't get pitch off your hands. Before you picked up anything, you had to rub your hand in the dirt so your hands wouldn't be so sticky. That was wicked fun. The shelter was dedicated on August 21, 1957.

Tools and Machete Fights

The first-years used single-bit axes. Second-years and up got double-bit axes and machetes. I still have my machete. They would do some damage! You could take down a small tree if you grabbed it maybe five feet up and you bend it, put as much tension as you can, and then you slash down at the bottom.

Another thing that was cool about machetes: We had machete fights. You and I would each have a machete, and we'd turn it so that the backside was out; then we'd crash those machetes, "Bang, bang!" The goofers—oh, my God, they didn't know that it's the backside that we're hitting. It's not

In August 1956, Ben English, who was known as Moses because he hiked slowly, encountered a donkey on the trail. The incident—immortalized in this cartoon by trail crew member Warren Lightfoot—gave him a longer nickname.
(Illustration by Warren Lightfoot, courtesy of Ben English, Jr.)

the sharp side.[20] We wouldn't do that to a tool. My machete has three or four dozen dents or nicks in the back from where the other guy would slash against it. It was a cool sound. You know, steel ringing on steel.

A lot of people thought—and still think—that the trails take care of themselves. Once, we decided we're going to make it so the goofers realize that trails don't take care of themselves. It was on the Ethan Pond Trail. We came to a very thick part of alders. Well, we made the trail a little extra wide, like maybe it was 8 feet wide and maybe 8 feet tall. It was a clear, beautiful, and wide trail. And then all of a sudden there was this wall of alders, and we left it vertical. We hoped people would say, "My God, maybe we're not on the right trail. Maybe it doesn't go any further!"

Moses, the Donkey Killer

Later my first season, I got a little something added to my woods name. The AMC had 12 miles of trail over on Katahdin. And every year, for one week,

[20] "Goofer" was a term used by people who worked in the mountains to refer to people who did not work in the mountains.

three guys would go over and patrol. We'd get in the Jeep and drive for six or eight hours to Roaring Brook Campground and spend the night there.

The next day, we'd hike into Russell Pond. There was a cabin in there, a real cabin with doors and windows. It was for the ranger, but we could stay in it.

The trail was an old tote road and it was pretty level. At the end of the week, on the way out, I remember I was in the lead and was leaning forward. When you come out of the woods you're in a hurry and you just want to get out to civilization. You lean forward, you're holding the bottom of your packboard on your hands to lift it up or steady it. Your eyes are down and you're looking where your feet are going.

Warren Lightfoot was right tight on my butt, and Joel was right tight on Warren's, right behind him. There were three of us just as tight as we could go. I mean, we were booking it.

I looked ahead on one of those straight stretches, and I saw a donkey coming toward us, packing in supplies for the ranger at Russell Pond. There were a couple of donkeys with a muleskinner. We just kept right on truckin'. I glanced up again and we were closer, and they were still on the trail. I figured the muleskinner is going to have the donkeys stop for humans. Maybe I took the wrong assumption. We got close enough, and Warren and Joel, they saw what was going on. We got even closer and I figured, *I guess I'm going to have to be the one to make a move.* It was pretty close. So I stepped aside. And Warren and Joel, they both stepped aside. And the donkeys swept past us. And the muleskinner, he didn't say anything, he just probably nodded or something. And then they just kept on going. At that point, Warren thought that was the funniest thing. He fell over laughing. He grabbed his gut, and he just laughed and laughed. He was howling. Joel was too. And he said, "Moses, I thought you were just going to run right into them." And Joel says, "Moses, the Donkey Killer!"

Trail Crew Changes

The trail crew first-years got $15 a week. The second-years got $20, and the third-years made $25. The trail master got $45, I think. And, of course, we got all our food, our tools, and AMC paid for the laundry.

Working for the AMC, you're paid in great spirits and fun and accomplishment, but your wallet doesn't get fat. So eventually, after my third year, my parents and I figured I guess I better get a "real" job. I didn't want to be trail master, really. But being a second-year and a third-year was kind of cool, because you knew the ropes. You knew where the trails were and you knew how to get to Dream Lake or the Reel Brook Trail without having to be told. And you didn't need a map.

Things have changed over the years. The trail crew members these days, they're more worldly. I certainly wasn't. I mean, these guys after their first year, maybe the next winter they've got an internship with the Micmac Indians on Cape Breton, and then the next year from where they're in college they're going over to India to help build trails or something. That was not me.

One of the big changes is having women on the crew; I mean, it's natural. We all live together. When you're on trail crew, you certainly have to be a definite makeup. They say you have to be able to live for five days in the woods close to each other's butts. If you can't do it, then you're not cut out for it. That eliminates ninety percent of the world.

And you stay in tents away from shelters, away from people. There weren't so many people in the woods when I was on crew. We stayed in shelters practically all the time. If we were working out on Franconia Ridge, we'd stay at Liberty Spring Shelter. The mountains are a lot busier now.

Not having a campfire is a big part that's different. You know, they used to say that campfire was the caveman's television. It's so neat to sit around a campfire. We used to cook on a fire for breakfast and supper. And it wasn't [called] dinner! It was supper. On trail crew, first-years got the firewood, started the fire, kept it going, and the upper-years did the cooking. And then, the first-years did the dishes. We built a fire at any shelter. The next thing we'd do is get a pot, get water in it, and boil it. You kept it going while you were cooking and eating, and then the hot water was there for the dishes.

If it was rainy, and it was going to be raining the next day and hard to get the fire going, well, you'd get wood on your way to the shelter. You get your wood, keep it in your pack, and keep it in your sleeping bag, to keep it dry. If you were a first-year, you had to get the fire going and keep it going. I still like campfires. I've got a fireplace built against the boulder, outside here. I just go down there and sit. Maybe sit and read. Maybe just lie down. It's cool to do that.

Now they use stoves, and we can't have fires. I couldn't be without a campfire. But the crews now—the trail crew doesn't miss it. They don't miss it because they didn't have it. Stoves, women, campfires, and staying in tents—those are all changes. But I don't think the type of person on trail crew has really changed. When trail crew alumni from the '50s and '60s and '70s come back, they say to the current crew, "You know, it's so great. Your names have changed, but it's so great to see that the feeling and the tradition and the excitement and the energy, the intensity of it, and the whole scene is the same as it was."

After I left trail crew, I worked at Camp Asquam, a girls' camp down on Squam Lake. I was the hiking counselor. That was pretty cool. I did two summers there, and then in '61, I worked at Christmas Farm Inn doing grounds. I didn't go back to visit trail crew much until the mid-sixties.

I guess at some point I realized that this trail crew thing had really made an impression on me. So, I began to drift back and visit Hutton or go into the trail crew cabin, which was built in '76. By the time I had gotten back, women had already come in. I wasn't an immediate observer of women joining, but I think it's great now. I mean, I don't know how it would have been in the '50s to have women on trail crew. Probably, they wouldn't want to have them on the crew just because of the formality of the expectations that boys and girls didn't go out to the woods together.

Becoming a Teacher

When it came time to figure out a career, I wanted to be a forest ranger or conservation officer or do something outdoors. I was told after my aptitude test that I wouldn't do very well in math, and that I would need a lot of math to be a forest ranger, which is a bunch of bunk.

So that was the street I was headed down, and all of a sudden, it was like that big wall of alders on the Ethan Pond Trail. That's the end of forestry for me. I didn't know what the hell I wanted to do in college. Business? I hated it. And I hated numbers. I'm still not good in math. Somebody said, "Well, why don't you take education courses?" So I did.

After college, I started teaching right away in Campton, New Hampshire. I've always taught seventh- and eighth-grade English and history. Every now and then I'd have a sixth-grade class, and every now and then I'd have a ninth-grade class. I was two years in Campton, and I ended up liking teaching. I taught for another thirty-two years, the last twenty being in Bartlett, New Hampshire.

Railroads

My interest in trains started when I was probably two, three, or four years old, when my mother and father used to drive me around eastern Massachusetts and southern New Hampshire. Where we lived, all the bridges had signs that read "Boston & Maine Railroad." My mother would say, "There's a bridge coming." I would get excited and say, "Boston & Maine Railroad!"

When I was in Whitefield with the trail crew, the B&M and the Maine Central were both there. There was passenger service on both railroads, plus freight trains. Driving through Crawford Notch, we'd see trains. Working on Webster Cliff, we'd look down and see those trains going through the notch.

My roommate in college was George McEvoy, and he liked transportation. We hung around the local railroad yard, maybe an hour here and an hour or two there. They liked us down there. We'd look at the trains, look at the cars. Before long they said, "You want a ride?" We'd move around the yard when they were shifting cars around. We'd get rides when they delivered coal to the woolen mill steam plant down in Sanford. Another day they asked, "You want a ride to Portland?" Well, we'd make sandwiches and go along. Once a month we'd ride.

I took pictures of railroad buildings and stations and bridges and section houses and things, as well as trains. I've always been interested in structures. I have a little shanty that used to be up at Crawford's. The railroad moved it down to Glen, and then they didn't use it anymore. I bought it for $5, and brought it up here. And so I have a railroad building out back. But that's nothing compared to Ray Evans who had seventeen buildings! Ray and I got along very well. We were good friends. I couldn't keep up with him on the trail, even though he was thirty years older than me.[21]

I was in the Pemi [Pemigewasset Wilderness] in '56, '57, '58. Working in the Pemi on trail crew was pretty cool. There was a great connection between logging railroads, the mountains, and the trails. Just what I love. I admired the Number 17 [railroad] trestle every time I hiked past it. Eventually, I decided to hike to the trestle for the express purpose of photographing it. That day

---

[21] Ray Evans grew up along the railroad tracks in Crawford Notch and went on to be a lifelong lover of railroads and the White Mountains and a friend to many hut and trail crews.

Ben English stands at the base of the fire tower on 4,700-foot Mount Carrigain on September 12, 1964. The view is north, over the Pemigewasset Wilderness. (Photo courtesy of Ben English, Jr.)

was August 14, 1960. When I arrived, I was dismayed to see that it had been washed out in the flood of October 1959, when the slides had come down in Franconia Notch, every notch was closed, and the Kanc [Kancamagus Highway] was washed out. After I had started teaching in Campton in 1962, one of the guys who worked at Rand's Hardware Store in Plymouth, Francis Boyle, gave me a couple of his photographs of the trestle after it had been abandoned. The track was on the top. They call them upside-down bridges.

Mountain History

No matter where you go in the White Mountains, it's been logged. I like knowing what was here before. For example, the Wilderness Trail coming out of the Pemi. People will say they went up Bondcliff and then they had that 5-mile slog coming out. But I say, "Wow, this is a neat culvert," or, "I wonder does that brook have a name," or, "Is this evidence of something over there?" I do the same thing on the Rocky Branch Trail. I like going up to Shelter #1 and back. I might even do it this afternoon. But, I look every time. I go, "Oh, yeah, over there on that rock, there's a drill hole." Or, I know there's a benchmark up there on that rock. Even though I've seen it a hundred times, I look forward to it. I look for landmarks along the trail.

There's an arrow sign on a tree on the Rocky Branch Trail, for example. But if you look straight ahead, it's all trees and raspberries. Why do we have to have an arrow there? Well, the arrow's been there since the time that was a log landing, back in the '70s or something. If people saw it, they might have been tempted to go straight. Well, the arrow disintegrated and, a couple years ago, the Forest Service put up a new arrow. It doesn't need to be there, but there has been an arrow there and so now there's a new arrow! So if I find an arrow or a pile of brush for a detour, I ask myself, "Why, what was that?"

Mountain Books

My mother's mother and father, Ida Rachel James and Walter James, they tramped around the mountains between 1899 and 1926. They lived in Portsmouth, New Hampshire, and Waltham, Massachusetts. They came up probably three times a season, originally by horse and buggy and later by train. They went to Sandwich and Chocorua, because that wasn't too far from Portsmouth. Later, by train, they went to West Ossipee, Madison, North Conway, and Bemis—later called Notchland—in Crawford Notch, so they could get to the Davis Path, which was one of their favorite places. They began to come to the White Mountains by automobile in 1918, after they purchased their first car. They could come farther in the same period of time that it took to come by horse and carriage or by train.

They took copious notes. Then, when they got back to civilization, they wrote their notes into stories. My grandfather also had a camera. He started with plate glass negatives and then film negatives, and developed his own photographs. [My grandparents] made journals with the stories plus his photographs. If you asked me what inspired me to write and take pictures and be interested in the mountains, I'd say it's because of them.

One day, I was talking with Mike Dickerman from Bondcliff Books in Littleton [New Hampshire]. Mike knew that I liked mountain literature and photographs. I told him about the journals that we had, and he said,

"Well, bring one over." So I took one of my grandparents' journals over and showed it to him. I thought it was worth pursuing. And Mike confirmed that immediately. He basically said, "Let's stop all the work that I'm doing now and get these into print." Up until that time, those journals were passed through the family without much thought. They just migrated from house to house, from bookcase to bookcase.

My sister Jane did all the digital restoration of the photography. She made them printable. My wife, Judy, retyped the earlier stories, which were handwritten. (Later, my grandparents used a typewriter.) The results were the *Our Mountain Trips* books. I certainly learned a lot about my grandparents. I mean, not only where they went, but how they thought. They were very sharp, educated writers.

I remember going places when I was on trail crew in the '50s that my grandparents had hiked or tramped back in the early 1900s, like Shoal Pond or Carter Notch. [When I told my grandparents], they'd perk up and we'd have a brief discussion about the changes that had taken place in the intervening years.

Changes

My grandparents spent some time just loafing. We don't do that these days. Life was slower, then. We don't relax at home, and I don't know if people even loaf anymore at the huts. Geez, these days, we have to be at the parking lot at such-and-such a time.

It's not just in the mountains. It's society. Sometimes I have to be somewhere for something, I'm always thinking, *Crap, I gotta leave now, so hurry along.* I can't take time to look at a bird's nest. People get up on the top of Carter Dome, and they'll even say, "I ate three handfuls of Gorp and then I left."

Maybe they don't know any better. Maybe they don't have the wherewithal to comprehend that if they stay here for an hour and a half, they might see something, or the weather might change, or somebody nice might come by. They have to hurry down. Oh, and they set their stopwatch—and I don't mean trail runners. I mean, you know, regular goofers. "Oh, I made it down in an hour and fourteen minutes!"

Maybe they think the thing to do is to get up there as fast as they can and get on their cell phone and call, "Hey, I'm up here now!" I sound like I'm cynical, don't I? But maybe that's what they want to do too. I guess what's lost is the slowness and the feeling of just standing up there, putting your foot on a rock and looking down from Carter at the Wild River Wilderness. Think about what used to be down there in logging days, the fire in 1903, all this stuff.

Vibram soles are another change. Vibram soles just destroy trails. It's like tenderizing meat with those hammers with all the bumps on them. It softens the trail and then it rains like it did yesterday and the trail goes down the hill. There's more trail wear, for sure.

And Justice Douglas's article about the huts. That brought in so many more people.[22] And then came the interstate highway system and light-weight equipment. People can just put a tent on their back and go.

Visiting the Crew

I hike in as often as I can to see the trail crew—on a good day; I do not like sticky, muggy weather. I'll just go into the woods, visit, eat lunch. They thank me just for showing up.

When I go visit the crew, I often go in by myself. Sometimes I take in a cantaloupe with me. I have my machete from the trail crew days with me. They know that when they see the machete sticking out of Moses's pack, there must be something inside the pack and it's not ice cream.

I tell them, "I don't come in to inspect your work. I want you to be proud of your work. Show me your work. Explain to me what you're doing." And they do. They'll say, "Oh, these rocks were over here and I set this here. You can't see that rock underneath. That's the base rock. If you dig down about four inches...." And they'll dig down. There it is, right there. They're wicked proud of their work and they show it to me with that sense of pride.

Two summers ago, I had a stomachache. It wouldn't go away. I went down to the hospital, and after a bunch of tests they said, "We'll make you feel better. We're going to take your appendix out!" That was Sunday night.

---

[22] A *National Geographic* article in 1961 highlighted Supreme Court Justice William O. Douglas's trip through the AMC huts. Many people credited it with increasing interest in—and use of—the hut system. See page 89 for George Hamilton's story of escorting Justice Douglas on his hike.

On Tuesday afternoon, I came home. They told me that I couldn't hike for six weeks. I said, "That is not an option."

I was out here mowing the lawn, and a truck drove in the driveway. I recognized the two trail crew. They said, "Hey, man, how are ya? We just drove down to the hospital and they said you went home. We brought you something." They brought this huge wood chip from an ax cut. It said, "Get Well Ben" and all of them signed it. Junior, who was trail master last year, told them on their Kinsman patrol, "Whoever chops the biggest chip, that's going to be for Ben." That's an example of the relationship.

Then, Junior got hurt later in the summer. He ended up down at Memorial Hospital. Whenever anybody is in the hospital, I'll go visit them. Well, I had a chip. I wrote, "Junior, get well soon. Moses" and then the date. I took it in to him in his hospital room. Geez, he just about cried, you know. It was cool. Wicked. I'm telling you all this because that represents the feeling of the relationship.

Trail crew has probably shaped or created a whole life for me. My association with the current trail crew each year—the relationship that I have with them, that we have together—is unbelievable. I still hang around with them, and they come here and visit. Every New Year's for the last ten years, we'll have a brunch for whoever shows up. Judy and I get a mess of food, and some of them bring food. Some of them lie on the floor, some play cribbage, and some sleep beside the stove. Some of them go outside with their skis or sleds or snowboards. Others just sit around. It's very meaningful. And when I go into the woods now to visit, they say, "Oh, it's so awesome to have you come in and just talk with us, or just sit and watch."

What's special is the connection between the present and the past. It's the connection between young people and old people. An old man, in this case. It's the continuation of the camaraderie and the tightness and the love for each other.

Ben English, Jr., continues to visit with the AMC trail crew at their work sites, at AMC's Hutton Lodge in Pinkham Notch, and at his home in Jackson, New Hampshire. Whenever the ground is snow-free, he can be found hiking throughout the woods of the White Mountains.

Casey Hodgdon

A Gentle Mountain Man

Casey Hodgdon holds a cluster of prisms while working with Brad Washburn on his Presidential Range mapping project in the summer of 1983. The prisms reflect light shot from a laser survey instrument set at a far-off distance. The light beams reflect back to the theodolite many thousands of times to average into a very accurate distance. The cluster means this was a very long shot; normally only one prism is needed. (Photo courtesy of AMC Library & Archives)

I N THE LIST OF PEOPLE WHO HAVE BEEN IMPORTANT in recent White Mountain history, some are famous, while others have made their mark quietly, without much recognition. Casey Hodgdon isn't famous, but he "did it all" with a down-to-earth, unassuming passion for the mountains. He worked for the Appalachian Mountain Club under Joe Dodge, as a weather observer atop Mount Washington, and as a range patroller for the U.S. Forest Service. He was also responsible for much of the legwork behind Brad Washburn's famed map, *Mount Washington and the Heart of the Presidential Range* (see page 3 for Brad and Barbara Washburn's story). Few people have more on-the-ground knowledge of the White Mountains' high peaks, knobs, and crannies—or a greater love for these hills—than Casey did.

Casey was also the vigilant keeper of the memory of Lizzie Bourne— the second recorded victim of Mount Washington's harsh weather. Casey's love for the mountain and his admiration for Lizzie seem inextricably linked as part of the mountain's unforgiving and beautiful history. When we talked with Casey in 1994, he grew serious and reverential as he described Lizzie's last moments and the loss her family felt upon her death, as though she were somehow a part of all of our lives: "She had a lively intellect, a joyous heart, and strong affections. She was to her kindred inexpressibly dear."

Maybe Casey is best summed up by a longtime friend who put it this way: "There's nothing highfalutin about Casey. He's the most selfless, unassuming person you can imagine—and the best friend you could ever hope to have."

In His Own Words

I was born down in West Lebanon, New Hampshire, just below Hanover, but my ancestors came from up north. My father came out of West Milan and my mother came out of Groveton, New Hampshire.

My dad was a locomotive engineer on the Boston & Maine Railroad. He used to run the big passenger trains right through Randolph Valley. When I was a little kid, we'd come up to visit our relations in Groveton. I remember looking up to the Presidential Range. It was like looking at Everest or McKinley! It was always a great historical and spiritual feeling. As a kid, I had access to the Baker Library at Dartmouth. I used to read everything I could about the mountains.

I got out of high school in 1952 and went to Concord Commercial College, a little business college. But I always wanted to work in the mountains. So, in 1953 I started writing letters. I wrote to the Crawford House, the Mount Washington Hotel, and the Mountain View in Whitefield. All I wanted to do was wash dishes in a hotel in the mountains. I got all these rejections back; they'd all already hired their crews. But I also wrote a letter to this outfit I knew about, the Appalachian Mountain Club, Joseph B. Dodge, manager. He answered back and sent me a mimeographed form to fill out. At that time the AMC really didn't mean anything to me. I knew vaguely that it was about mountain climbing and huts, because I'd read about it in books.

Joe Dodge sent a message through a friend of my dad's, who worked as station agent in Gorham; I remember my father had it on the front of the stack of train order sheets. It said, "Joe Dodge will see your boy for an interview." I rode up to the AMC with my dad in the train, and Joe interviewed me. In those days, Joe had a little office, upstairs in his house, not like it is now.

Joe said, "I don't know if I can use you in the huts. You don't look too rugged." I'm not very big now, but I was even smaller then! He said, "I tell you what. We've got this campground down the road, Dolly Copp. I'll put you down as a general crew member." During the Korean War, the government was facing big cutbacks, and they couldn't operate Dolly Copp Campground. There was a lot of hootin' and hollerin' about it. Somehow, the AMC got involved and ran Dolly Copp during the war. I thought, *OK! That's all right.*

We closed Dolly Copp down in September, and I went back to school for the winter and graduated that next spring. The next summer, I was back at Dolly Copp, and that fall I started working for Joe at Pinkham. He was going to put me at Tuckerman's the following spring. But in the late fall I walked into Berlin one day, and there was a sign out front of the City Hall: Uncle Sam Needs You. I saw the navy recruiter, joined the service, and went back and told Joe, "Gee, Joe, I joined the navy!" Of course, Joe was an old navy man, so that was all right in his book. I spent forty-two months on an old destroyer, out of Newport, Rhode Island. We were in the Atlantic, the Mediterranean, South America—all over. We even went to Basra, Iraq.

After the service, I came back and Joe rehired me. That was December of 1958. He told me, "I don't know if you'd heard or not, Casey, but I'm retiring. I'll be leaving here January 1." I was one of the last ones he hired.

Working for Joe was tremendous. It was easy them days. You didn't have everything that the AMC is involved with today. We just had the huts. It was like a family at Pinkham.

Casey Gets His Name

It was Joe Dodge who gave me the name Casey. Russell is my real name. My dad died in '54 and I had some of his stuff, including his railroad watch. I used to wear it like my dad: in my pocket and the chain out so I could pull it across. I was real proud of it.

Joe Dodge got the biggest kick out of that watch. One morning I was in the kitchen, running a stainless steel, steam dishwasher. Joe said, "Hey, Casey, how ya doin'? You got the 6:05 under control?" He kept it up for two or three mornings like that and then the cook, Fred Armstrong, said something like, "Here, Casey, you want to wash this up fast for me?"

They used to say if Joe Dodge gave you a nickname, you had it forever. Joe Dodge gave me that name. It's a nice name, and everybody knows me by that.

The Mules

I was never a muleskinner, but I got involved with the burros because we used them to supply the huts. They were quite practical in their day. We used them to get the huts open and to bring in bulky items, such as bags of cement, lumber, or a toilet bowl.

They rebuilt Madison Hut with mules. I think at one time they were running around forty. But when I worked there, we only had about ten of them. There was Poison, Tapioca, Rocky, and Smoky. Smoky was the one who folks used to feed cigarettes whenever the crew came around. He'd even drink out of a bottle. The donkey corral was in back of Pinkham, up where the lodge is now. I'd load the mules onto our '57 Chevrolet truck. You could get ten of them in if you packed them sideways—an ass this way and then a head this way. They were balky and could get mean at times.

We used to run them up to Carter, Tucks, Madison, and Galehead. We had a corral for them in Franconia, for when we were using them to supply Greenleaf and Lonesome [huts]. There was another corral set up for them at the foot of Beechwood Way, in Randolph. The muleskinners got a big military tent and the regular setup, with the stove and so forth. I recollect that, on the Valley Way, a good rugged hut boy could out-pack a burro.

The transition away from mules was interesting. I didn't have any great sentimental feelings or anything. I just sort of took it in stride. Helicopters are expensive, but they can move a pallet in four or five minutes up to Madison. It would take the donkey and the hut boys two weeks to do that. They get refrigerators up to Madison, where you could never get a refrigerator before.

To the Summit

I went from the AMC to the [Mount Washington] Observatory in '60. Gordy Miller was the chief observer then. They had a couple of fellows leaving, and they needed someone to do bottle washing and a little cooking. He came down the mountain to Pinkham and asked me right there. "You gonna stay here this winter, Casey?" I said, "Well, I suppose." He said, "We could use somebody on the mountain." So he interviewed me. We had a good talk; I wasn't really all that fired up about it, but I said, "Yeah, that would be a change. I'll try it." I went up and stayed five or six years.

It was just pretty simple in those days, and the weather observations— why, there was nothing to them. You learned after a while. I passed my examinations and got my airways certification. I started out as an observer, then I became acting assistant chief observer. There were four of us: Gordy Miller, chief observer; Willy Harris, Guy Gosselin, and myself. We stayed in the old observatory for two weeks at a time, then you had a week off, then you were up for two weeks, then you had two weeks off. It was all averaged out to 19.5 working days a month, or about the same number of days off that folks had in the valley.

It was a long stretch up there, two weeks in the wintertime in that little building with shortwave radios and electronic gear. But it was a rather relaxing atmosphere. The winters were enjoyable. It never bothered me, even when I was up there for three or four weeks straight.

We worked hand in hand with the AMC. We were always down at Lakes of the Clouds Hut. See, Lakes didn't have a radio in those days; they had an old, hand-crank phone. I used to repair that line a lot. The line went up to the summit. There was one at Tuckerman's too.

My son Travis was born while I was up there working on the phone lines. I'd go out in the back of the observatory where the line came out up under the old toilet tanks, pick up the phone line, and just start following it along in my hands. If it was blown apart, you knew where to fix it. Sometimes, it was just a little telltale bump or break in the line that I'd feel in my hands. I'd go down the summit cone in back of the TV antennas. The line crossed under Davis Path in a little two-inch pipe, near the intersection of the Crawford Path. Then it pretty well ran parallel to the Crawford Path, on the east side of the trail, crossed over the trail, and got into that pucker brush at the top of the Ammonoosuc Ravine.

Travis was born at 3:26 in the afternoon. I was probably down in that pucker brush, swearing and pulling phone lines. Finally I got to the Lakes. After making line patches, I went in to the Lakes phone, gave it a crank, and hoped somebody answered. Which Guy did. He said, "OK Casey, look, can you come back up the mountain?" I said, "I can—but I was gonna stay for supper." "No, you'd better come up. I need you here." "What's happened?" "Oh, nothing. I'll tell you when you get up here."

So I ran. There was Guy standing there and a couple of guys from the Cog [Railway] and from the TV station I knew. Guy says, "Congratulations!" and gives me a cigar. I went down in the car.

My wife took it in stride in those days. She was just a young thing, so she figured that's the way life was, but we talk a lot now about just how she did it. She was lucky she was a local girl so she had her friends around. It might have been selfishness on my part. I just thought it was great up in the mountains. Now I look back, and I think maybe I shouldn't have been on the mountain at that time, but that's the way it went. They were great days up there. I would have never believed in my wildest dreams as a young kid down in West Lebanon at fifteen years old, reading everything I could on the Obs,[23] that I would work on top of Mount Washington.

With the Forest Service

The observatory was steady work, but you couldn't raise a family on that. I left and went to work for the U.S. Forest Service [USFS] in the summer of '66. At first I was just summer help; then I got on the Civil Service roster as an official government employee and I started building retirement. Backcountry patrol was my job. Boy, I liked that! I'd hike Madison to Lakes

[23] Common nickname for the Mount Washington Observatory.

and back, and then down to Mizpah [Hut], after it was built. In the fall, I assisted in the closing of Dolly Copp—the Forest Service was back running it again—then I'd be in the woods marking timber until March.

I can remember when I was first on range patrol, looking down from the Great Gulf headwall and counting all the tents down in the Great Gulf. That was par for the course. You went out and talked with all the nice people at night. "Where can we pitch our tent?" "Well, right over there, in back of them." The tent strings would be crossing each other! It's all prohibited today. There was a lot of damage, especially down in the Great Gulf. I remember prior to the new wilderness regulations, which went in around 1964, there was no control at all. The place was heavily overused. Around by the upper shelters and the new shelter by the bluff, the land was really beaten up and desecrated.

Years later, after I had left the Forest Service and was working for Brad Washburn, we started mapping the Great Gulf. *Where are the people?* I wondered. I was amazed at how it had grown up. I never would have believed it if I hadn't seen it. I'd figured it would be a hundred years before you'd ever get that back, and in ten years' time it had really grown in. You go up to where the old shelters were now and it's all grown in around there.

Forest Service was changing a lot. Like the AMC, it was becoming more involved with the public and user permits. We had to go to law-enforcement school. The U.S. Forest Service has never been considered a law-enforcement organization. Now it has become one.

I left the Forest Service in 1976, after eleven years. I really didn't want to leave. The primary reason I left was because of my family, you know, being laid off for two months in the spring every year. With family demands, I eventually had to take a steady job with the Town of Gorham Highway Department and that was the end of my USFS career.

Working with Washburn

After leaving the USFS, I said to myself, *Well, I probably won't be doing much more hiking.* Then I ran into Brad Washburn, and he recruited me into the survey crew to work on his Mount Washington map. I was very lucky to work on the map. I was local, I was available, and I had the knowledge of the mountains and the trails. I'd never really formally met Brad, but I knew about him because I'd read his books on Mount Washington and about his climbing Mount McKinley. He was pretty impressive.

He had just started the map and he wanted a target put up on top of Mount Adams. I remember it was one of those freaky gorgeous November days, with people running about the range in T-shirts. The target was one of those steel ones that used to weigh thirty-five pounds. "You got a pack for it?" "Yeah, I got a pack for it." "OK, I'll give you a radio." So I got this target out of Madison Hut and put it up on Adams for him. He was over at the Halfway House on Mount Washington. I talked to him on the radio, and we got some bearings. And somehow or other that was it. I just suddenly started working and it became an eleven-year thing.

Brad would come and have supper here. My wife was very good about it. At first she was hesitant, because of me taking off all the time. But then she got to know Brad and Barbara. They're wonderful people. We've had many a meal right here at this table. The map was made right out of this house. We had telephone calls back and forth for eleven years.

Ninety percent of it was legwork. We used Joe Brigham's helicopter just a small percentage of the time. I've been to practically every one of the survey stations, helping to set them up. On the trail, you had to walk backward a lot of the time, and a lot of nights coming out with a headlamp on your head.

It was originally planned we'd measure all the trails with a wheel, but we never did because if you ran over a rough trail like the Gulfside, it would pick up a lot of inaccuracies. So we used 100-foot tape. I'd say ninety-five percent of all the trails were measured with 100-foot tape—sometimes time and again! We'd have a little error, Brad would say, "Something was not coming out right with this. Look at these figures we've got, but it shouldn't be this way." I remember doing that, don't know how many times, 'til he finally was satisfied.

Some hikers wondered what was this all about. I suppose you can see their point. Once, Brad and I went down to the Southern Peaks. There was a fellow and a woman on Monroe. We said, "Nice day," or something like that. I took out my tape and started writing numbers down in my book. It's all quiet, and the fellow says, "What are you trying to do? Leave your mark in the White Mountains?" I start to explain it's a very important map project, and I get to tell him all about triangulation stations and all that stuff. I could tell right away that that target really rubbed them the wrong way.

Casey (left) poses with Brad and Barbara Washburn while working on the Presidential Range mapping project, 1983. (Photo courtesy of AMC Library & Archives)

Things like that never bothered me. I wouldn't want to see a hotel built on top of Monroe, but something like that wouldn't bother me one bit. But it's interesting meeting people who have a different aspect on things. Some of them get pretty extreme; I mean everything would be out of the White Mountains and stripped down. For example, I love the cog railroad. It surprises me the people who think it's a terrible thing and should be outlawed and off the mountain.

"The Other Woman"

When I first worked at the observatory, one day in early May I was making a trip around the summit on my last day. I went up against the railroad tracks, and there was an old memorial sign to Lizzie Bourne, just kind of leaning there. It was the funniest damn thing: Something just kind of grabbed me and I started to wonder who she was.

I asked Colonel Teague [owner of the Cog Railway], "Would it be all right to build a new memorial?" So I took Lizzie's old sign down to my house. I had it in the cellar and, when we had trouble with the sewer pipe under the toilet, I flipped the sign over and shoved it up in there so the thing wouldn't come apart. That's the same sign that's up in [Senator] Judd Gregg's office in Washington, D.C., right now. Anyway, I made a brand-new one to replace it. I traced it out with stencils and painted it by hand with a fine brush. It took quite a while to do it.

About the time I started this great infatuation with her, my wife came home one day and said, "You know that girl you're interested in? Bourne? Well, there was a picture of her on television today."

"You don't mean Lizzie Borden?" Everybody gets them mixed up. A couple of days later I went down to Portland, to F.O. Bailey's Antiques Appraisers and Auctioneers. They took me way upstairs into the garret of the place, and there's Lizzie's portrait pushed up against a dirty old window. It's by Charles O. Cole, who apparently was a famous portrait painter out of Maine. It was painted after her death from a daguerreotype. Years later, I actually acquired that daguerreotype. I gave it to the Mount Washington Observatory Museum. It's now in the Valley Facility in North Conway.

They want $375 for it. I said, "$375?" He said, "Yup." It's one of the few times I really thought on my feet fast. I said, "All I've got on me is ten bucks. Can I put it as a down payment?" He said, "Sure!"

We didn't have any money, but I had a good name. So I went up to the bank and I talked to one of the guys. He said, "You want $375? Don't worry about it, Casey." So I got my first-time-ever loan out from a bank.

I started learning more and more about Lizzie. This nice woman, Barbara Kimball, who was the curator of a museum down in Kennebunk, helped me find a lot of letters. Lizzie's buried in the Hope Cemetery in Kennebunk. There's a huge cemetery, but something almost took me right to where she was buried. Part of the inscription on the stone is what I painted on the memorial sign. It's from "Excelsior," a Longfellow poem about a boy that climbs in Switzerland in the Alps and dies up there. I think Lizzie's father must have changed the "he" to a "she":

> *Here in the twilight cold and gray*
> *Lifeless but beautiful, she lay.*
> *And from the sky, serene and far*
> *A voice fell like a shooting star.*

She was twenty-three years old when she died up there on Mount Washington. A lot of people used to joke she was run over by the train, but she died in September 1855, fourteen years before the Cog was built. They built this tremendous monument when she died. People stood there in the old days and got their picture taken. If a person died on the mountain today, they'd probably forget about it in a couple of days.

Lizzie was there with her uncle George W. Bourne and Lucy Augusta, her cousin. They decided they would hike to the summit and spend the night at [the] Tip Top [House]. They started out as they do today, too late in the afternoon, about two o'clock or two-thirty, and started across from the Glen House. They finally made it to the Halfway House. Of course, Mr. Myers would talk to them and give them the old spiel about it being late in the day. "Why don't you stay overnight and head up tomorrow morning?" "No, no, we're going to go up." Lizzie was the persistent one.

The letters that Mr. Bourne and others wrote said they had gotten up 6 miles and were experiencing no difficulties at that time. In fact, two of the Spaulding boys, who were going down to the Glen House for the night, encountered them at that point, and their report was that they weren't in no trouble at that time. But imagine after that, you can almost picture it: You get above that point and suddenly you start getting into the wind. Lizzie had a hard time going; she had a new bonnet which was whipped from her head and must have gone over into Huntington Ravine or someplace. She was greatly distressed at that, but finally darkness closed upon them. Mr. Bourne left them for a while and proceeded up farther, probably to where the corral is now. They couldn't have seen the corral because if he had he would have known how close he was to the summit. But they had no conceivable idea.

They were in the fog, cold, and they're lucky it wasn't a triple tragedy. In a letter, Mr. Bourne wrote how the girls sang songs, and he talked to Elizabeth—Lizzie—and said, "How are you doing?" She said, "Nicely, thank you," and those were her last words.

In the letter he mentions how they pulled the shawl over her and weighted it down with rocks, and then "they moved some distance away and spent the night."

The following morning they looked up, and, with the weather breaking, there was Tip Top. So Mr. Bourne ran up and banged on the door and told

Casey Hodgdon keeps a vigilant watch over Lizzie Bourne's monument, 1994.
(Photo by Jonathan Kannair, jonathankannair.com)

what happened during the night. They all ran down and got Lizzie. They tried to revive her, but to no avail. She was long gone. One account talked about her beautiful black hair in the wind and the stark and staring eyes.

They packed Lizzie in a box they made, and brought her down where she was met by a horse and team at the 2-mile mark because the road was only done to that point. The letter I read from her father said she looked as beautiful in death as she did in life.

Four or five years later, in August 1861, the road was finished. Judge Bourne didn't die until September 23, 1873. I'll take the sign up again this spring. I'm going to go over the lettering: "Aged 23 years." The old ones had it down as twenty years, but that was wrong. She was born June 20, 1832. I usually get the monument up before Memorial Day. I don't know who will do it after I'm gone.

Looking Backward and Forward

I stayed in the White Mountains because I really liked it here. Of course, I was fascinated by stories of Everest and the Matterhorn. I remember a *Life* magazine back in '47 which had a big article on the Matterhorn. That article fascinated me to no end. The great fall from 14,000 feet to the glacier below. And McKinley! I read about Brad Washburn, never thinking that years and years later I'd meet him. But the history of the White Mountains has always intrigued me.

I left the AMC in the mid-sixties, and about that time everything changed—helicopters came in, radio communication, and the new AMC programs. I could see it changing when I was at the observatory. Joe's house was torn down, the new office was built, and then the new Pinkham trading post came a year or two after that.

I'm glad I worked in the old days. There's probably people working at the AMC now who thirty years from now will say, "I'm glad I worked there then; boy, look at it now." But you go up there now and there's so many people around. What's it cost now, to stay in a hut? Something like $50? I remember back when I was on range patrol it was $8.50 a night. I can't afford to stay in the huts for fifty bucks a night, but I can't argue about it. I suppose in this day and age there's a tremendous overhead for operating the huts. It's probably a justifiable, break-even price.

I try to keep pretty open-minded. I remember the summit the way it was, when I was up there with the old hotel. I wish it was the way it was before. But, there again, I keep saying to myself, this is the way it's got to be. You've got to keep up with the times and the vast multitudes of people. You can't operate the way we operated thirty or forty years ago. So I accept it. Of course, every now and then tears trickle down your cheek and you think, *Gee, the old days.* It's too bad it's this way now. I'd like to see it the way it was with a hotel over there, old Tom the cook, the people who worked there, and the chambermaids. Those great old sentimental days I'll never forget.

I still hike a lot. I walk the railroad tracks all the time. I walk from Gorham to Randolph and back. I measured it with my measuring wheel. It's 43/100 miles each way. I walk to Berlin a lot and my wife will pick me up. That's 492/100 miles.

In my wildest dreams, as I think back now, I've done everything there is: I've worked on the summit at the observatory, AMC, Dolly Copp, range patrol for the Forest Service. What more could you have?

People have come and asked, "How would you like to go back and do it all over again, except you can have all kinds of money, but you won't live that kind of life?" No, I don't think I'd do it. I'd go right back and do the same thing again.

Upon retirement from the Town of Gorham, Casey Hodgdon worked as a docent for the State of New Hampshire's Division of Parks, at the Tip Top House on Mount Washington. He remained active until a few months before his death, often walking the rail trail from Gorham to Randolph, or the old Hogan Road from Gorham to Berlin. He died at the age of sixty-seven on June 15, 2002.

Without Casey, the Lizzie Bourne monument has not had a dedicated caretaker, instead being maintained by the Cog Railway with the support of volunteers.

Bill Arnold

A Lifelong Caretaker

Bill and Barbara Arnold stand on the back deck of their house in Randolph in 2011.
(Photo by Ned Therrien)

NESTLED BETWEEN THE RUGGED NORTHERN PRESIDENTIALS and the wild Kilkenny Range, perhaps no town better represents the spirit and landscape of the White Mountains than Randolph. High alpine cabins and shelters are within walking distance of the town, and in the valley lies what is said to be the densest network of trails anywhere in the United States.

Bill Arnold spent his summers in this unique setting, wandering the trails around town, in an era when allowing your child to take risks and experience independence was more acceptable than it is today. "It was great. We just walked everywhere. You'd go right where you wanted on the trails," said Arnold. "We had friends in the valley and we'd just shoot down the EZ Way or Bee Line and come home at the end of the day. And our parents—I don't know if they knew where we were or not. We didn't get in trouble, and certainly we were in good shape."

Those childhood walks on the trails were just the beginning. Arnold became the youngest-ever caretaker for the Randolph Mountain Club (RMC). That, in turn, led to seasons with the Appalachian Mountain Club (AMC) at Pinkham Notch—including the great winter of 1968–69, when the snow never seemed to stop. There was so much snow, avalanches were a common occurrence, and the crew at Pinkham resorted to running a snowblower on top of the lodge roof. From there, it was on to backcountry patrol for the U.S. Forest Service and seasons spent fighting forest fires out West. "Being a Forest Service ridge-runner was right up there on the list of great jobs," said Arnold.

Through his many years in the backcountry, Bill has maintained a lifelong commitment to search and rescue in the White Mountains, while also working to foster a sense of self-reliance among hikers. We spoke with him in 2011 at his home in Randolph, New Hampshire.

In His Own Words

I was born in Medford, Massachusetts, in 1946, but we moved to Cincinnati, Ohio, when I was three years old, and I have a lot more memories of there. I went to various schools in Cincinnati and Dayton, Ohio, and even Niagara Falls, New York, and I went to college at Paul Smith's in the Adirondacks for a semester. I studied forestry.

We had been coming to Randolph to this house since the summer before I was born. My father was an Episcopal minister. When he was in seminary, my father had bad hay fever and he had a professor who said, "Oh, you ought to go up to the White Mountains. They don't have any allergies up there. I go to this little town called Randolph and I have a house there. You ought to go up."

So my parents came up here and they stayed at what's now the Grand View Lodge and ended up buying this house in 1939. That was the end of the Depression and I know they got it cheap.

So I've been coming up here summers all my life. I became really good summer friends with another kid up here, Peter Bowers, and we spent a lot of time hiking and a lot of time fishing. Jack Boothman would send us to these secret fishing holes[24]—we were maybe eleven, twelve years old—and we were allowed to go up to Castleview Rock alone. This was in the late 1950s.

It was great. Especially as we got to be teenagers, we basically just had the run of the town. Before we could drive, we just walked everywhere. You'd go right where you wanted on the trails. We had friends in the valley and we'd just shoot down the EZ Way or Bee Line, and come home at the end of the day. And our parents—I don't know if they knew where we were or not. They didn't really seem to care much. We didn't get in trouble, and certainly we were in good shape from being out on the trails. We'd go hiking a lot, go fishing.

The hotels were around when I was a kid—the Mount Crescent House and the Ravine House were going. They were the center of things. Some of the little summer homes never even had a kitchen. People staying there would take their meals at the Mount Crescent House. We'd get our mail there. The post office was in the valley and the Boothmans would pick up the mail from there and bring it up to them. We'd eat meals at the Mount Crescent House occasionally. That was kind of a big deal. They had the buffet every Saturday night, and Jack Boothman would always save the end slice of the ham for the RMC Crag Camp caretaker, who used to be down on a Saturday night.

---

[24] Jack Boothman was a resident of Randolph, a North Country fixture, and a friend to all in the community.

My mother and my sister and I would come for the whole summer. My father didn't have his whole summer off, so he would fly—back then you could fly right into Berlin—or he would take the train because the train would stop right here at Randolph station.

Becoming a Caretaker

When Peter Bowers and I were fifteen, we spent a big part of the summer up at Crag Camp. It was a great, great place to be in the summer. Ash Campbell, Jr., was the caretaker there, and we were up there a lot of the time. We helped cut the firewood for the stoves, painted, and did a lot of work. We put some money in the kitty, but we did a lot of work too.

There were no radios then. We used flashlights. We'd all go out on the porch at nine o'clock, put all the flashlights together and flash down to the valley. Our parents would be down in a car and we'd see the headlights blink back and forth and then they'd know we were up there safe and we'd know that they were down here.

Ash was supposed to come back as the caretaker of Crag Camp in the summer of '63, but at the last minute, he didn't. I can remember very well the day getting a letter from Klaus Goetze[25] saying that Ash had turned down the job and that they decided that they would offer the job to Peter and me together. We were only sixteen, but somehow Klaus figured two sixteen-year-olds would equal a twenty-year-old or something like that. We were offered the job at $20 a piece per week.

I can remember getting the letter and just being—just wild. What more could you want when you're sixteen years old back then? Being the Crag Camp caretaker was better than being the president of the United States. I mean, it was like right up there with God—you just had all the power in the world. You were away from your parents, but then close enough so if you got in trouble, they were here—and all your friends were around all of the time, and there was a lot—I don't know if status is the word, but it was just the best job in the world, and no one was nervous about us being up there.

There was no Gray Knob [cabin] caretaker and that was the first time RMC had two caretakers. We kept an eye on Gray Knob and the Log Cabin

---

[25] Klaus Goetze was a longtime RMC president. To this day, the club is run by volunteers.

and the Perch but we stayed at Crag Camp. I went up there in mid-June and stayed up through the summer. Peter and I would alternate days off so I was up there alone some of the time.

We didn't collect money. Back then, you didn't have to pay. There was a metal box bolted to the wall, and it had a sign over it with a picture of a cat that said, "Please feed the kitty." So part of it was to get people to donate money and keep it clean and neat, and there were projects that had to be done like painting and patching, putting the roofing cement on the leaky roof and cutting firewood.

Handling the crowds was probably our weakest spot because we were young. Back then, you got a lot of the camp groups. It was crowd control. I can still remember the biggest night we had was thirty-eight people. People sleeping on the tables, under the tables, in the kitchen, on the woodstove—I mean, you'd pack 'em in everywhere.

A couple of times we had some minor rescues. The way you do now, where a group will come in late and say, "Oh, we've got two more people up there someplace and we don't know where they are." We'd go out with a Coleman lantern and we'd find them. It'd be cold and windy and wet, but even at sixteen, we knew our way around the mountains so well that we could find them.

Packing for RMC

After we caretook Crag Camp, I spent a couple of summers helping RMC out on the trail crew, when somebody was sick or they needed somebody extra. When RMC remodeled Crag Camp and Gray Knob, I did a lot of packing of the materials: flooring, roofing, shingles. Everything went up on your back—there were no helicopters then. This is back when AMC was still using the mules. We talked about mules. Decided it would be pretty hard getting them up the Spur Trail, and I think the higher powers decided people—teenagers—were cheaper than mules anyway. We got paid maybe thirty-five cents per pound.

I probably did three summers of that construction packing. I'd start out with maybe fifty, sixty pounds and then get up to eighty and then go over a hundred probably two or three times a week. A hundred pounds would take me probably three and a half, four hours. Then I'd rest a little bit and have lunch and then come down in forty-five minutes.

We'd pack from Coldbrook Lodge, the home of [Jack and Gwen] Boothman. They had a scale at the camps and the caretakers were in charge of weighing the loads when they got in, and they'd keep track and let the powers in the valley know how much everybody packed. I was pretty much the main packer. My goal through that whole time was to carry more than my weight up there, which I eventually did. I carried up a cast iron sink and a pump and a bunch of other stuff. I weighed 115 pounds and the load was 132.

After that summer, I went to Paul Smith's College, but I had to leave, due to health issues, which I had all through school. They really flared up and I thought, *I need to get out of school and just get my act together.* The school said, "You can come back any time you want, but you need to get healthy." So I found myself sort of wondering what to do next and ended up here.

Life at Pinkham

I went to Pinkham to work for AMC in late summer of '67, after just sitting around a bit. Of course, I had worked for the RMC and I knew the White Mountains. Bruce Sloat [AMC huts manager] hired me, saying, "When can you start? How about tomorrow?" I said, "OK." Back then they'd pretty much hire anybody anyway, and if you actually knew where you were in the mountains, well, that was a big plus.

The very first job at Pinkham was working on a dam on the Cutler River that used to be for hydropower. It was full of boulders. Sid Havely was on construction crew and he gave me the task of going up there and sloshing around in the pool, and hauling these rocks out. It was hard work. I always remember my first day's work and thinking, *Well, is this what it's going to be like?* But this was September now, so the huts were just closing. Back then you'd do breakfast at Pinkham for the guests, then we'd close a hut and come back and work supper.

The summer hut crew thing was not for me. I learned when I started working at Pinkham in the wintertime in '67, the winter crew at Pinkham were very, very different people from the summer hut crews. To a point where there was friction. The summer hut boys would come up at vacations and want to stay in the crew quarters at Pinkham while we were living there. They'd be up partying and carrying on—I mean, I don't blame them; they were on vacation. We weren't.

The scene at Pinkham then was way, way, way different from now. We all lived together. It was all like family, which isn't to say we all got along. It was a lifestyle of just living with a lot of different kinds of people—no matter whether you got along or not, you had certain things that had to get done. Marty Child was the hutmaster at Pinkham when I started. But, after November, Marty said, "I'm leaving. I'm going to New Zealand. I'm out of here." I said, "Okey-dokey, I can be hutmaster." I'd been there only what—two or three months? But, the hutmaster's job was just to make sure everybody was doing everything.

Four or five of us did the basic meals and lodge work. There were Bruce and Mary Sloat, and two cooks, Mel McKenna and John Chadwick. A few others would come and go. The AMC had a hard time hiring then. Bruce had a deal with Antioch, and they'd get two or three or four students from there who would come in and work for three months at a time, then they'd leave and a new busload would come in. Commander Marvel would meet them out front with his gun strapped to his side—"Welcome to Pinkham."

Commander Marvel: I could go on for days about him. He was assistant manager of the hut system, under Bruce. He always insisted that he be called Commander. His name was Robert Marvel. But, after a while, I didn't think twice about it. He was Commander Marvel. He was a retired navy commander, from Bartlett, I think. He was sort of the authority figure for us kids, and that didn't always sit very well with us. He had worked down in Antarctica as a commander of a base. He was very, very, very, very conservative, which was an interesting mix, because there weren't many other conservative people working at Pinkham.

He must have started in '65 or so, and he left in the early '70s. But he made a big impression. We had "Der pans" in the huts, and "Der barrels," both named for the Commander. Der barrels were 55-gallon drums that were painted green. This was before carry in/carry out. There were huge crowds in the spring on the weekends up in Tuckerman's. They were way more out of control than they are now. One job we always did every Monday was go and empty the Der barrels into the truck. The barrels were right down in the middle of the parking lot at Pinkham. They'd be emptied Friday, and by Monday morning, they'd be buried in trash. It was actually a good job because it was ninety-nine percent beer bottles and every twentieth one would be full.

Kibbe [Glover] was there in those days too. He was great. I feel sort of honored because I think I was one of the relatively few people that could get along with him. He had been in World War II. I guess he went through a really nasty time on some islands in the Pacific.

Kibbe loved the girls! That was back when Pinkham had a little snack bar and coffee place. People would come in, sit down, and actually talk and visit and put up their maps and plan hikes. We sold coffee and sandwiches and Kibbe was always hanging around there—that was in the Trading Post. He was a good photographer, and he'd find the pretty girls and come out and start taking pictures—*click, click, click.* The trick was that most of the time he didn't have film in the camera because why waste the film? So then there'd always be somebody that would be yelling, "Kibbe, you got any film today or not?" And he'd go off grumbling.

When I was at Pinkham the Vietnam War was going on, and there were guys who had gone off to Vietnam. I think the whole time they were gone, some of them were thinking about coming back to the White Mountains. Probably, in some respect, that sort of kept them going. A few of them would come back to Pinkham even in the middle of the winter and want a job, and we would try our very best to hire them back if we could.

We would hire them on which is pretty interesting because we were a pretty radical antiwar group then and very much opposed to the war. But then you'd get these veterans that would come back and you'd get to actually know them one on one, and it was a whole different thing. Some of them were fine, and some of them had all the classic symptoms that you read about—up all night screaming and the heavy drinking, and they obviously had seen some really, really bad things. Living in a group like that was probably as good a thing as anything for them.

Joe Dodge

Joe Dodge [who had retired in 1959] came into Pinkham when I was working there. He used to come up every Friday 'cause Mel McKenna was the cook. Mel would make doughnuts every Friday morning, and Joe would come up and get doughnuts and have a cup of coffee. Mel found out eventually that Joe was feeding the doughnuts to his birds, and all of a sudden, he got cut off.

Right about that time [in 1969], they rebuilt the Trading Post. When I started at Pinkham, it was the old log Trading Post, which was a classic building. Of course, it was in rough shape. The roof would leak, and I can remember on rainy days lining up buckets right on the front counter where we worked, catching the water coming through the ceiling. The basement was full of water too. The building wasn't big enough for the needs, but it was really, really sad to see it go because it was a classic. It was a log cabin. It was kind of dark but the new building—and I still call it the new building—certainly doesn't have the same ambience as that old one did. The old Trading Post was very, very welcoming and cozy.

There were bullet holes in the logs in the back of the dining room wall. Apparently Joe Dodge and his friends after dinner would sit back with a couple of drinks and shoot at the squirrels as they ran along the inside of the logs. Even in my time, we were pretty horrified that such a thing could happen.

Joe was retired, but he'd come up for a visit from time to time. It was great. He was just like one of us going back and visiting now. He'd tell stories. He was still Joe. Still kind of cantankerous, and he wouldn't stay that long. He'd have a cup of coffee and then head out. This was in the old log building, of course. The new building was built in '69. I remember Joe came in once when the new one was built. Came in once. Had a cup of coffee, looked around, and he never came back, as far as I knew. He probably did some time but not that I saw while I was there.

1968–1969: The Big Snow Winter

The winter of '68–'69, it just snowed and snowed and snowed. I was staying in a little house at the end of Mount Crescent Road [in Randolph] on my days off, and it was like living in a cave. The windows were buried. I had steps going down into the door and I had to duck my head under the little porch roof.

Roofs caving in was the big issue that winter. At Pinkham, we shoveled and shoveled and shoveled. We hired extra people to shovel. They hired a big front-end loader to bucket out the snow in the parking lot. It kept getting stuck, so they had to have two so one could always pull the other one out. We had a snowblower up on the roof of the lodge that we put up on blocks so we'd just shovel snow into it. This was two stories high, but it got

Bill Arnold, second from left, rests on a 1971 winter hike with, from left, Gordon Campbell, Chris Campbell, and Jon Frueh. Arnold later helped dismantle the metal Quonset hut seen in the background. (Photo by Jon Frueh)

so the banks on the side were so high the snowblower couldn't even blow off it. Eventually, it died because we were working it so hard.

There was just no place to put the snow. Wildcat [Ski Area] was shutting because the gondolas were hitting the snow. They'd have to dig them out. It just kept coming and coming. There was some kind of rescue every Sunday, and some in between. It was all hands on deck. There were some really wild rescues.

I went from early October of '68 'til mid-June in '69, working in the snow the entire time because I was up working for AMC in Tuckerman's a lot in the spring. We'd do breakfast at Pinkham, then go up. We had huge, huge crowds. This was before there were any camping regulations. There were people drunk all over the trails, camping everywhere, just piles and piles of beer bottles all the way up the trail. We'd go up mid-week with garbage bags on because it was a nice day for a walk. So you'd take your garbage bag and fill it with beer bottles. This was before carry in/carry out.

There were a lot of people, and conditions were so different from what they were used to because of the snow. I'm glad I was young because I can remember being completely exhausted at the end of every weekend between the big crowds coming up and the rescues.

Search and Rescue

I started getting into search and rescue during the winter of '68–'69 while I was working at Pinkham. I'd done a little bit with the RMC, but when you're at Pinkham, you're the only show in town—that was it except for Forest Service at Tuckerman's. Brad [Ray][26] and Rene [LaRoche] were up at Tucks. It was basically the two of them. So whenever anything was going on, it was AMC. You'd never think twice about not going on a rescue. We'd leave one person at the front desk to work the phones and the cook and that was it. Supper for the guests would be late, or the cook would fix the meals, and the guests would just wait on themselves. There'd be dirty dishes when we got back, but you never would consider not going on a rescue unless the conditions are just too bad, or you were sick.

There was a school group from Phillips Academy, up on Mount Adams. A poor kid just slipped and fell. Didn't slide very far but he hit his head and died.[27] The group got him down. They broke into Madison Hut and sort of laid him out there. Sent somebody down for help. It was on a Sunday [February 9, 1969], during one of the many, many huge storms, just snowing feet after feet. I can remember leaving Pinkham at dusk with a new Crew Cab four-wheel-drive pickup. Had it loaded to the gills with litters in the back and everything. We met Forest Service and Fish and Game at Appalachia with all this stuff. It was just snowing as hard as you can imagine.

We started up the Valley Way and Paul Doherty was there.[28] He was working for Fish and Game and had a deal with Polaris snow machines where they would give him a brand new Polaris snowmobile every year. It was the hot machine. But, it just went 20 feet and he buried it and that was it. He was all upset. Jack Boothman was there on one of his old snow machines, and just went *putt putt putt* right up the trail. Jack and Paul were good friends but there was a lot of rivalry over the snow machines. Jack got probably three-quarters of a mile up the Valley Way before he had it buried. Then we came along on snowshoes and eventually passed him.

We went up and brought this poor kid down. It was rough because there was a whole school group and they were obviously very upset. We came

---

[26] See page 163 for Brad Ray's story.
[27] See "Accidents Report," *Appalachia*, December 1969, XXXVII no. 4, page 657.
[28] See page 213 for Paul Doherty's story.

back to where Jack's snowmobile had been and it wasn't there. "This is the tree, this is the corner!" We know it's here. There wasn't even a bump in the snow. It was just completely buried in maybe four hours. We had to dig it out, then haul it out. But that's the way that winter was. It just kept snowing.

The biggest rescue, most tragic rescue certainly in terms of numbers that I've ever been on, was the Cog Railway, which was in the fall of 1967.[29] Something like seventy-five people were hurt and eight people were killed. I was young. There was a little kid who died that was like three years old and I can remember having to pick him up. He was the age of my nephew at the time. That's a lot when you're twenty-one. That rescue was probably a life-changer for me.

We headed up the auto road with a truck full of litters, blankets, and people. The first on the scene was the observatory, along with Doctor Appleton, who was up visiting the Obs[30] that evening. It was pretty much AMC, and Forest Service sent a bunch of people.

The truck kept overheating on the road because we had it so loaded down. By the time we got up there, it was dark. We were up there most of the night loading up injured people and then eventually bodies. They put the bodies on a flat car to come back down on the train. I ended up spending the night at the observatory. Their phones were ringing off the hook. We went back down to the site early in the morning with coffee and doughnuts. Rene LaRoche and Casey Hodgdon [from the Forest Service][31] spent the night there at the scene because there was stuff strewn everywhere. Governor [John] King came up the next day. I actually caught a ride down the auto road with him.

I've been on a lot of rescues since then and five plane crashes too. They'd almost never turn out well, although one crash was over on Mount Cabot where we took up hiking boots and walked them both out just fine.

We here in New Hampshire and the White Mountains, we're very good at search and rescue. People get hurt, we get them out. And I can't tell you for sure how it compares with the rest of the country or the rest of the world, but I think it's pretty favorable and unfortunately, I think that's part of the

---

[29]   See page 177 for Ellen Teague's story. She was the owner of the Cog Railway.
[30]   Common nickname for the Mount Washington Observatory.
[31]   See page 111 for Casey Hodgdon's story.

problem. You know I've heard people say to me, "Oh well, if we get hurt, we'll just call you, Bill, or call the Forest Service, or we'll just pick up the phone and dial 911." They know someone's going to come. I don't know what you're going to do about it. Are you going to say, "No, we're not going to go"? It's the same old question.

Cell phones have changed things a lot. They just made it way, way too easy to call for help. I'm sure it's part of the problem. In the olden days if you got hurt, you didn't really have any choice but to get yourself out of it. The very last resort really was to send someone down for help. That's all you had. Now, the very first resort is just to pick up your phone and call for help. It happens often enough now that people just get to thinking, *Oh, geez, it's been two hours. Where the hell have you guys been?*

I think it has changed the experience. In my youth, part of being in the mountains was that you were just out there on your own, and if there was a problem, you dealt with it. That was part of the experience. That's why you went to the mountains or the woods. You were just one on one. With a cell phone, it's just all completely different. That's not just here in the mountains; it's just the way our world is.

The big thing now is who's going to pay for search and rescue. Certainly, there're more volunteer groups and more individuals than there ever have been, but it's also costing a lot more. Fish and Game certainly is more involved than they used to be for whatever reason. When I was doing it, even twenty years ago, you didn't really think about the money. Somebody had to but it was mostly all just volunteers. Of course, you've got a lot more fancier, more expensive equipment now too.

I think volunteers could be used more now, and I think there should be a mechanism to at least make it easier to reimburse them for equipment—and maybe mileage—from the New Hampshire Outdoor Council. I think the state of New Hampshire, just like any other state, should be ready to ante up and pay for search and rescue. I mean, we've got the mountains. They attract bazillion tourists and tourists are bringing in a lot of money.

We're talking about $150,000 a year for search and rescue—not really all that much in the scheme of things. Whether you take it out of meals and lodgings tax or take it out of the tolls, or take it out of your gas tax, or whatever—if we're inviting these people up and we're taking their money, one way or another, then we have to ante up a little bit. It's got to cost a little bit from the state.

I think the Forest Service needs to take a bigger role. I've said for years that certainly that would be the most fair. If your federal taxes are paying for search and rescue, then the guy from Massachusetts is paying as much as the guy from New Hampshire, and that makes it a little more fair. The Forest Service, one way or another, is in charge of the national forest, which is most of the White Mountains. They're charged with managing them. They should be doing a lot more in search and rescue, both in manpower and financially. They haven't for years and years and years. I don't think it will change, but ideally it should.

I don't think a required hiker fee is really that doable. Partly because the Forest Service already has one. So what are you going to do, require two permits, one from the state and one from the feds? I think really the state needs to cough up the money.

Going to the Forest Service
In the spring of '69, I came back to the RMC. I worked at Gray Knob that summer of '69 and I went back to Pinkham in the fall of '69. In '70, I applied for a job with the Forest Service. They knew me. I'd worked with Brad [Ray] and Rene [LaRoche] on rescues and at Tuckerman's. Back then at Pinkham we had a policy that any Forest Service, Fish and Game, State Police, highway crew—any of those guys—could come in for a coffee or a meal, anytime. I applied for the job and got on as a seasonal. John Bailey was my boss and I worked on trail crew, and we worked hard.

The first part of the summer was clearing blowdowns and brushing—a lot of brushing—on Forest Service trails. And then the second part was erosion work. We worked on the Valley Way, all the Carter trails, [Mount] Moriah, Shelburne Trail. There were about four or five of us on the crew then. John was in charge. I was sort of unofficially second in charge even though it was my first year working with the Forest Service. I knew the mountains better than any of the others.

I went back to AMC in the fall of '70, and in '71, I went back with the Forest Service, but now I was backcountry. They called us backcountry ridge-runners then. Next to being an RMC caretaker, being a Forest Service ridge-runner was right up there on the list of great jobs. You'd just hike around the trails all day. There was a certain amount of trail maintenance. You'd have a storm and there were trees down, then you'd take your ax with you and cut them out of the way. Put up signs. Maybe repair bridges. Cleaning water bars. Keeping track of the Quonset hut at Edmands Col [below Mount Jefferson]. Painting the yellow rocks on top of the cairns on the Gulfside Trail. The top rock was always painted yellow with highway paint. It was always a windy day, of course, when you were doing that. Anything that needed to be done out there, we did it.

By now, we had radios and repeaters that sort of worked. Sometimes [the equipment] worked, sometimes it didn't. It was a little primitive. With a little experience, you knew all the places you could talk to and from, and places you couldn't—which was most places.

Marking Timber

There were a lot of Forest Service jobs that weren't nearly as specialized as they are now. They'd bring me on earlier in the spring and try to keep me on longer in the fall. I became part of the timber-marking crew. That was great work.

I learned that fall is the great time of year to be out in the woods. All of us have been dealing with crowds in the mountains, one way or another, whether you're working in a campground, or backcountry, or whatever. So then, all of sudden, you're out in the Kilkenny with nobody around except for the rest of the crew.

I would start out tallying. We would have a crew of four, or five, or six. There'd be Brad and Rene and Norm [Rheaume, the timber-marking boss] and John Bailey, Bob Doyle, and there must have been a couple of others maybe. It sort of varied from day to day.

The forester would lay out a sale—a certain area that was going to be harvested—and he'd write a prescription on just what types of trees he wanted selected from that area. Whether it was going to be clear-cut—which we did a few [of] then—or selective. And if it's going to be selective, what are you selecting? Then he would give you the spiel. The first day working on that particular sale, we'd all get together and he'd tell you what he wanted. You'd pay attention to it, but eventually he would leave and you would all look at each other and say, "What did he say?" And it would either be, "Take it all,"

Bill Arnold visits the Randolph, New Hampshire, Fire Department in 2011.
(Photo by Ned Therrien)

or "Take some and leave some." We didn't really dwell on it but we kind of had a sense of what he wanted.

You'd wear these tally-whackers—counters—and with the saw logs, you'd be calling them out all the time, counting the trees you're marking. "Yellow birch. Red maple. Sugar maple. Fourteen-inch." You'd paint the tree and you call it out and the tally person would be marking it down in the book—in the cold and the snow and with cold fingers. And then every certain number of each species, the tally person calls out, "That's a sample." If that particular tree that you'd marked is a sample tree, then you'd have to measure it. You'd figure the number of saw logs in it, the number of pulp logs, any defects, and so forth, and that all got entered in. And so, you're getting an estimated value of the timber sale based on a random sample of all the different species.

We'd always have a lunch fire in the cold weather. You would toast your sandwich on the fire. We had our dogs with us. The dogs had packs on them and they carried the paint. As they'd walk around, they'd shake the paint all up—and if you needed more paint, you'd just call a dog.

You'd go across the sale in a line. There was a certain amount of pressure and a certain amount of yelling, because you're expected to keep up with the crew. Once you'd go across, you'd shift over, turn around and come back again and so on, so you're covering the whole sale, and if you got a sample, then the whole line has to stop while you're doing it. If it was cold, people would be like, "Come on!" People would start yelling at you. Brad or Norm—they could look up at a tree and click it right off. Some of us rookies, though, we had to use a clinometer and other ways to measure it and you took a little longer because you wanted it to be right. You had to be certified. You had to take an exam every fall to test your ability. Then the crew would get in the old argument about whether it's a red maple or a sugar maple or whether that is a defect or not. But, it's really good work.

The Forest Service would keep us on until the snow got too deep because you'd have to stump mark the trees.[32] We'd come in at the end of the day and they'd say, "Is the snow too deep yet?" Of course we'd say, "Oh, no." Because, if it was too deep, we'd get laid off. Eventually, somebody would say, "That's it." It was usually around Christmas time. I did that for years.

Young Adult Conservation Corps

Somewhere around '78, the Young Adult Conservation Corps came in, and I got hired on full-time to help run that program. I was full-time then for three years. I think the crew were sixteen to twenty-four years old. They'd show up at the depot in Gorham every day. I think we had to average twenty people a day, so we would hire more in the summer and less in the winter. It was kind of your typical government program. It wasn't real efficient. But, what is? We'd have ten or fifteen kids right through the winter and we'd go out every day. It didn't matter how cold it was. We cut snowmobile trails. We cleared wildlife openings. Timber stand improvement.

There were a few [participants] that had moved here from away, but most of them were local kids. Some had done some snowmobiling and hunting, but most of them really had never spent much time outside, certainly not in the mountains. This was a whole new thing for them, even

---

[32] A stump mark is a paint line below the cut level that leaves proof, after cutting, that the tree was meant for removal.

though it was right in their backyard. We would teach them how to use an ax, to use tools, to run chain saws, how to dress in the cold, be able to work outside all day long in below-zero temperatures and stay warm. Be able to work and come back tomorrow and do it again. It was a good program, and it really did get them out in the woods. I was still on the young side and I was going to straighten all these kids right out and save them from all the perils out there. Eventually I was just happy to settle on saving a few and the rest will be what they [will] be.

I still see them around. I see them in town regularly and, to a tee, they'll ask, "How are you doing?" or "Oh, you haven't changed a bit," and they've all changed and then they'll say, "Boy, those were some of the best years of my life. I know I didn't like it then. I know I was the biggest complainer."

There was some regulation that if you were supervising a certain amount of people, they had to send you off for supervisory training. They would send me off to these trainings, and I would ask, "Well, what do you do when you got a half a dozen girls who are all lined up crying when it's twenty below zero?" or, "What do you do when two of the guys are fighting it out with knives? You know, there's blood all over the snow." And, "What do you do when you come in from work on Monday and you ask where Joey is, and they say, 'Well, he's in jail for three weeks but he'll be back after that.'" This is all stuff that happened regularly, so the training didn't really help much. But it was a good program, and then they eliminated it.

Fighting Fires

As part of working for the Forest Service, I got pretty involved with firefighting, going on western fires. The first one I went on—I think it was in '76, a big, big fire on the Upper Peninsula in Michigan. With any of those fires, there's good times and bad times, but I really got hooked into that. As much as they would send me on fires, I would go.

I stopped because I turned sixty. Bruce Sloat always used to say, "Fires and search and rescue are for young people." I figured sixty is kind of getting up there. I remember the last fire trip very well. We started in Utah and ended up in Idaho. I did fine, but I was always the last one in line.

One of the Most Memorable Days

One memorable day with the Forest Service was in 1982 when there was a great hold-up at Carter Notch Hut. This guy walked in. "This is a stick-up!" Geoff Burke—who I knew well from when I worked at Pinkham—was up visiting one of the hut crew. Geoff decided to wrestle with this guy and Geoff got shot. I knew Geoff and I knew he'd wrestle with anybody.[33] Meanwhile, at the same time, there'd been a woman who walked into Wild River Campground and said, "I was in a plane crash two days ago somewhere back there in the woods and my friend, who was the pilot, is dead in the airplane." So they said, "Well, where is the plane?" She said, "Two days back there somewhere."

I came into work the next morning and was told, "Go up in the Carters. We're looking for a guy with a gun that just held up the hut, and if you see a burned-out airplane with a body in it, we need to know about that too." And I'm thinking, *I don't really want to find either one, you know. It's a nice day. I don't need to ruin it. I don't need to get shot. I don't need to find bodies.* So, I go up the Moriah Trail to the top of Mount Moriah, and there's a group up there with a woman who is celebrating [climbing] the last of her 4,000-footers. They're drinking champagne and having a great time. They offered me some, and I said, "No thanks." I asked them, "Have you seen anybody with guns or any airplanes or—you know—anything out of the ordinary?" And they answered, "No, nothing but champagne."

I eventually got a call on the radio that they'd caught the stick-up guy. I guess he had a friend at Wildcat and the police did their police hunting and caught him there.

The Forest Service found the plane. There was just a poor guy. He was burned in the plane and I had to go in the next day and help carry him out.

Frontcountry and Leaving the Forest Service

After [the Young Adult Conservation Corps], I went back to seasonal work for the Forest Service, back to backcountry and marking timber and more law enforcement. They had me working at Dolly Copp Campground two nights a

---

[33] Burke's leg wound was not life-threatening, but it, and the stress from the event, dogged him for years. See Chris Stewart's article in *The Resuscitator*, newsletter of the OH Association, Spring 2005.

week. I didn't really like that at all. In the backcountry, I did law enforcement, but it was all camping regulations. Every now and then, you'd have a group that would be causing trouble somewhere out there, but you'd deal with them.

At the campground, Friday nights were always the worst. You'd have people driving up, setting up their camp, getting drunk…. There was vandalism in the bathrooms and just stuff that I didn't feel I needed to deal with. I just didn't like that kind of work. I'd rather be out on the trail.

I always used to say about my time with the Forest Service: "I'll keep doing this until it's not fun anymore." I could tell I wasn't going to get on full-time and that was always my plan from the first summer I started working on trail crew. They'd bring in people from somewhere far away and I'd often have to train them. Then, in the fall, I'd get laid off and they'd be there.

So, I left the Forest Service in the late '80s. I found a job with Dave Fuller working construction, through the winter. I was always on the [Forest Service] fire crew, though. I kept my fire qualifications up, signed on as a seasonal, and then they would call me.

Becoming a Different Kind of Caretaker

In the late '80s, I started caretaking work in Randolph. A lot of the old houses I worked on were Boothman cottages. John Boothman [Jack's father] was very much a developer, and he had it nailed. He owned a lot of land in Randolph, and he would sell one or two or three lots a year only to the "right people," in his judgment. This was around 1910 or thereabouts. So now they've got two college professors and then you've got a minister over here. John Boothman would build the house and he would pretty much tell the people the house he was building. The owner of Mount Crescent House needed water and so did all the houses here on the hill, so he started the Mount Crescent Water Company, which he built and maintained with his crew. Then you needed something for all these people to do. He was one of the founders of the Randolph Mountain Club. His crew built a lot of these trails, or maintained them anyway.

I ended up working for the descendants of the people Boothman built houses for. These houses now have been passed down through the generations. Randolph's unique and it's because of the John Boothman factor. They used to say we have more miles of trails per capita than any other town. I don't know. It's a good story. There's a lot of trails, any way you look at it.

RMC Camps

[In] '67, '68, somewhere in there, the RMC decided that they should have someone on the board of directors who was either a caretaker or a trail crew member. I was the one. I've been on the board off and on ever since then.

Somewhere in the early '70s, I was put in charge of the RMC camps.[34] By then, the use in the White Mountains was really picking up. There was more and more use and abuse. There'd been talk over the years of RMC having a winter caretaker. We were having people go up on weekends for a couple of winters. They'd sort of collect money. Sometimes they'd spend the night; sometimes not.

I had thought long and hard over the years about having a winter caretaker and had decided, in my mind, that it would have to be the right person. The person would have to be kind of crazy. He'd be the first one to spend a whole winter in a little drafty cabin on the north side of Mount Adams just below treeline. That's pretty rough. And I had gotten to know the guys in the state park on Mount Washington because I worked for the Forest Service and I was up there all the time. Mike Johnson was the manager. Mike Pelchat was the assistant manager, and at some point later in the summer of 1976, Mike Johnson said, "Geez, you guys ever thought about having a winter caretaker at Gray Knob?" And I thought, I know this guy. He's crazy. And I was right. I talked to the RMC board of directors and we came up with a salary and hired him.

Turned out he'd never been to Gray Knob. I got an Ashley woodstove. Not too, too heavy. His first trip, he started up there with a woodstove. He made the turn at Mistake Junction, turned off Lowe's Path, ended up at The Perch, with a woodstove on his back. So he took sort of the long, scenic way to get there. But he made it.

He had to be crazy, because he really had to be ready for anything. I mean, we knew there were parties going on up there. So he had to be able to handle parties, had to be able to handle the weather, had to be just ready to deal with anything that came along.

I've been doing radio call at 8 P.M. with RMC caretakers since 1976. There are a lot of stories. But there's a classic involving Albie Pokrob. He

---

[34] RMC calls its two shelters and two cabins "camps."

was caretaker at Gray Knob for quite a while. Albie is a great guy, so it's easy to tell stories about him. He'd gone several nice, clear spring days without seeing anyone at all. I don't remember the schedule we had him working then, but they didn't get days off as much as they do now. I talked to him once after he'd gone several days without seeing anybody. "How's it going, Albie?" "Oh, it's going pretty well." "What'd you do today?" "Well, I went out for a hike and I counted two-hundred-and-something snow fleas in my footprint." And I was thinking, *Well, Albie, maybe it's time for a day off.*

Changes

In my mind, the big change over the years is that the number of hikers really peaked in the '70s or early '80s. Back when you had heavy trail use and everyone was in Vibram-soled shoes, that caused a lot of environmental damage. If you have less people, then you just don't worry about it so much. The biggest change I've seen is communication. And the biggest part of that is cell phones. It's not true just in the mountains—it's everywhere. The idea of just going off and not being in touch. People now, they're just horrified at that thought.

Obviously there's a lot more concern about the environment. I think some of it gets a little over the top. When I worked the first summer at Crag Camp, back into the mid-sixties, you threw your garbage over the edge of King Ravine, and most of the AMC huts did the same kind of thing. There also was the can pit, and you could go down there in the evening and you'd hear the raccoons and the porcupines mushing around, and you never would consider why you would not do that. The toilet was sort of right in that general area. Sort of hung right off the side, almost. And, then the whole environmental movement came in and carry in/carry out—which is good. I mean, look at something like Tuckerman's. They didn't really have a place where you threw your trash. You just threw it. So now we're not throwing garbage into the ravine.[35] We're packing it up and hauling it down the mountain and taking it to the dump and dumping it in the dump.

---

[35] AMC changed its waste practices in the mountains in the same era. See "Goodbye Back-country Dumps, Hello Tent Platforms," *Appalachia*, Summer/Fall 2006, LVII no. 1.

Of course, we didn't have as much plastic then. Really, how much environmental damage were we doing? It's a judgment thing. But it sort of makes me wonder. I mean, obviously the thought is right. You want to take care of the woods and the mountains. You don't want to misuse them. You don't want to have piles of beer cans on the trail, but I think sometimes it can get a little carried away. That's just our society.

Proud

I'm probably most proud of the fact that I found a way to make a living here. This is a lifestyle that, in a way, I sort of fell into. But I also chose it. Some people will say things like, "Well, this is a nice place, but I can't imagine living here and coming all the way up this hill in the snow and the cold. How do you ever survive?" And, of course, I'm thinking, *How do you ever survive down there in the city?* I can't imagine it. Things will be changing. I've got to start slowly cutting back on work here in town, but I know I'm not going to just cut things off. I'd probably go crazy, and people are going to keep calling me anyway.

I'm proud that I've been on a lot of rescues and I've probably helped some people out. I like to think that I helped put out a few fires. I'm glad that I met Barbara. That's worked out great. She likes to be here now. She's retired from the school system. We've been married over twenty years, and they have been the best years of my life—no doubt. My stepdaughter, Alex, has also been a great addition. She's married and living in Washington, D.C., with her husband, David, and two children, Henry and Della. I never thought much about being a grandfather, but now that I am one, it's wonderful!

I'm proud of just being able to live here, and I feel like I've contributed to the town. I've always felt that it's anyone's responsibility to somehow contribute to society, whether it's your local town or whatever, whether it's volunteer work or something else. You try to leave the world a little better than when you started—whatever that means.

Bill Arnold continues to live in Randolph, New Hampshire, with his wife, Barbara. Working toward retirement, Bill is enjoying spending time on Cape Breton, Nova Scotia, and with his stepdaughter, son-in-law, and grandchildren in Washington, D.C.

Fran Belcher

AMC's First Executive Director

This portrait of Fran Belcher was painted by portraitist and courtroom sketch artist Melven H. Robbins (1918–1999) in 1990. It hangs in the library at AMC's headquarters in Boston. (Image courtesy of AMC Library & Archives)

D URING HIS DAYS IN THE WHITE MOUNTAINS, Fran Belcher's skills and interests were perfectly in sync with his time. The earliest years occurred during the legendary Joe Dodge era. Joe, longtime manager of the high huts system of the Appalachian Mountain Club (AMC), made an enormous impression on the young high school student and bestowed the nickname that would last the rest of Fran's days: Foochow (see next page). Fran noted that, "Joe started at Pinkham when it was laissez-faire. He sort of took advantage of this position and built himself up as the mayor of Porky Gulch, and rightfully so; I think anybody would. It was the frontier in those days."

In later years, Fran's devotion to AMC and his business skills were both called upon when he served for nearly two decades as the organization's first executive director. Those were critical times as AMC made its transition from an informal, mostly volunteer organization, to a dramatically larger, more influential entity. Though ultimately positive, in his view, these changes were not entirely without some loss. "The AMC has grown immensely," he noted in the fall of 1993 during an interview at his home. "It's no longer the friendly family. It can't be with sixty thousand members. I think you have a lot of little enclaves of friends.... But, I think the AMC today is what I would have hoped for and expected."

His mountain days also overlapped with the reclamation of the logging railroads by the forests. Thankfully for Fran, many relics were still quite evident, and he explored remote sites with great zeal and a keen eye. Well known for his uncanny memory and his immense knowledge of AMC and White Mountain history, he wrote *Logging Railroads of the White Mountains* (AMC Books, 1980) based on years of research and field trips.

A scholar, a writer, and a leader, Fran was also a man of great humor. His longtime friend and AMC colleague Fred Stott noted, "He loved to laugh and registered his enjoyment with a high-pitched giggle that was part sound and part facial expression. Whenever he passed by the portrait of Joe Dodge that [used to hang] at 5 Joy Street [AMC's headquarters in Boston] he always raised a hand with a quietly voiced greeting of 'Hi Joe.'"

In His Own Words

My family had a history of climbing mountains. In the 1890s, my grandmother worked at the Profile House in Franconia Notch. She climbed Mount Lafayette and Cannon Mountain. My father got to go climbing along with his brother, and then we all started climbing. We went up to Lake Winnisquam on summer vacations, and from there we climbed all the Belknaps, the Squam Range, Sandwich Range, Moosilauke, and ultimately, we climbed to the huts.

I was a senior in high school when I was hired by Joe Dodge. Joe came down to Andover, and he really got a crowd. He told all these exaggerated stories about the North Country. Joe was in his heyday at that time. He was flamboyant and very colorful.

I went to work at age eighteen in the huts. I was considered young. I was just going into Dartmouth. We were paid twelve dollars a week—six or eight dollars plus board.

Working for Joe Dodge was great. Back then, he was a splendid boss. You could do the wrong thing, and he'd let you get away with it until you learned a lesson from that. He backed his kids one hundred percent. Joe gave me the name Foochow. We had a man—a Chinese person who came from Canton—who was a guest at Pinkham. This fellow and I got talking. That was when Joe heard that I was born in Foochow, China.[36] One day Joe was up working in the cooler house, and he screamed, "Goddamn it! I got a new name! Hey, Belcher!" He came in and said, "You're Foochow! That's your name!"

I spent 1934 and '35 working in the kitchen at Pinkham, when it was a three-man crew. The next year I was assistant hut manager. That was the year they turned buildings around and did a lot of construction at Pinkham. The current lodge center building was built in '34, and in '35 the two buildings that were originally there—the log cabins—well, one was turned around parallel with the other one, and it was connected and made the Trading Post. That's now the old trading post.

---

[36] Foochow was the Americanized name for the city of Fuzhou, China. Fran's parents were working as missionaries at the time of his birth.

Fran Belcher (right) stands with Massachusetts Conservation Council Chairman Warren M. Little (left), presenting the Environmental Award to Franklin S. Browning of the advertising firm Humphrey Browning and MacDougall, 1975.
(Photo courtesy of AMC Library & Archives)

It was a very colorful job. They had a crew of local people from Berlin [New Hampshire]. Some of them became very good hutmen over the years, but when they got paid, they'd end up in Gorham or Berlin getting plastered to beat hell, and we'd have to go down and bring 'em back. Then they might not work for a day or two.

A Presidential Skyline Drive

Those were also the years when they were planning a highway through the Presidentials. I think the Green Mountain one was going to be the first and the Presidential one second. That was in '33 and '34. "They had the whole thing surveyed. It took at least two years, maybe three. It was a work project. The crews were paying guests at Lakes and Madison [huts].

We have a map at Joy Street of the Presidential Highway Skyline Drive. It was the baron of the Crawford House that was pushing the highway.

Well, Louis Cutter, Sr., got the map, and the project was canned by Cabot, Corcoran, and Cutter. Tommy Corcoran—we called him Tommy the Cork—just said, "No dice." He once told us, "There'll never be a gas pump at the Lakes of the Clouds!"

AMC's First Executive Director

When I got married in '36, I got a job with the Boston & Maine Railroad. That was in the middle of the Depression. You've got to remember this: Any job was a job. I ultimately became a claims agent, handling accident investigations of people who were injured, employees who were injured, crossing accidents, and so on. I worked out of the Boston office and was transferred to Concord, New Hampshire, where I was for two years. I traveled all over the North Country by train, sometimes by caboose. The hills were right there. It was marvelous to be in that atmosphere.

The mountains became a part of my life. The associations that I had with hutmen have been lifelong; 'til death do us part. I'd been a member of a fraternity in college, but you never were as close to those guys as you were working in the hut system. You live with them, you work with them, and I think to some extent, Joe started up an *esprit de corps* that tied us all together.

The AMC in those days was like a friendly family. I had served three to four years as an officer of the club before I became executive director, so I knew the other officers. I knew the amount of devotion that they gave to the job, the responsibilities. Most of them were very challenging people. You couldn't go to sleep at a meeting!

Here's one example: Bob Morgan was president of the Boston Five Cent Savings Bank. I first served on the council when he was president of the AMC. He was very insistent that we start exactly at 4:15. At 6:15 he left, because he had to catch a train. He was a no-nonsense guy. I've sat through council meetings since then that have gone on forever, but Bob Morgan could see where we were going, and say, "All right gentlemen, this is the way it's going to go."

Then there were the likes of Miriam Underhill. She lived up on Randolph Hill, with her husband, Robert.[37] They were just superb people, brilliant.

---

[37]   See page 86 for George Hamilton's story of working with the Underhills.

From B&M to AMC

I left the B&M for a very good reason. Management had changed and Patrick McGinnis, who was a rather noted nut on railroads, took it over. He came from the New Haven Railroad and had a history of wrecking railroads from Georgia to Virginia to New Haven.

It just so happened that AMC was looking for somebody at Joy Street,[38] when somebody turned to me and asked me if I'd take it. I was executive director of AMC from 1956 to 1975. I was on the Executive Committee, and they canceled the committee, knocked me off, and turned around and hired me! My salary was $8,000 a year.

The activities of the club were great. I didn't have much to do with it. They were run by volunteers. One of the important parts of my job then was to work with the volunteers and make sure they set the policies, and I carried them out.

We didn't have much staff. There were two girls there when I went in, and one of them immediately resigned. The other ultimately resigned, and there was even one day where I was the only employee there. We built up from there. The club took a risk in hiring me because of the costs. But I wasn't costly by a long stretch, I'll tell you!

They had a woman in there a long time, Adelaide Meserve.[39] I think she was there from about 1906 until 1951 or '52. Addie was a one-person institution. She had assistance at times. She brought in a girl to succeed her in '49, but things fell apart. The problem was that the club officers in the period up 'til then were people like Charlie Blood, who was treasurer for twenty-five years. Blood was a lawyer on Beacon Hill and was able to devote half his time to the AMC. He wasn't alone. There were some others from time to time; they were the people who were able to do the work that should have been done by staff.

The break came after Miss Meserve retired. Jean Patterson took over, and some of the people who came along in the various council jobs couldn't devote the time that the others had, so there was a void. Al Folger, for example. He was assistant councilor of trails. I was councilor of huts. I couldn't

---

[38] AMC's headquarters is at 5 Joy Street in Boston, Massachusetts.
[39] AMC's sole, and longest-serving, employee at the time.

A Mountain Leadership School group gathers at Madison Spring Hut, circa 1967. Fran Belcher stands on the left. (Photo courtesy of AMC Library & Archives)

devote the time that some of my predecessors had, and Al Folger couldn't because he was working for a bank. There were others. I know that Ken Henderson was the editor of *Appalachia* at that time. He was terribly upset because the office wouldn't give him any help. You can see the difference in the journal from the time he edited it to when the Underhills were editors, when they began to get assistance from Joy Street.

Working with the U.S. Forest Service

We worked pretty closely with the Forest Service. Cliff Graham, one of the early forest supervisors, was a very interesting guy. I knew Cliff reasonably well. He was supervisor when the Forest Service had no money. We took over Tuckerman Shelter—the first one—because they couldn't operate it. It was built by the Civilian Conservation Corps and operated by the Forest Service up until the war.

We took over the Brickett Place[40] in Evans Notch in about 1948. Starting around 1955, we took over Dolly Copp [Campground] and ran it for six

---

[40] This brick farmhouse was run as Evans Notch Hut by AMC from 1948 to 1959, before the Forest Service took over operations.

years. We had a big dickering session about the terms at Dolly Copp with Cliff, Joe [Dodge], myself, and Don Allen. The Forest Service didn't have money to operate these places or to hire the personnel.

The huts and Pinkham operated under a use permit. Except for Madison, of course, where we owned the land. In the case of Lakes, we already had an OK to build it from whoever owned it before the Forest Service took it over. Carter was the same way. There had been a camp in there before us, and ultimately we built our property with Mac MacGregor.[41]

We had individual use permits on all the huts on Forest Service land: Greenleaf, Galehead, Zealand, Lakes, Pinkham, and Carter. But it was not one permit. Each hut was on its own, individual permit. It was difficult because they kept coming up for renewal. They were three-year permits. In fact, in my time we put them on thirty-year permits, all of them. That was worked out between George Hamilton,[42] the Hut Committee, and [Forest Supervisor] Gerry Wheeler.

Occasionally things did get touchy. I remember Joe Dodge went in and sawed off a lock on a gate at Zealand, so he could go on further in. There were those sorts of things.

The AMC's relationship with the Forest Service was quite different back then. I remember the forest supervisor, Gerry Wheeler, saying things to me like, "Christ, you don't go to Pinkham Notch Camp, you go to Joe's place." Gerry never stayed at Pinkham, and I think it was partly because he never felt at ease there. Gerry always stayed over at Philbrook Farm, in Shelburne. He had places he stayed where he didn't have to politic, and that was one of them.

You have to realize, Joe started at Pinkham when it was laissez-faire. The AMC, of course, was there before the Forest Service, and the Forest Service was in the background. We invited the Forest Service. But Joe sort of took advantage of this position and built himself up as the mayor of Porky Gulch, and rightfully so; I think anybody would. It was the frontier in those days.

One of our big concerns was the condition of the building at Pinkham. It was hardly worth putting people up and charging them, particularly in

---

[41] Red Mac MacGregor was one of the first managers of the AMC hut system and the person who hired Joe Dodge.

[42] See page 81 for George Hamilton's story.

the off-season. That's where Gerry Wheeler helped out. He made sure that we did something. People liked Pinkham, but Gerry was concerned about safety—fire hazards and that sort of thing. So, he worked with us and came down and spent time at Joy Street. Gerry was very concerned that Pinkham was put together with staples and glue and that Joe wasn't really paying attention to the needs. Gerry Wheeler used to say baling wire and Scotch tape held things up! And we had to spend a lot of money. Joe was a great one for putting everything off. He'd come in with an emergency request for money for maintenance. I remember once, he wanted $4,000 for Lakes of the Clouds, at short notice. At the time, we were going through a change in our budget, whereby we wanted to know ahead of time what was coming.

Another problem was that in 1954 and '55, Joe Dodge had several spells, physical spells, where he collapsed at the bottom of a trail, timing ski races. He collapsed one time at a Hut Committee meeting in Boston. Joe had all sorts of problems with his stomach, and he was finally ordered to go see somebody and get a physical. He was sent to a hospital in Boston. Then the Hut Committee sat down with Joe at a meeting at the hutmen's cabin, and he was told that he was going to have to retire.

Logging Railroads of the White Mountains

The inspiration for *Logging Railroads of the White Mountains* came from spending my days off around Zealand Hut in 1934. It was pretty funny country in those days. It was very barren. You had to walk all the way from Route 302 to get to the hut. You could see the signs of the fires that had scorched that area. On one occasion I went over into the flats with Dr. William May, who was a former AMC president. We were looking for signs of the railroad. That was when it was a meadow; now it's a swamp. We dug up all sorts of relics. Apparently, there was a roundhouse there, a logging camp. A lot of it we carted back to the hut.

Somewhere along the line, I picked up the rumor that J.E. Henry was a bastard, and when he got through in there, he lit everything and burned it up, intentionally. This is what you picked up in Twin Mountain, locally, but it wasn't true.

It was Bob Monahan who started my interest in logging railroads. He was a forester at the Forest Service in those days. He said, "Nobody's ever checked it out; why don't you do it?"

I let it sit on the back burner for a while. I had tried to do some looking around, but I couldn't put my finger on dates and people, and where these things went. Lo and behold, when I went to Concord for the B&M, I found all these fine records. I found all sorts of things. I've given quite a few of them to Dartmouth College.

Then I went to see Governor Sherman Adams, and I had a meeting with him to see if he approved, and what he suggested. He said to me, "I've always wanted to do this. I'm qualified to do it, but I'll never get around to it; I'm in politics. Go ahead. You have my blessing." That was to do the research. He gave me several ideas, people I should see. One of the things you have to worry about when you go to see people is how truthful they are. What did they observe? How accurate are they? He knew that from dealing with people. The people he sent me to were very accurate.

I spent three days up in the Pemi [Pemigewasset Wilderness] with Harry McDade just after he'd moved to Littleton,[43] and Francis Boyle. The Boyles had a cabin up there at Stillwater, but nobody knew about it. It didn't exist on anybody's records. But the Forest Service tried to get it torn down. I was really casing the joint at that point, in the early 1960s. I knew at that point that I was going to be writing a book. It wasn't that I was trying to make any discoveries, it was more confirming things that I knew or thought I knew. Francis's father was Billy "The Bear" Boyle, an engineer on the logging railroads, and I got a lot of color from him—as much as anything else out of that whole trip!

It was a different era, then. They lived by their rules and by the laws of their time. And we've learned a lesson from them. I mean, that was the time of Rockefeller and other people running around, making oodles of dough, and ultimately the Sherman Antitrust Act and the Interstate Commerce Commission Act became law. And we got the Weeks Act. We can thank J.E. Henry and others for the notorious ways they did business. It doesn't mean there won't be someone who comes back and tries to do it again, though.

Parting Thoughts

The AMC has achieved a lot over the years. I guess I'm most proud of the fact that the club is healthy. I won't say we're wealthy, but we are wise. It's

---

[43] See page 41 for Harry McDade's story.

a big job today, to keep the whole thing going. We've done a tremendous amount of things over the years.

The AMC has grown immensely. It's no longer the friendly family. It can't be with sixty thousand members. I think you have a lot of little enclaves of friends. It'll be hard for anybody at the top to see out into the pasture. The cows may be out there, but you may not be able to see them, you know? But, I think the AMC today is what I would have hoped for and expected.

As for the future, I can see AMC being bigger. I can see us doing more public service. Education is one of the big areas that has many manifold angles to it. For example, the workshops we run. George Hamilton and I were the first ones to put together the first Mountain Leadership workshop. We ran some offbeat workshops too, having to do with technical climbing— Mountain Leadership Grade III, I think it was. Bill Putnam was very much involved. We didn't have leadership training inside the club until we went outside and brought people in. It was Gerry Wheeler who had an awful lot to do with getting something going. I know we did those early workshops with some trepidation at times, but my God, here we are. Education is more than just workshops now.

I'm pretty happy with the way the huts are going these days. It's a little confusing, though, if you go in there when they're busy at Pinkham. I've been there on a couple of occasions recently when, God! I'm glad I didn't have to put up with it!

We've also got to maintain good relations with the federal government and the state government. I've seen many of the changes between various White Mountain National Forest supervisors and various administrations. I think they're fairly level. You and I don't have to worry too much about them unless we get a president who wants to knock everybody's head. I think we have to maintain these good relations.

These days, I spend a fair amount of time at Joy Street at the library. I've had my brain picked by quite a few people in recent times. One thing I should mention, I have to give an awful lot of credit to my wife, who has supported me in all this. It wasn't a one-person job, by a long shot. We, the two of us, have attended a lot of club events in particular, but other things as well—outside affairs. If one person had to do it, it would have been difficult.

The White Mountains are friendly country. It's close enough so you can see it all from Mount Moosilauke, one of my favorite mountains. It's cohesive. It's close enough so you can understand it. The AMC, we were the first mountain club in this country, the second conservation organization, although the word conservation wasn't coined until the twentieth century. "Conservation" was part of our daily dozen. You took care of your backyard.

A revised edition of Logging Railroads of the White Mountains *was published in 1994. Fran Belcher died on May 17, 1994. He was seventy-seven years old.*

Work in the Whites

Previous Page
Top: Peter Limmer (Photo by Ned Therrien)
Bottom: Arthur and Ellen Teague, with New Hampshire Governor John W. King on the right (Photo courtesy of Anne T. Koop)

Brad Ray

The Avalanche Watchman of Tuckerman Ravine

Snow ranger Brad Ray puts an arm around his rescue dog, Tuckerman III, in 1999.
(Photo by Ned Therrien)

I**T WOULD BE HARD TO ARGUE** that there is anyone who knows Tuckerman Ravine better than Brad Ray. For over forty years, Brad was a U.S. Forest Service ranger who spent his time observing, working, living in, and thinking about the ravine and surrounding areas on Mount Washington's eastern slope. Whether they know it or not, thousands of hikers, skiers, and climbers have met him and shared in his expertise. Tens of thousands more have read his avalanche forecasts. His work, along with that of others in Tuckerman and Huntington ravines, has saved many from injury and death.

But Brad's depth of knowledge and understanding of the mountains extend well beyond the glacial cirque of Tuckerman Ravine. From his days growing up in Berlin, New Hampshire, where he spent every minute he could "upriver," to his backcountry work for the Forest Service, Brad has acquired an extensive knowledge of the region that, when blended with his thoughtfulness, dry humor, and modesty, embodies the best values of the North Country's mountain ethic.

During his days as a snow ranger, when snow started to swirl from northern New Hampshire's wintry skies, Brad began to pay close attention to the avalanche conditions. Long before his official workday began, the mix of snow and ice and rock and forest that rise above Pinkham Notch would appear in his mind. "You start thinking about it when you're still in bed and your eyes are closed. You can hear the wind, and you can hear the pelting of snow or rime crystals that rap upon the window.... You're accumulating information all the time," he said. That information became part of Brad's official avalanche forecasts, and it formed the seeds of the advice he dispensed in person daily. To this day, Brad still pays close attention to conditions on Mount Washington, frequently sharing his expertise and advice with today's snow rangers.

In the interest of full disclosure, the interviewers would like to point out that Brad and *Mountain Voices* co-author Rebecca Oreskes have been married since 1995. We spoke to Brad at their home in 1999.

In His Own Words

I was born and brought up in the mill town of Berlin, New Hampshire. My father was superintendent of the Riverside Mill—he made paper. He worked a lot of hours and we didn't see too much of him. My mother was a housewife. I grew up in what was called Norwegian Village, where most of the Scandinavians lived. The rest of Berlin was mostly French, with some Russians on "the avenues" and Italians down in Cascade Flats.

The remnants of turn-of-the-century logging were still there, but I missed the heyday when all the loggers and river drivers would come out of the woods in the spring, and Berlin would turn from a quiet, peaceful village into, "Oh, no, here they come. Let's get all the women off the streets!" But I do remember my father would often visit some of the beer joints along Main Street, and there were a lot of loggers hanging out there. I also can remember as a young teenager helping throw pulpwood off logging trucks into the river. You had to be careful not to go in with the wood!

Growing up, we always went upriver—north along the Androscoggin. I never went south. I think I was well on in my years before I even went to Conway. My father was a woodsman, a hunter, and a fisherman, and there was nothing to offer down below. My life was in the woods.

I joined the Marines while I was still in high school and did basic training at Parris Island, South Carolina, and advanced infantry training at Camp Lejeune, North Carolina. I was six months active and six months reserve for six years.

Starting with the Forest Service

In 1958 a new ranger came to the Androscoggin District of the White Mountain National Forest, Rick Goodrich. I knew the Forest Service was hiring, so I just went down and signed an application. Rick was a former marine and I was a former marine; I think probably that's why I got the job.

I worked at Dolly Copp Campground as a "laborer three"—I cleaned toilets, threw trash in the truck, dug holes, and did whatever else was asked of me. One dollar and fifteen cents an hour. I remember my first check, for two weeks worth of work: $75. I was living high on the hog then—I thought that was really something!

In a few years I was foreman of the summer crew, then assistant administrator and finally administrator. I worked at Dolly Copp for eighteen years.

In the winters, I started working up in Tuckerman Ravine with Leavitt Bowie, the first official snow ranger. (He'd started up there in '52.)

When they told me I'd be a snow ranger I really had only a vague idea of what I was getting into. But I knew working in the ravine was outdoors, and that's where I love to be. It was interesting, it was different, and it was also kind of challenging.

I learned to do avalanche forecasting from Leavitt; from reading "the book" [the original *Avalanche Handbook*]; from going to the National Avalanche School in Alta, Utah; and from on-the-job experience.

Avalanche Control and Shooting Ice

In those early days we did a lot of what we still do today: avalanche forecasting and first aid. We also used to open and close areas of the ravine when the avalanche danger was high. We had a chart that we went by, which listed all the contributing factors to an avalanche, and each had a point scale. When the factors added up to fifty or more, it would be dangerous enough that we would have to close that area. We'd post the area with signs, and then we'd call down to Pinkham on a crank phone to tell them what we found.

Another difference in those early days is that we would shoot ice for avalanche control. Guns were a big part of our life in the beginning up there.

Right about that time they were developing an "avalauncher" out West. It was a great big, Rube Goldberg kind of invention, fired by compressed gas. We got one and started doing our avalanche control in Tuckerman in the winter of '65–'66. We would set the avalauncher up at the snow rangers' quarters at Hermit Lake, and we would fire into the ravine from there. Being the youngest man on the crew, I was the one elected to go up into the ravine to make sure that nobody else wandered in while we were shooting. They would shoot right over my head—most of the time. Sometimes they were very close to me—I could hear rounds clattering off the rocks, somewhere on my right; I would dive to the left. It was very exciting.

One particular day I was up in the ravine, and I heard an explosion which didn't come from where it was supposed to come from. I turned around and looked back down, and I saw that right outside the snow rangers' quarters there was a big billowing black cloud of smoke, indicating powder burning. I ran down and found both Rick and Leavitt pretty cut up from shrapnel.

There was shrapnel in the building, and shrapnel had split the trees. It turned out there was a leak in the barrel [of the avalauncher], and it had pushed that rocket up the barrel far enough so that the chain pulled the fuse igniter while the explosive was in the barrel. Rick and Leavitt were in the hospital for a while, and they both lost their eardrums, but we were very lucky no one was killed.

Before the avalauncher, we had tried to use a Browning automatic rifle to knock down ice and have the ice start an avalanche. Unfortunately, it didn't have much accuracy. You'd pull the trigger and it would keep shooting—it was hard to hold it in one place.

We also tried a .50-caliber machine gun that we mounted on the Connection first-aid cache. That wasn't at all effective. Even when it was on slow-fire, it was firing fifty rounds a minute, and, don't forget, you had to lug all those rounds up there—they were heavy. The bullets were made to shoot down airplanes and were a half-inch around and five inches long. They were pretty impressive.

I have a picture of us shooting the .50-caliber up in the ravine, hoping that a big bunch of ice would come down and start an avalanche. Then I have another picture of the Connection cache after an avalanche wiped it out. We were still learning!

We were pretty confident with the .50-caliber; we knew exactly how many clicks it took to screw in the gun barrel. Well, it turned out we didn't know it very well, because we blew that up also. Leavitt and I were shooting it when one of the bullets blew up. No one was injured, since most of explosion went up in the air, but once again shrapnel was flying around us. We decided not to use that anymore.

Finally, we tried dynamite. That was really hairy! Some of those places up in Tucks are pretty steep—nearly vertical. We would go up there and lower ten sticks of dynamite down over the ice and tie it off. That was kind of exciting! With all that dynamite on my back, I probably would have been safer staying a marine.

We had used the .50-caliber and blown that up. We had used the avalauncher, and we'd blown that up. I kept joking that maybe we should get a .75 recoilless rifle, but, with our record of not being very precise and blowing things up, I didn't think the guys on the summit would appreciate it. Also, Twin Mountain's right on the other side, and they wouldn't appreciate having a live round coming into the middle of town. In any case, that was the end of our blowing things up for avalanche control.

We'd gotten to realize that shooting ice for avalanche control just didn't work. So, we only shot down ice using M-1 rifles just to control icefall. It

Brad Ray (left) and Rick Goodrich try to improve avalanche conditions by shooting the ice with a .50-caliber machine gun on the Connection first-aid cache in 1964. (Photo by Brud Warren)

wasn't unusual for us to shoot many tons of ice in the morning before skiers got up there—ice we brought down under controlled conditions which would've come down later under uncontrolled conditions when a lot of people were there. I think it was valuable, but Forest Service politics ended that.

I had one close call when I was shooting ice. There were three or four of us in the ravine at Lunch Rocks, and we were taking turns with the two rifles because one rifle would get so hot the wood would start burning after shooting two hundred to three hundred rounds of ammunition. I remember very carefully looking up and thinking, *No ice is coming down; good enough.* And the next thing I know, I find myself about fifty feet downhill on my knees. My first thought was, *Oh, my God, the gun went off and I probably shot somebody*. But the gun was still pointing up in the air, like my Marine Corps training taught me. I looked up at Lunch Rocks and there were four or five guys standing up there, all looking down as if to say, "Is he still alive?" I had gotten hit in the side of my head by a basketball-size piece of ice.

Snow Rangers Today

Right now there are three of us from the Forest Service working full-time as snow rangers, and one part-timer. We work seven days a week. For safety reasons, there need to be two snow rangers on duty at any time.

Today, we don't open or close the ravine. We just give people our best advice. A typical day starts at 7 A.M. at the Forest Service garage at Pinkham Notch. We get out our Snow Cat and drive directly up to Huntington Ravine, so we can catch any ice climbers who may be going up.

We once thought that avalanche forecasting for Huntington would be just like avalanche forecasting for Tuckerman, but they're just two incredibly different ravines to forecast for. They each have their own unique snow conditions.

When you test snow stability, you're looking at how much snow fell, how quickly it came down, what the density is, and what kind of a surface it's landing on. Wind direction and wind velocity are extremely important, as is the new-snow type, to name just a few contributing factors.

I ask the new guys who work for me, "When do you start looking for signs of avalanche?" And they'll say things like, "Well, when I get there and I start looking through the binoculars." Not true. You start thinking about it when you're still in bed and your eyes are closed. You can hear the wind, and you can hear the pelting of snow or rime crystals that rap upon the window.

Through the night you probably heard the snowplow go through once, twice, three, or even five times. So, already you have an idea of what's going on. It's already in your mind. You're accumulating information all the time. By the time you get to the bottom of Huntington Ravine, you should already have a very good idea of what's really happening.

At about 8 A.M., the summit forecast comes over the radio, and that gives us information like wind speed and direction, how much new snow there's been, the density of the snow, how long the storm has been in progress— all these things are very important. After we've been up to Huntington, and

Brad Ray posts the day's avalanche conditions on Huntington Ravine in 1999.
(Photo by Ned Therrien)

once we have that information, we can do our forecast for the eight gullies in Huntington Ravine. We call the AMC, and they post it down below. Then we go down to the Harvard Mountaineering Club cabin and talk to everybody we see to be sure they have the latest information. We post an avalanche bulletin at the cabin and update our sign, which has slats that go in next to each gully saying "low," "moderate," "considerable," "high," and "extreme."

Once that's done, we go right to Tuckerman, where we repeat the process we did for Huntington—look at the ravine, change the signs, write up a bulletin, call AMC, and talk to people. Finally, we update our web page, and fax and e-mail the bulletin out to a lot of cooperators.

I've found over the years that the majority of people respond very well to our avalanche bulletins. I think people know that we make pretty good calls, so they take our advice. We also appreciate dialogue and questions. If hikers or climbers want to respond to us, we love to talk to them. In all our avalanche bulletins, we never just say, "The avalanche danger is moderate." Instead, we say, "The avalanche danger is moderate for these reasons." We try to let them know what we're thinking. It's an educational process. We're giving people a reason for what we're doing. I know I hate to have somebody say, "No, you can't go there," for no reason at all.

Most avalanches in this particular area are direct-action avalanches. They usually happen during a storm or immediately after one. We get twenty to twenty-five significant avalanches that we can see a year in Tuckerman. I'm sure there are more that we don't see. What's unusual in this area is that we get a lot of our snow after a storm, when the wind shifts direction and comes out of the west or northwest, blowing most of the snow right into Tuckerman. Typically, we have about 55 feet of snow each year, at the deepest spot in the ravine. The most I've seen is 85 feet, in 1969.[44] It was great skiing into August that year.

The point of all this effort is to try to save lives. The only reason we're up there is public safety. And that was the original idea, I think, when they built the first building up there in 1938.

Accidents

Catastrophes, I've always thought, are just around the corner. We get big crowds up there, and some people who have no idea what they're getting into. They'll go into the ravine when we have it posted as high avalanche danger. On the positive side, we're seeing a big change today, with people being more prepared. We see people today who wear helmets, have shovels on their backs, and carry avalanche transceivers.

Our accident rate is basically a flat line, even though we're getting more and more people up here—thirty-five to forty thousand people every winter/spring. We usually have about twenty-five serious accidents a year.

---

[44] See page 133 for Bill Arnold's story about the snowy winter of 1968–1969.

I used to count the fatalities I've worked on, but I gave that up a few years ago. I think probably it's up around thirty or thirty-five. Some are avalanche fatalities, when people are climbing and not realizing the danger. One of the biggest things that gets people in trouble on Mount Washington is the weather. They say Mount Washington is home to the worst weather in the world—and I can almost believe that! I've been up there with winds well over 100 miles an hour and a temperature of thirty below zero in winter. I was the last one to talk to a couple of guys who were going into Huntington in those conditions. The last thing I said to them was, "Stay warm, guys." We found them three days later. Frozen solid.

People ask me how I can stand all the accidents, all the stupid people. The accidents are unfortunate and they're always going to happen. But there's always the good stuff, and that's what you've got to concentrate on. You can't save everyone, and I guess I learned to live with the accidents and the fatalities a long time ago. But I really feel sorry for the father or the mother who comes to Pinkham, when we have to tell them we're sorry, but we think their son or daughter is in serious trouble, or they're missing and we're looking for them. Or they've died.

Some people will say, "Why didn't you have a sign that told them they shouldn't do that?" or, "Why didn't you have a fence there that they couldn't go beyond? Why don't you close it?" We can't do that. If we started closing areas again, I would stop working there.

People have a right to go into the mountains. What happens when someone gets killed on the highway? What are you going to do? Close the highways? Let's say ten people get killed in an avalanche in Tuckerman Ravine next week; what are we going to do? Close the ravine? That's not the right thing. There are so many thousands of people who want to enjoy the mountains that you can't close it off to them. You shouldn't even restrict it.

Every time you go into the mountains, it's a calculated risk. And that includes every person who goes out there on a rescue as well—everyone has to make that decision: Is the risk worth it? As a search leader, I always have to weigh the risk of sending a rescue party out versus waiting for better conditions. I won't put anybody up there to look for people until I feel that the calculated risk is in our favor.

People have to assume responsibilities before they go out, but it's our job to let them know what the risks are. It's a very dangerous area, and you can't go there and expect not to be at risk.

The Mount Washington Volunteer Ski Patrol

The ski patrol was formed back in 1938, I believe. There were a bunch of folks who decided that there were so many people going up to Tuckerman that they needed to have a patrol there. So, the Mount Washington Volunteer Ski Patrol was formed. When I started working up there, there was still one member of that original group, Swampy Paris, and he was the ski patrol leader. A dynamite guy. People called him the "Mighty Mite" of the ravine. Swampy was a small guy—he weighed in at about 125 pounds, soaking wet—but, boy, he could get people to pay attention, I'll tell you.

The patrol's still active today, with a lot of good people on it. There are about sixteen active men and women. Their primary job is to assist the Forest Service in providing information about avalanche and icefall danger, and caring for accidents in the ravine. It's a unique ski patrol in that skiing is not a prerequisite—we would rather have a technical ice climber on the patrol than a skier.

"Tuckerman"—the Dog

There are three ways of finding people buried in the snow: Number one is with an avalanche transceiver. The second most effective way is with a trained dog. And the third method is with probes. I've been training my dog, Tuckerman III, as an avalanche rescue dog. A dog can find a person buried in the snow eight times faster than twenty people.

To train a dog for avalanche rescue, you need to have a dog that's capable of being out in the elements and feeling comfortable in a winter setting. And you need a dog that likes to play. That's one of the requirements, because you have to make a game out of the searching. I start off by having someone hold the dog while I go jump in a hole in the snow that I've just dug while the dog was with me. Then the other person will let him go and the dog will come running over to me, and I'll play very hard with him. So the dog thinks, *Well, this is fun. I find him buried in the snow and I get to play.* Next, I'll go jump in the hole with another person, and Tuckerman will find us and get to play. That way he gets the idea that no matter who he finds, he's going to play a game. After a while, he gets to the point of thinking, *Oh, this is great. I'm going to go find somebody.* And then you give him a search command. And he'll think, *OK, the command means we're going to go find people buried in the snow.* You work on that, and you have to keep making it harder and harder.

Tuckerman is a German shepherd. They're very popular in Europe and they've been proven to be excellent search dogs. And I just think German shepherds are among the most beautiful dogs there are.

The Tuckerman Scene

When I first started in the ravine, fewer people would ski over the lip of the headwall. It's an awesome sight and very steep—almost vertical.

Over the years, people have gradually done more and more. Brookie Dodge [son of legendary White Mountain figure Joe Dodge], after he came back from the Olympics, skied Dodge's Drop. He was the only one who'd done it. Then, for a while, you'd see somebody who was really good who would do it. These days, people do it pretty regularly. A friend of mine from Canada showed up one year with a broken leg; he had two ski poles and one ski. So I said, "You're going to go up and try a little bit, huh?" He said, "Yep." And he did—he went up and came down Dodge's Drop, with one leg in a cast. He made it look easy!

I've also seen a lot of funny things. One time, there was a guy skiing down and he lost his ski—but you always see people losing their skis. Then he lost his boot. Well, sometimes people lose their boots, so that wasn't too unusual. Now wait a minute, there's more than a boot there; his leg is attached to the boot! He ended up down at the bottom of the ravine and his leg and his boot are up on the hill. It happens he had a prosthesis, but it took me awhile to figure that out!

Today, people do everything up there—skiing, snowboarding—and most of them do wonderfully. A few years ago I saw a guy on skis, on the ice in the center of the headwall, and I thought, *This guy's lost. He doesn't have any idea where he is and he's going to kill himself.* And he came over and he skied that ice beautifully. Then there were six others right in back of him. The next five skied it fairly well. But the way it works up there is, there's always one who leads everybody, and he's the best, and the guy after him is almost as good. The guy after him is almost as good as the guy before him. So, finally, you get the last guy, and he's not really good at all. He doesn't even know what he's doing there. The first few guys do a really good job of skiing the ice and then the last guy comes down bouncing all over the place.

With everything I've seen up there, I think the scariest moment I've had was May 17, 1969, at 1 P.M., when five tons of ice came crashing down through Lunch Rocks on a very busy day. The ice broke up into chunks that weighed a ton, chunks that weighed ten pounds, and chunks that weighed hundreds of pounds—refrigerator-size, car-size, baseball-size, basketball-size—you name it, it was all coming down through the crowd of people. It was carnage. We had eight casualties right then—three broken backs and others with miscellaneous problems. I remember people walking into the snow rangers' quarters, and you couldn't get past the litters, with people waiting to be taken down the mountain. Luckily there were no fatalities.

The nicest memories I have are of the people who come up the mountain and really appreciate being in a unique place. They've brought their children with them and are showing them what a great place it is; they're able to explain to their kids where they're going and why—icefall danger here, avalanche danger there. "We'll ask the ranger what he thinks, where we could go today." They're having a really great experience. I think that's the best thing for me, especially when you see people teaching their young ones.

The Future

As for the future, there's new emphasis on recreation in the Forest Service, but I guess I should have been born in Missouri—you're going to have to show me; you're not going to tell me about it. You're going to have to show me that that's going to change, because I've heard it so many times I won't believe it 'til I see it.

The Forest Service is in the process of downsizing. Our Year 2000 organization calls for a lot less than we have now and we've lost a lot of good people already. Everybody who works in recreation in our district is pretty stressed out right now.

We have to keep fighting to get dollars for the Tuckerman program. Management moves around quite a bit, so every couple years you've got to sell the program to them again because they have no idea what you're talking about. It's difficult to do. The way things are going in the Forest Service, I feel less secure that we're going to have a snow-ranger program in the future.

We're trying to start Friends of Tuckerman, a group that would get together all the folks interested in the ravine and help us figure out how to continue what we've been doing and make it even better.[45] We want to make sure that there'll be a snow-ranger program in the future, and that the ski patrol will have the equipment they need to do the job up there. We hope that a Friends of Tuckerman program will help us become more self-sufficient.

As for the White Mountains, I think they're going to be as good as they are now, if not better, in the future. I have this hope that somebody is going to realize that our natural resources are important, and important to the public. I don't know when a groundswell of people like me will say, "Wake up. Let's put some money into our programs and run them well." I guess that's what I hope is going to come. I think people have to realize, if they haven't already, that the White Mountains are a very special place. If somebody wants to tear it down, there are folks who won't stand for that.

The best part of my job for me is helping people. That's what I enjoy. I enjoy doing that outdoors. To be in Tuckerman Ravine, telling people what the avalanche and icefall danger is, how to avoid it, where to go, what to do—how to have a really good time with a minimum of risks. Having people appreciate our help and say, "Thanks a lot. We really appreciate your information." That to me is the reward I get for doing the job.

I guess I've worked in the ravine longer than anyone has ever worked there before. People ask me how much longer I'm going to be there. Well, I like to think I'm just mid-career now.

Brad Ray retired from the U.S. Forest Service in 2002. Unable to stay away from Tuckerman Ravine, he joined the Mount Washington Volunteer Ski Patrol and can still be found sharing his knowledge and love of Tuckerman on many spring weekends. He's currently working on a memoir about his fifty years working on Mount Washington. Tuckerman III died from complications of degenerative myelopathy in 2008, after eleven years of living and working alongside Brad.

For up-to-date avalanche bulletins and Tuckerman Ravine information, visit mountwashingtonavalanchecenter.org.

---

[45] Friends of Tuckerman Ravine was founded in 2000.

Ellen Teague

Groundbreaking Owner of the Cog Railway

Ellen Teague stands in front of the Cog Railway in Bretton Woods, New Hampshire, June 1994. (Photo by Jonathan Kannair, jonathankannair.com)

I N OPERATION SINCE 1869, the Mount Washington Cog Railway preceded by more than four decades the creation of the White Mountain National Forest. A miracle of engineering to some, a blight to others, the 3-mile-long railway has indelibly shaped the face of Mount Washington. For forty years, Ellen Teague was a driving force behind the Cog, one of New England's best-known mountain attractions.

Ellen Crawford Teague, an indirect descendant of the famed Crawford family of New Hampshire, was raised in relative privilege in an upper-class Philadelphia household. In 1942 she married Arthur S. Teague, the Cog Railway's manager. Together they ran the railway, purchasing it in 1962. After Arthur's death, Ellen became the Cog Railway's first female president and treasurer.

In addition to the difficulty of being a business owner at a time when women were not expected to seek power, Ellen suffered a series of major tragedies in the mid-sixties. In 1967 her husband died, and only two weeks later her teenage daughter Lucy was killed in a car accident. One month later, on September 17, tragedy struck again when one of the Cog's trains derailed, killing eight people. While these grievous hardships clearly affected her life, she referred to them only as "my tragedy," preferring to focus on happier memories. Ellen ran the Cog Railway until 1983, when she sold it.

It didn't take long after meeting Ellen at her home in Whitefield, New Hampshire, for this interview in 1994 to realize she was a woman of uncompromising strength and determination. In addition to the challenges of running one of New Hampshire's most famous tourist attractions, she raised six children.

Savvy businesswoman, wife, author, mother, lover of Mount Washington. Few people adored the railway more than Ellen Teague.

In Her Own Words

I was born in Philadelphia in 1913. My mother was a Philadelphian who taught Bible at Agnes Irwin School. My father was a doctor and his father and four brothers, and the fellow before him—all doctors from Ayrshire, Scotland.

I started private school when I was five years old. It was a different age (I'm eighty-one in April): I belonged to the Penman Club; we had horses; we had paper chases and we had hunts; we had teas; we went to private schools. We went to Miss Henley's Private School, then the Wharton School, and then the Agnes Irwin School. I graduated in 1930.

We did everything that our type was trained to do. We made our debuts and did some stupid things, but we did it to be polished women. When we were kids, Father taught us how to write papers and how to form letters. Father would set a table, and then we'd clear it and say, "Now this is the way a table should be set." It was all about etiquette, of learning gentility, I suppose.

I went to school and university in Philadelphia to become a nurse. I went to Thomas Jefferson University and graduated in 1935. My father taught me never to refuse a medical case. I got involved with caring for a woman whose husband had died and she went into shock. So I got her in an ambulance and went down to Atlantic City. The change of the ozone, I think, brought her around. Next morning I walked in, and she looked at me and opened her eyes. Well, I was with her almost a year and a half. They used to come up here to New Hampshire, to the Mountain View in Whitefield—people used to come up here for a month or two months—and she'd ask me to go with her. I didn't want to leave my hospital, but it seems that you get involved with people and you stay with them. That's how I got to know New Hampshire.

I went with her down to Florida too. It was there I happened to meet Henry Teague, the man who owned the Cog Railway at the time. He was 6-foot-4, weighed about three hundred and some pounds, drank beer, smoked cigars, and he would take over when he came into a room. He had a table next to our table. Henry Teague said to me one night, "I have a friend coming. Would you like to meet him?" I thought, *Well, my gosh, would I like to meet him? I didn't know whether I wanted to meet him or not!* But I did meet him and that's what got me involved. A year and a half or two years later, in 1942, I married Arthur Teague—no relation to Henry. Arthur was the manager for the railway that Henry Teague owned.

When Arthur went overseas in World War II, I came up here, and I worked with "Uncle" Henry on the railway. I helped with the gift shop and the cabins. After he was discharged, Arthur wanted to go to the University of Virginia. He did go, but Henry Teague said, "After the war, you've got to open the railway for me." My husband said to me, "It's up to you." Well, I

Ellen Teague stands at the Cog Railway with Miles Lacross in 1972.
(Photo courtesy of Anne T. Koop)

liked my own way too—I was twenty-nine, you know, when I married—
and I wanted to do my own thing. But I let him just make his decision. He
wanted to run the railway, because Henry had been good to him. So we
came back, and I got involved.

My husband was a wonderful, wonderful fellow. He was a good husband,
a good family man, and excellent in business, engineering—he could build
anything. Locomotives, houses, he was a natural. And medals. He won two
Presidential Citations; the Silver Star; the French Croix de Guerre; the sec-
ond-highest British award, with General Montgomery. He was easygoing; he
never wore any medals. He hated them. I divided them among my six kids.

The Cog Railway

The beginning of the railway was in 1866. It's the world's first cog railway.
Sylvester Marsh designed the first locomotive with the vertical boiler and
got a patent on the cog mechanism back in 1861.

Henry Teague owned the railroad for twenty years until he died in 1951.
He left the railway to Dartmouth College because he was a Dartmouth

graduate, but Dartmouth didn't want to own the Cog. It was a liability. So [Governor] Sherman Adams, Art, and I went down to Dartmouth College. Sherman Adams wanted that Cog Railway too! Sherman and I, later on, used to dicker a little bit, but we were like brother and sister, you know.

Nevertheless, Sherman backed out and John Meek, a friend of ours and the treasurer of Dartmouth College, said that if Art would put down so much he could have the railway. I forget what we put down, but we borrowed $10,000 from the bank. We didn't have any money; heaven sakes. But we said we'd pay so much a year, which we did. We bought the Cog in 1962, and I paid it off, I guess, in 1980. It took me a long time.

The Cog Railway would not have survived without political pull. Governor [Walter] Peterson and Governor Lane Dwinell supported the Cog, and I kept in with those I felt had more strength and ins, people with pull.

The hardest part of running the railway was trying to teach ethics, responsibility, and friendship. We were like a family. And if anyone didn't do right, we told them. It's a different age today, and they had a hard enough time in my day!

My work at the Cog Railway at that time was to keep things as best we could morally—for the dignity of the railway—which wasn't easy. Down at Fabyan's, we had that hotel there that was "red light." My husband and I went down and we had dinner with [Governor] Mel Thomson. I told him what was going on, and he said, "I'll fix that!" He closed the place that same night.

I also ran the Summit House [hotel] for a while. I had thirty-three employees up there. It was interesting, and I went up quite a bit then on the train. I didn't brake, because you don't want to get in there and be a roughy! But you ought to be able to use the train brake. My kids did it. The girls can throw the switches, and actually some of them are faster than some of the boys.

A Woman's Place
I did a lot of things at the railway: I worked in the office. I worked in the kitchen. I worked in the dining room, if I had to, getting buffets done. I met many of the politicians. I met all the buses and I would talk to the people. But as a woman, you didn't want to stand out.

I was used to men because all my first cousins were males, and we did a lot together. To me, it was easy. But a lot of people don't accept women.

They still don't. I think it was difficult for some of them, when my husband died and the board elected me president and treasurer. Jitney Lewis, my husband's assistant, said, "I wouldn't work for a woman." But that's past history. I think people have to grow up and accept women today. The women today need the money because the expense of living is terrible. And there's no reason why they shouldn't work, if they work together and understand each other; but dominate, no, I don't think women should dominate.

My husband was an example to me. I was proud of my boys and girls at the railway, I was proud of the workers and the way they worked: conscientiously.

My strongest memory is all these little steam engines and the building of the Colonel Teague locomotive number eight, and my men who worked in the engine shop. I used to go down there, watch them, and just see the construction. The upkeep of the locomotives took a heck of a lot of work! People don't realize that.

On a typical day, I'd awake at five. I had to get a bath before I'd start. I'd go up in the parking lot and talk to people, and I'd go up in the gift shop and see people at breakfast. I'd go in the kitchen. I always did the ticket office too. I made the rounds. Then I went up to the office and I'd make my rounds again, keep my eye open to the trains on time, the schedule. It was marvelous. Some mornings I'd go in the parking lot, and I would talk to the people coming in. I just wanted to know the people. We had a lot of people that returned. Because, if you give courtesy, you get business. It was a regulated railroad at first. We were only allowed to charge $8 for a ride.

We never took a vacation until the year before Arthur died, when we went to Spain, Paris, and northern Africa.

I was challenged by our life with the railway. My husband threw responsibility at me. I did the best of my ability for the railway, and whether I proved worthy was up to my public and my men and women.

Neighbors on the Mountain

White Mountain National Forest Supervisor Gerry Wheeler used to come by very frequently. He was a friend of mine, but mostly my husband's. We used to go over the boundary lines, and Gerry would sit and talk. We had a sign up there, and we would watch for fires. We went to the forestry meetings, and it was like one big family.

Arthur and Ellen Teague pose with New Hampshire Governor John W. King (on right), circa 1966. (Photo courtesy of Anne T. Koop)

But there have been radical changes since then. Changes to the atmosphere, the type of people. The world has changed. It's a radical age. It's a different world, and you have to adjust to it.

I loved Joe Dodge. He loved Mount Washington. He loved the forestry, and he loved these people.

Then there's Doug Philbrook.[46] It was always very competitive with Doug. But we've always been friendly and gotten along with the carriage road and worked with him.

I like the old summit building, and I'm sorry they ever tore it down. But Sherm Adams wanted to have something in his memory, and he got it.[47]

Selling the Railway

I was president of the railway after my husband died in 1967. I operated it for sixteen years before I retired. It was tragic, selling the Cog. I was seventy, and there comes a time. My children were all gone. A woman at seventy, continuing? No.

---

[46] See page 201 for Doug Philbrook's story.

[47] The Sherman Adams Summit Building atop Mount Washington serves as the headquarters of Mount Washington State Park. The building was opened in 1980.

I had been working every single day. I worked through November. Then I did the books and the writing and the hiring and all that stuff in the winter. That's enough. When you get to seventy, it's time for the young to take over. I love the young. This world belongs to the young. We've had our day.

North Country people bought the railway. That's extremely important to me.

A Final Word

I went through a lot of things. I don't know how I ever survived. I guess I'm just a strong woman. My father taught me to face reality, facts. I know when anything happened, we always had to do what we had to do, no matter what. I remember a lot of things we had to do we didn't want to do. I think you have to accept things; whether you say some people have sickness, a disease, it must be terrible, but you have to face it. You're born with a determination.

I also had a lot of wonderful people to help me; I had the strength of my background, my religion, and my friends—and I had a good lawyer, Jack Middleton.

I have enjoyed my work. There's nothing else like New Hampshire, the White Mountains—they're gorgeous. I think Mount Washington intrigues people, not only with its wind velocity and the type of climbing—just think of the people who have been on Mount Washington. That's extraordinary to me.

The Cog has a future, a definite future. There's the extraordinary history, the intrigue of the unique locomotive. The Cog Railway has all this history. It's rugged. The Cog stands out in New Hampshire. It's something that New Hampshire needs.

Ellen Teague will be remembered for her love of both mountains and people. A longtime family friend said of Ellen, "No words can totally describe her love of the mountains and the people that lived in them. She taught me at a young age to hold fast to your beliefs and always help others." In her later years, Ellen spent time with the local Weathervane Theater in Whitefield, established a scholarship trust for young equestrian horse riders at the Lancaster Fair Horse Show, and attended St. Paul's Episcopal Church in Lancaster. Ellen Teague died on July 13, 1999, at the age of eighty-six.

Karl Limmer

A Bootmaker Birthright

Francis Limmer's skilled hands work on a new pair of ski boots, circa the 1950s. (Photo courtesy of the Limmer family collection)

FOR SOME PEOPLE, Limmer boots and the White Mountains are inseparable. Many White Mountain hikers wouldn't think of wearing anything other than a sturdy pair of "Limmers," the famed handmade boots from Intervale, New Hampshire. There was a time when Limmer boots were part of an Appalachian Mountain Club (AMC) hut or trail crew unofficial "uniform," and a first summer paycheck would immediately go to buy a new pair of boots. The first snow rangers in Tuckerman Ravine and members of the Mount Washington volunteer ski patrol in the 1950s all wore Limmer boots. Today, they remain the boot of choice for hardworking trail crews, hut and shelter staff, and other backcountry workers, and because of their unique look, they are recognized immediately by hikers around the world.

The boots are still made by hand in Limmer and Sons Custom Shoemakers shop in Intervale, just north of North Conway. At the time of our interview, Karl worked alongside his cousin Peter Limmer. They represented the third generation of Limmer shoemakers, upholding the family tradition. The company remains a small family business. In an era of instant gratification and "cheaper, faster, and lighter," Limmers are a happy anachronism; a buyer must now wait three years for a pair of custom boots.

Hikers—sometimes joined by their four-footed hiking companions—come into the shop for the final tracing of their custom-made boots, to drop off their boots for repairs, to try on a pair of stock boots, to buy laces or boot grease, or just to share tales of the trail. The comforting smell of leather and boot grease permeates the shop. This is a scent so familiar to many White Mountain hikers that it might be the valley equivalent of the call of a white-throated sparrow or the roar of arctic winds through alpine tundra. The walls are covered with faded, stapled photos, showing Limmer boots and their owners in locales as far-ranging as Everest Base Camp, the AMC huts, Katahdin, and the Aiguilles of Chamonix.

It's hard to imagine any other outdoor gear for which people have such a strong emotional attachment. Men and women have worn them at their weddings; some people have been buried in them. There are probably those among us who would have chosen to be born in them, if that had been an option. After AMC hutman Ben Campbell died while hiking in Scotland, his Limmers were nailed to the crew room wall at AMC's Lakes of the Clouds Hut. One of Guy Waterman's last wishes was that his Limmer boots be placed in a cairn alongside his son's, deep in the White Mountains. (See page 53 for Guy's story.)

We interviewed Karl Limmer at Limmer and Sons shop during the summer of 2005.

In His Own Words

This is the family business. My partner and first cousin, Peter, and I are the third generation of our family in New Hampshire to do the craft of hand bootmaking. Our shop has been here since 1951.

Our grandfather, Peter, was one of twelve children. He emigrated from Germany in 1926. At seventeen, he had been drafted into World War I and sent by the German army to fight on the Russian front. He got captured, was in a prisoner of war camp that fifteen thousand guys went into and five thousand came out of. He always said that it wasn't brutality [that caused the deaths], it was starvation. At that time, the Russian people were starving and they couldn't justify feeding their prisoners better than their people.

He finally escaped from an island in the Black Sea and made his way back to Germany through Russia. It was quite a challenge. Everything had broken down, and there were armed factions that didn't necessarily have uniforms that you could see. He says they'd come upon you with their guns on you and they'd say, "Who are you and what's your side?" If you said the wrong thing, they just shot you. I guess he was able to say the right things all the way back home. He had been gone from home for six or seven years. Like a lot of guys that have seen hard times in war, though, he didn't talk about it.

Before he went into the service, my grandfather had mastered his craft as a shoemaker. You did that by middle school. The teachers and your parents decided if you were an academic or if you were a crafts-bound person. They decided for you. It was determined that he should be a shoemaker.

He started by sweeping the floor. He told us he even ended up straightening out the shoe tacks, because they were so frugal they used them over again. It took seven years of living with the shoemaker, under the guild system, for him to become [an official] "master shoemaker." I think it was 1921. We have his master's certificate here on the wall. It was during this time that he met my grandmother. They were married on March 9, 1919.

Peter Limmer, Jr., and Francis Limmer take a break in their shop, circa 1970. Paper boot patterns hang from the ceiling. (Photo courtesy of the Limmer family collection)

Along about the time of the Depression, Hitler's name started to come up in politics, and my grandfather saw the handwriting on the wall. He didn't want to be involved in another war. He was definitely not into what the Nazi Party was into. Most of the Bavarians weren't. You see, my family is from southern Germany, the mountainous region. They were laid-back, southern farmers. They were more interested in having a beer and just living life and enjoying their countryside.

So, my grandfather and grandmother landed in Boston in 1926, along with two-year-old Francis (my dad) and four-year-old Peter (my cousin Pete's dad). They had no family in Boston at the time; they didn't have any money and couldn't speak English. So they naturally gravitated toward Jamaica Plain, which was at that time a German enclave. It had the support system. The language was there, the food was there, and the community helped them out when they first got here. My grandfather did a lot of house painting until he started shoemaking, and my grandmother did a lot of house cleaning.

In the 1940s, World War II came along, and my father and my uncle were both drafted. My father went into the U.S. Army and subsequently into the Tenth Mountain Division. My uncle was in the U.S. Air Force. He stayed stateside during the war. My dad saw action in the Italian Alps at Riva Ridge. In a very short time, his unit sustained some of the highest rate of casualties of any outfit during the war. After the war, many of the guys from the Tenth Mountain Division settled in the Mount Washington valley to promote the infant ski industry.

My dad, Francis, met my mom in 1946 when he was in Boston. My mother was doing seamstress work. She learned to be a seamstress when she was in Germany, and she was there during the war. She saw a lot. It was something that she didn't talk about a lot, just like the soldiers. My mother and father were married in 1950.

After the war, Uncle Peter went back to visit Germany, where he met his future wife, Marianne. They were married in 1953, and Marianne came to America in 1954. Like my mother, Marianne was in Germany during the war and she saw a lot as well.

Moving to Intervale

During my grandparents' twenty-four years in Boston, my grandfather started his custom shoe and ski boot business. My grandfather and grandmother made traditional Bavarian-style side-tie shoes. In 1950, my grandfather moved his family up here. We actually have the ad for the land—Pete has it up in front of his workbench. I think it was in the *Boston Globe*, which advertised this place, with thirty-eight acres of land.

I think it was a unanimous decision. Both my dad and my uncle were avid skiers. They were outdoor, athletic types, and this area reminded my grandfather of Bavaria, where he was from. He was always a little homesick. One of the things I remember him saying when I was a little kid was, "There were times when we first moved over here that I sat at Revere Beach and looked out over across the ocean and said if I could swim all the way back I would."

When they moved up here, the business was pretty well established. But they weren't making hiking boots yet; they were making dress shoes and ski boots for the MIT and Harvard crowds.

Around 1950, while skiing in Tuckerman Ravine, my dad and uncle met Howard Head, who was working on a prototype metal ski. I think Pete might have one of the first metal skis ever sold, ones his father bought from Howard Head. They're Head skis that are serial number 325. Those are collector's items these days. Of course, everybody thought he was crazy to make skis out of metal. But we know how that worked out.

The Birth of the Limmer Hiking Boot

I think the family began making hiking boots right around 1951. I don't know if I could say they had the foresight to know what the outdoor recreation industry would turn into. But it was certainly fortuitous that they ended up here at the time they did, and that they were in this business.

The business involved ski boots throughout this whole time. They sustained the ski boot business until about 1965, about the time that the plastic ski boots came out. To be honest with you, I think it was somewhat of a relief, because skiers were kind of like complainers, you know? I think they wanted their equipment to be magical and to take the place of physical conditioning! I can remember my dad coming home on Sunday evenings and saying, "All they do is come in and say it hurts me here and it hurts me there."

It was about this time that our hiking boot reputation was starting to grow.

The Next Generation

I didn't really come into the business until about 1967. I graduated from high school in 1970, and for two or three years before that, I would take the Bartlett bus from Kennett High School [in Conway, New Hampshire] and get off at the end of Route 16A or right here on the street and just come in after school. It gave me pocket money.

I did have a choice, though. My mom and dad told me, "If you want to go to college, it's there for you. But if you want to be a shoemaker, that's there for you too." I'll tell you right now as a hand shoemaker you're never going to go hungry because there'll always be people who can't buy shoes [off the shelf] and you'll always have work. And that's true.

I felt a sense of tradition, a sense of security in the job. Even at that age, I realized it was going to be a good opportunity, that somehow or other I would end up owning a share of the business and have that job security for the long term. My cousin Pete is four years younger than I am, so I'm sure he felt the same way, but he was four years later coming in.

Pete grew up right next to the shop here. Earlier on, our family would celebrate all the holidays together. We were more like brothers than cousins.

My grandmother passed away in 1968, and my grandfather passed away in 1971. It was really hard on my father and my uncle. For years afterward, there would be customers coming in and asking for them, and each time it was kind of an emotional rub. When you work together like that for your whole life, it's a big loss.

By 1972, I was working pretty much full time. It was difficult to live at home and work with your father. If there was a problem at home, it carried over to work. I think it's natural for your parents to have higher expectations of their own kids than they would others'. So there was a little bit of roughness in the relationship there. But I worked as an employee until 1979, when I struck out for different scenery, a different life. I lived in Vermont from 1979 to 1985, doing shoemaking there. I realized, though, that it was going to be a lifetime struggle to just get established. I had in mind to have a family and own a home, and I didn't see that coming from the [Vermont work] anytime soon. But I befriended the lady who is now my wife, Marie, over in Vermont, and we moved back here in 1985.

The Business Grows

From about 1965 on, we got more and more popular. The word was getting out. There were a few articles. The *Boston Globe* had done an article, and would do more over the years. Each time they do one, the volume of business increases. Our reputation travels by word of mouth. It's slow, but extremely effective.

When 1974 came along, the *Wall Street Journal* did an article on our business. That's when it really exploded. At that time, our backlog was probably six or eight months. Within six months of that article, [the wait for a pair of boots] was three-and-a-half years.

We were the first outdoor shop in town. Starting around 1965, you could buy ice axes, crampons, climbing ropes, pitons, and carabiners here. In 1975 or so, my father and my uncle decided to get out of that business. They had that lengthy boot backlog, and the old saying is: "Shoemaker, stick to your last." The "last" is the mold that the boots are made over.

During that period, it was always just the family who worked in the business—my grandmother and grandfather, and my mother, aunt, uncle, and father, and then my cousin and me. Everybody had a specific job. My

From left, Trevor Limmer, his father, Peter, ace repairman Ken Smith, and Karl Limmer work diligently in the family shop in 2005. (Photo by Ned Therrien)

grandfather cut the leather for the uppers. My mom and my aunt shared the sewing and the secretarial work.

Back then, the business had low overhead. They didn't have help to pay or insurance benefits to offer. They just kept putting everything into the business. I can remember seeing my dad's paycheck in the early days, and it was something like $65 a week. That was for probably a fifty-hour week.

My dad and my uncle were...how should I say this? They gave good deals and then complained that they weren't making enough money. Our boots have always been a good value. I can remember more than one customer writing a check to pay for boots and saying they should be more expensive. Now when do people ever buy anything and tell the vendor that they would be willing to pay more? In the retail business, it's a little more justifiable to just add your margin and that's your selling price. Tradespeople, craftspeople tend to be more modest about their craft. They're good craftsmen and not necessarily good businessmen. I would put my father and my uncle into that category.

A Shoemaker's Hazards

In about 1995, I came down with contact dermatitis, due to exposure to the chemicals in the glue. It's a problem I still have. We used to use acetone to wash our hands off at the end of the day, and there were no such things as material safety data sheets. You didn't know what the risk was. My dad was sensitive to it too. His hands had dried, cracked skin on the palms when he was my age. So after twenty years of fooling around with that stuff, I became sensitive to it. Pete never got sensitive to it. He's the only bootmaker right now. One of our staff, Ken [Smith], who does repairs for us—we now consider him a master boot repairer—he has a problem with that stuff too, if he's not careful.

Limmers Today

Our boots evolved from White Mountain hiking. My grandfather always made good boots, but when he saw a weak point, he tried to fix it. For example, how many seams are there? How many inches of stitches are on the boots? Our present-day boots have only a third of the seams that are in the older boots. Fewer seams mean fewer inches of exposed stitches to abrade and fall apart, and better waterproofing.

The climate here is not very different from the climate in Bavaria. What is different is the type of hiking. The mountains in Europe are much newer. This is a theory of mine as to why, say, Italian boots have pointed toes. It's not because Italians have pointed feet. It's because of form following function. You hike in a lot of places, over passes and on trails that are just gravel paths. But when you go to a summit and you're using toeholds and handholds, then you're actually doing rock climbing. So, that's why you've got a pointier boot. Here, the majority of the distance that you travel is not on that severely abrading stone, but you can still take whole hikes where you're on rock all the way.

The real foundation of our business has always been what we call the core users, the professional outdoor people—the New Hampshire Fish and Game conservation officers, the AMC trail and hut crews. When people see our boots on those professionals' feet and their ankles are hurting them, they think, *Well, I should buy what the pros buy.*

For years, the state of New Hampshire has had Limmer boots—black and shined—as part of their official dress uniform. Their purchasing agent, it's been said, says, "If we fire them, they give back their gun and their boots."

Over time, people coming up from downcountry have seen a lot of change between Conway and North Conway. We're proud to be able to say we're one of the only places that you'd still recognize if you haven't been here for twenty years. Our reputation was originally developed and continues today by word of mouth. People believing other people who have the product and aren't being paid to say, "This is a good thing"—it's more effective than paid advertising, where you're trying to create an aura.

I've become very thankful as I get older—maybe because I'm also a little wiser—for what our parents and grandparents did and what we were more or less bequeathed as a blessing to carry on.

Today, my cousin Pete and I are the co-owners of two different companies. There's Peter Limmer and Sons Inc., the traditional company that's been around since 1950. And then there's Limmer Boot Incorporated, our wholesale side that has developed a line with the Meindl Company in Germany.

Around 1995, I had to stop making boots because of a reaction to the boot glue. I do the administrative work for Peter Limmer and Sons and whatever a job entails that day for Limmer Boot Inc., whether it be placing orders, taking orders, packing, shipping, receiving.

In the Peter Limmer and Sons hand shoemaking side, we have Ken Smith who works for us. He's my age, fifty-three, and has been with us for about eight years now. He's a self-described master cobbler and proud of it. He does an excellent job. Ken does pretty much all the repair work, as well as retail sales.

Then we have Trevor, Pete's son, who just started within the last month working on repairs. Once his skills are established with hand tools he can start on bootmaking. He seems to be doing quite well; he seems to have a knack for it. But at sixteen, he's just at the beginning. Trevor is basically doing the same thing that Pete and I did—working after school, before graduation—that's how I got my spending money. Hopefully he's going to be carrying on the tradition of the next generation, the fourth generation.

I have a stepdaughter and a stepson. My stepson worked here for one summer, and he went to college and is now a clinical social worker. We have four grandchildren ranging from almost seventeen to just over a year. My wife and I also have two foster boys that we're going to be adopting; they're four and a half and they probably won't end up in this business, but they may—if they're interested. Being a bootmaker is kind of like skiing or riding a bike. You don't ever forget how to do it. So even in fifteen years if I'm still around and they wanted to learn it, I could teach them.

A Visit from Merrell

In the early seventies, this guy came into the shop and said, "Hi, I'm Randy Merrell and I want to be a bootmaker. Can you hire me?" My dad and my uncle said, "Oh, we're not looking to grow the business," and they had in mind that my cousin Peter and I would be coming into it shortly anyway. But Randy hung out for a week or so. At home in Vernal, Utah, he had taken his father's garage and taught himself how to make cowboy boots. He was a very smart guy and obviously pretty motivated; he kind of hung out here in the shop. He went back out West and started making handmade hiking boots.

My dad and my uncle never really expressed any animosity for the fact that he came out with a boot that a lot of people said looked like ours. If you know how to make cowboy boots and you know how to make a pattern it's not that hard to make a hiking boot. I've always considered other shoemakers to be contemporaries, not competitors.

A bunch of years later, two fellows—one of them was a marketing guy right out of school and the other was a venture capitalist—approached my dad and my uncle with a proposition of developing a line of boots. My father and my uncle said, "No," once again. "We're just going to stick to making boots." They said, "You know, there's a guy out in Utah, his name's Randy Merrell. He might be interested." That's how Merrell Boots got born.

One time I got a call from a guy out West saying, "You're going to be really mad—there's a guy out here selling Merrell boots, saying they're the Limmer boots of the West." I wasn't mad. It shows we're the standard.

Building a Pair of Limmers

We make about 250 pair of custom boots a year. That comes out to be approximately a pair for every working day. We repair slightly more boots in a year. The wait for a custom pair is now about three years.

The leather for all of our boots, the uppers, are made for us in Germany by the same people that make our stock boots. They have a very high-quality leather. It's a top grain, which means it's the outer layer of the hide, it's the tightest grain, the toughest grain, the best quality, and they only use the butt and top of the back and shoulder. It's a very small piece, maybe a couple of meters by a meter on a very large animal. They use mountain cows that are out in the weather so the leather is tougher. In this country, we produce the same rawhides because of the beef industry, but I have a suspicion that perhaps the rawhides aren't as good quality because of the fact that the cows are treated with so many chemicals.

It takes about twenty-four hours to make a custom pair of our boots. I would say it's right around eight hours of actual labor. The rest of the time is dry or set-up time. We work on six or eight or ten pair at a time. If you do the same process to six pair, by the time you're done with the sixth pair, then the first pair is ready for the next step. But if you had to make one pair of boots, it would probably take twenty-four hours of elapsed time to get them made.

When a person places an order for custom boots, we take an initial tracing. This helps us order supplies. When we get to making the boots, we do a final tracing. The customer has to come to the shop for this. People come from all over the country for this. Some of them plan their vacations around it.

After the tracing, we choose a last, which is the mold that the boots are made on. It's a kind of a stylized foot representation. We've got probably one thousand pair. You choose a last that matches the length, the volume, and the width, or the taper from forefoot to heel, as well as any other attributes that make a person's foot unique. Then we add or remove material to make an exact match.

Every piece of leather is different. On a pair of boot uppers, we use leather from the same hide and, ideally, from the left and right side. Being a natural fiber, no two pieces stretch exactly alike. When you're cutting, one of the skills is not only having the upper pattern at the same attitude so that the stretch tendencies are going in the same direction, but you have to look out for flaws in the leather. It's kind of like wood that would have a knot—or the grain—that might or might not work in the piece that you're building with it.

Then it's the lasting process. "Last" is a noun (the foot model); "lasting" is the verb, the act of pulling the leather over the last. Leather is God's gift to man, being a perfect material for shoes because it has this very moldable nature to it, especially when you apply water. So, you pull it over the last wet and let it dry. You can take the nails out and pull the upper off of the last; it will still maintain that curve around the toe and around the heel.

The next trick is to make the left look like the right, a mirror image. The lacing fixtures have to line up across the pair as well as vertically from toe to heel.

Next, we choose a pair of our oak-tanned leather inner soles. We hand cut them to fit around the shape of the last. Then we choose an upper. One of the things that's really taken the strain off of us being able to produce 250 pairs a year is that the uppers come pre-sewn from the Meindl Company in Bavaria, the same leather as our standard production, or "stock" model.

So anyway, the boots have to dry overnight, and then we begin to attach the upper to the inner sole. The adhesive that we use for attaching the lining is contact rubber adhesive; you roughen the leather up, and it has to be dry for it to adhere. We glue the lining in, from the ball of the foot around the heel and to the ball of the foot through the arch. You have to be very careful. If you don't pull the leather tight to the last, the boot's going to be too large; if you pull the leather too hard, it will tear. This is the step where you really build up your hand and arm muscles. Pete and I both have pretty stout handshakes from doing that for many years.

Next, the heel counter gets inserted. It provides the arch support and keeps the heel aligned over the sole. Once the heel of the shoe is completely lasted, we repeat the process with the toe lining. Then comes the box toe, which is sort of like fiberglass. It's like a powder that is bonded to the cloth, soaked in solvent to make it soft and workable. This step is called the string lasting, which forms the reinforcement for the toe of the boot. It automatically pulls the pleats in. You know just how hard to pull it and in what direction, so the little wrinkles are out of it to the bottom of the inner sole. The whole goal here is to get all of the wrinkles below the welt line so that they don't show when the boot's completed.

In a factory these steps that I'm describing are done in a matter of minutes, sometimes even seconds, with a thermally activated adhesive. Some of the equipment actually has refrigeration built into it to cool the adhesive quickly and speed up the production process. Doing it by hand, you have to wait for the leather to dry. We use an acetone-based celluloid cement. It bonds two pieces of leather together and also dries stiff.

After another eight hours to dry, we trim the excess off with a knife, grind it on our finishing machine to further take out any inconsistencies, then draw the outer upper leather over. By this point, you have three plies of material in the heel and toe, to establish a support and protection system.

The last part is the actual lasting process, pulling the leather over the last. What happens next is everything's fixed to the inner sole, as I've already described, down to the level of the bottom of the inner sole, and then the tacks and nails that have been put in there while the glue is setting up are removed. The outer upper leather only is turned just a little more than ninety degrees back out so that it's in the same plane as the inner sole bottom. That forms the Norwegian welt of the boot. And then there are two mid-sole layers. We used to use an all-leather mid-sole. But there are a few things that have come out over the course of time that have actually been better mouse traps, and one of them is this leather fiberboard that we use now. We use a very high quality. It's a latex-impregnated leather fiberboard that's about an eighth of an inch thick. The fiberboard is attached with contact rubber adhesive and the first of two rows of stitches.

Then we embed a half-length steel shank in the first mid-sole and add the second mid-sole layer of composition rubber, another eighth of an inch thick. The layer of composition rubber material is attached with another row of stitches, contact adhesive, and a very thin strip of leather, about a quarter of an inch wide, to complete the welt. In the trade, we call this a storm welt. A storm welt provides protection for the first layer of stitches and it helps to keep the boot sized. After stitching, the extra material is trimmed off along this welt, first with a knife and then with sandpaper, for the finished edge.

The boot soles are paired at this point; then an appropriate size Vibram sole is chosen, held on with the contact rubber adhesive and our signature screws; then the heels are put on with adhesive and nails. That takes the night to dry. Then they're trimmed and the edges of the soles are completed by applying black wax melted onto the sole edge. This is called burnishing.

When we're lasting, all the tacks go through the inner sole into the last so that there's a bunch of little tiny tack holes after the tacks are removed on the bottom of the inner sole. We have a special tool that basically just closes up the holes after the tacks are removed. That's it. After the insides are finished, the boots get a shine and they're done.

I like to describe a well-fitting pair of boots as kind of—in effect—an extra set of muscles and tendons surrounding your muscles and tendons, a sheath of extra support for the heavy duty nature of walking over rocks and uneven ground and carrying extra weight.

Photos on the Walls

There's a picture on the wall in the shop of Base Camp in the Himalaya with Mount Everest in the background. That picture was the first that started the tradition of people sending us photos. I think probably that picture has been

Samples of Limmer boot models line the shelves in the store, 2005.
(Photo by Ned Therrien)

there since the early seventies. Now it's just kind of a tradition that customers will send in a picture. And it was just like, "Oh, look at that, this person was here with their boots," and, "Oh, you know, we're going to go to the Great Wall of China next summer and I'll take a picture for you." What's interesting is there's a fair degree of anonymity that's involved because there's hardly ever faces—just boots and views!

We've got one out there of somebody sitting in an outhouse and then, as far as unusual goes, there's one that was taken in Swanton, Vermont, at the second-to-last Grateful Dead concert that they had up there. The caption on the photo reads, "Jerry's gone, but our Limmers rock on!"

Based on the pictures, a lot of people have been married in Limmer boots, and I know some have been buried in them—well, I think you've got to have comfortable feet for eternity.

A Unique Craft

I don't know if I could really put my finger on it in words [why Limmer boots are so special to people], but I can perhaps draw a parallel. It's kind of like the same thing as when third-generation customers come into our shop to get boots from the third generation of our family, because the expectations for quality—and for the product—after these fifty years remain the same. I think it is partly because being a small family business makes it very personal and personable. One way or the other, whatever may come up in the way of product failure or fitting problem, we always try to have it come out in a fair and equitable way. (Although, our reputation sometimes does at the same time create unrealistic expectations like people who think that boots are guaranteed for life and that we resole them for free and that kind of thing.) But I suppose it's—and this is a hard thing for me to talk about because it's kind of like I feel too modest—I suppose it's become a tradition, a New Hampshire tradition, just over the course of time.

One of the things that I really like is when a person calls up and they get either Pete or I on the phone and they're absolutely amazed that they have somebody by the name of Limmer talking with them. I think that's a tremendous asset for us. Even if we got to be quite a bit bigger, I don't think there'd be a time when Pete or I wouldn't pick up the phone. It makes me feel good when people say, "You guys are really kind of mavericks in the world of business today."

It's a unique craft. I'd like to think, in a way, that our family is kind of an embodiment of the fact that a person can come here from another country as an immigrant with nothing and get ahead. America is still a place where if a person wants to work you can get ahead. And it's darn few places in the world that that opportunity exists to the degree it does here. I think that's something we should all be proud of.

I wouldn't dare to say what the business will be like in fifty years. I would hope that we would still be able to maintain the level of customer satisfaction and quality in the product that we have today. It would be amazing if it were still a family business—it would be over one hundred years. The Meindl family, in Germany, is eleven generations in the bootmaking tradition. Pete's son, Trevor, is the fourth generation of the Limmer family—so we're working on it!

Several years ago Karl Limmer and his cousin Peter Limmer decided to divide the Limmer boot businesses so that Peter is now the sole owner of Peter Limmer and Sons, maker of custom boots, and owner of the retail store walk-in location for the Limmer production footwear models. Karl is now the owner of Limmer Boot Inc., the retail mail order business. Ken remains the boot repairer. Trevor still works at the shop part-time in winters. He and his younger brother run a landscape business in New Hampshire. Hikers throughout the world continue to wear and love Limmer boots.

Doug Philbrook

The Auto Road's Tourism Advocate

Doug Philbrook, on right, poses with his invention: the log de-barker (circa the 1950s).
(Photo courtesy of Andrea Philbrook)

MOUNT WASHINGTON, highest peak in the Northeast, is known for its wild weather and its history as an attraction for hikers and tourists alike. Few figures loom quite as large in the mountain's recent history as that of Doug Philbrook.

A burly man with a northern Yankee's no-nonsense approach to conversation, Philbrook's eyes would light up when he talked about three things: the Mount Washington Auto Road, which he managed for more than twenty years; his collection of books, maps, photographs, and ephemera, spanning more than two hundred years of White Mountain history; and his wife, Andrea. Each of these was a passion, and each was related to the others.

The rest of Philbrook's story traced a variegated life that included a stint working in the logging camps of northern New England and Quebec during the transition from workhorses to power equipment—from never-ending pots of pea soup in dirty bunkhouses to chain saws and power de-barking machines.

Philbrook spoke to us at his home in Gorham, New Hampshire, in 1994. There, surrounded by White Mountain art, Philbrook lived with Andrea, just a few miles from the Glen House and the base of the Mount Washington Auto Road.

In His Own Words

My mother gave birth to me down in Boston, but my father's family came from New Hampshire. They owned the Philbrook Farm Inn in Shelburne. So I used to come up here holidays and every school vacation. That's how I got my start, you might say, in New Hampshire.

The Philbrook Farm Inn goes back to 1861. It's the oldest operating inn owned by the same family in the United States. In my den, I have the first dollar bill I ever earned. That was earned on the farm. I got paid by the day, fifty cents a day.

I worked up here some while I was in school, and when I had finished my schooling, I came back to the inn. It seems very far away from me now… I've done so damn much since then!

I would hunt and fish and hike when I was up here. I was an ardent woodsman, fly-fisherman, and hunter and trapper. I just plain enjoyed living in the woods, camping. The family [still] has a camp down in Shelburne. I lived there one year—all through the winter! At that age you're just crazy!

I remember we'd be so happy when Labor Day came because, back then, the day after Labor Day all the tourists left the hills. You had this feeling of something being left all to yourself again. I remember distinctly that sensation of having the country back.

I moved back and forth between the North Country and other places a couple times. Now, understand, this was back in the mid-1930s, when jobs were damn scarce. Nobody was working. At that time I heard that the state police were taking applications, so I managed to get on with them; that was my first full-time New Hampshire job. There were forty applicants and half of them were college graduates. It was a miracle that I wound up on the top of the heap!

I started out working south of here, but I just pushed to get transferred up north, and I worked for the state police for three years. You'll notice everything I ever did, I did for three years! Crazy! But the only reason I left the state police was because of the war.

Logging Research and the First Chain Saws

From the state police I went into the shipyards; from there I went into the Marine Corps for the remainder of the war. After the war I came home and worked for Herman Schanche and the Northeast Pulpwood Research Center, a research organization with an office right here in Gorham that was supported by Brown Company, Oxford, International, and Great Northern. Mechanized logging was coming into being, and they needed people to research, develop, and help implement all these new techniques.

At first I was just a field man, going out and studying logging operations and helping companies develop improved techniques in the woods. I did this all over the Northeast, from Pennsylvania up into Quebec. The big push was to mechanize the woods, because labor was suddenly in short supply after the war. The new equipment was primarily tractors, for skidding logs. The power saw was just starting to show up in the woods then too.

The companies were all modernizing their logging camps. There was all kinds of new stuff. Never had electricity in the camps until then. It was a transition time. Of course, I realized that because that's what I was there for—to help them change.

It was also the end of the real logging camp days. Life was still pretty damn crude in those camps, but I just saw the tail end of what was some real rustic stuff. For example, in the bunkhouses, everyone slept under one blanket. I mean, whole bunks! The blanket was a big old mill felt, and it may sound like a nice, comfortable blanket. But it was anything but that; those mill felts were heavy, itchy, and pretty damn smelly.

The bunkhouses were heated with buck stoves. They'd have a vessel of pea soup on the stove that they'd keep going all winter long. One of the things I always liked to describe was when they started up a camp in the fall. They'd cook up the pea soup in a big oval-shaped wash boiler—you see them in antique shops these days. Every time it'd get a little thin, they'd dump in another bag of split peas. If it would get too thick they'd dump in a bucket of water. We all loved pea soup! That was back when they made *real* pea soup.

Anyway, I used to report back to the companies that were part of the Northeast Pulpwood Research Center, and pretty soon I became the manager. We were trying to improve the transportation and methods of handling the wood. In those days, it was strictly old-fashioned—they were still using horses, the same way they had done for dozens and dozens of years, and they still had those crosscut saws for felling trees and bucksaws for cutting them up.

Of course, there were people in the logging camps who resisted the changes. Change is uncomfortable. But it wasn't only the men who were reluctant to change; it was their bosses as well. And sometimes they were right. When we brought the first chain saws into the woods, they were always breaking down. The saws would all give up, just quit. You'd go into some camps and there were a bunch of those big saws—we called them two-man saws—hundreds and hundreds of them hanging on the wall; their bosses had told the men just to put them away. They weren't like the little light one-man chain saws we know today. One guy on one end was the power plant, and the guy on the other end of the blade was five feet away. When the one-man saws first came into being, they were damn revolutionary.

I remember the day when I was told to stop wasting time playing around with these damn power saws! But we didn't quit—we just kept playing with them! Chain saws had to become more reliable before they could be used in the camps. This happened gradually. But once you could give them a good product, the workers were a lot more productive than when pushing a bucksaw. Of course, one thing we've forgotten today is how productive these guys were with a bucksaw. But they spent half their lives sharpening their saws!

Of course, pulpwood had to be peeled and we had to get rid of the bark. Because of that, nearly all the cutting was done in the springtime when bark is easier to remove. All the scientists involved were trying to improve on this phase of processing. My counterparts in the mills were developing new techniques, gradually learning how to pulp hardwood, as opposed to softwood. Back then there wasn't a market for hardwood pulp the way there is today.

It was during that time, in the 1950s, that I went to Sweden. The Swedes were trying to develop a mechanical method for de-barking the wood. I could write a whole book on that—the different methods for getting rid of the bark. This led to my joining an equipment manufacturer down in Nashua, Improved Paper Machinery Corporation, to develop a de-barking machine.

And this work with the pulpwood industry led to my going with the Oxford Paper Company in Rumford, Maine. I became their—they had a fancy name for it—methods development engineer. I was really a logging engineer, and I became the guy at Oxford who managed the introduction of the new equipment and techniques. In those days, there were two factions coming up: us younger guys, and the guys that were college-trained foresters. One of us was eventually going to work up into the management of the Woods Department, but there were a lot of politics. So I quit Oxford Paper Company, not knowing what I was going to do.

I worked for Mack Truck in Portland for a while. This couldn't have delighted me more; if I had to be in a city anywhere, Portland was my favorite. And so that's how I got into the trucking industry. I was a rep for Mack Truck. I think I was with them three years!

Return to the Whites
Then came the auto road. The centennial anniversary of the Mount Washington Auto Road was coming up in 1961, and the tourist industry group White Mountain Recreation Association decided that this anniversary was significant enough that they should use the road as a means for publicity, and see how it worked. The association came to me knowing I was associated with the road, because my first wife's family was the owner. Why the hell did they come after me? They had to get somebody as director of the centennial celebration.

It was the formative years of what later became the White Mountains Attractions Association, and I had already been active in this fledgling association. Somehow or other, the idea of being director appealed to me. I was willing to give up my job and move back up here to the North Country. It took me a year to get the centennial celebration going.

Another New Wave: Snowmobiles Come to the North Country

After the celebration, I left the auto road and went into the small-equipment business, selling and marketing snowmobiles. It was through Paul Doherty,[48] the Fish and Game warden, that I became interested. At that time, there was a lot of activity with snowmobiles in the North Country. There was a fellow down in Freeport who was looking for a new partner for his business, so I joined him.

But the public wasn't buying snowmobiles because of the expense, and the machines were always breaking down! As the distributor, I was on the road all the time back in those days—morning, noon, and night—to help get them repaired. But it didn't take long for people to start using them commercially, like Fish and Game, and then gradually they became popular for sport.

The Auto Road

I didn't come back to the auto road until '65, when the manager of the road, Charles Sullivan, died and the road ownership had to find somebody to replace him. They knew of my close association and my interest and so forth, but it came as a total surprise when they came to me and asked if I'd take over and help them out.

When I took over, I thought God had meant for me to do all the jobs that I had had in this lifetime so they would prepare me for this one, because everything I had done before turned out to be very important in managing the auto road. The work varied a lot from season to season. The road isn't operating in the wintertime, but managing an operation like that, there's a lot you can do year-round. So I was busy promoting the business during the winter, and in the summertime, I'd be working fifteen hours a day, seven

---

[48] See page 213 for Paul Doherty's story.

days a week, for six or seven months. I was always looking for ways to improve the management and operation of the auto road.

At the beginning of this period, I started up the Glen House again, so I had a hotel to operate in addition to the auto road! No wonder I was working fifteen hours a day! I didn't have a day off in years. There was a lot of crisis management, and details, details! Hundreds of details. It was no picnic. But I didn't mind all the work, and I tripled the road's business. When I first came here, we had four stages [vans that take visitors up the road] and now we have, I don't know, eleven. Things have changed since then too. There are twice as many tourists now as when I came here, and most people drive their own cars up the auto road. Only 15.5 percent take one of our stages.

But maintenance of the road was the biggest part of the job. It was horrendous. The road crew has shrunk over the years. We have much better equipment now, but in the early days it was very crude. We'd start as early in the spring as we could to try to control all the water we knew was about to come. The snowmelt plus the rainstorms meant that if you hadn't done everything to open up all the culverts and ditches to get that water running—well, you were in big trouble.

Every spring, the road literally had to be rebuilt! We used bank-run gravel back in those days. Just trying to get the best stone we could was quite a job. It was bony as hell, unfiltered, and every spring when we were rebuilding the road, I used to have to hire half a dozen extra guys for what we called the "stone force." They'd do nothing but spread the gravel out, forking the oversized stones off the road. The side of that mountain is built out of stones that we forked off the auto road! Eventually we added a rock crusher, eliminating the need for a stone force.

At that time, the culverts were made of stone. Some of them had been there since the auto road opened in 1861, and they were caving in, plugging up and giving us all kinds of troubles. So we gradually replaced those. I think we saved one good old stone culvert just for the sake of saving it so people could see what they were all like at one time.

And then there was the Halfway House [so named because it was halfway up the road]. The last time the Halfway House was occupied was when the navy took it over back in the '30s and '40s. They used it for developing and testing cold-weather equipment. The navy did a good job of trying to fix up the Halfway House, make it livable, but when they left, it fell into disuse.

We used to maintain the shed on the Halfway House as an emergency shelter. But the public didn't appreciate anything. People were breaking in all the time. I used to try to be kind enough to keep a supply of food and some firewood for the stove. But they'd run out of firewood and they'd use shingles off the side of the house. I think the stove was stolen finally. Then people built fires out there in the middle of the floor. We had to have a hell of a lot of maintenance work done on it. Plus, it wasn't safe anymore. We finally just reached the point where, in order to eliminate a hazard and a liability, I had the road crew burn it down in the wee hours of the morning. I hated to do it.

I've had excellent employees over the years. I didn't hire anybody who wouldn't stand out. I even ended up marrying one of them![49] The job of the stage driver was an interesting one. In a subtle and indirect way, I used to let them know that if they had some tall tales, well, I certainly wouldn't mind if they made them a little taller during their tour up the mountain. Part of my routine in breaking in a new stage driver was to make him ride with all the other drivers. That's how many of those tales got started, passed on, and improved upon from driver to driver.

A Passion for the Past

Back when I was living in Maine, I started to develop my interest in White Mountain history. I had several basic books which had been my father's, and I remember a time when I suddenly looked at them and thought, *Gee, that is interesting!* We had a copy of Kilbourne, and Crawford's.[50] I don't know what else. There wasn't much. Just the basics, but that got me to thinking, *What else is out there?* Pretty soon, I was a damn collector! I'm still collecting, but now the problem is nobody has anything left for me to find!

While I was collecting, I ran into some real odd characters. One woman had a big old safe in a storage room. She couldn't even tell me exactly what she had in the safe, but there were some old White Mountain maps. In the

---

[49] Doug's wife, Andrea, worked a variety of jobs, including chambermaid at the Glen House, waiting on tables, and working at the front desk.

[50] Frederick W. Kilbourn's *Chronicles of the White Mountains* (Houghton Mifflin Company, 1916) and Lucy Crawford's *History of the White Mountains: From the First Settlement of Upper Coos and Pequaket* (Hoyt, Fogg, and Donham, 1883).

The first Glen House hotel stood from 1852 to 1884.

course of my pursuing all kinds of items, I made it a point to stay in touch with her. After twenty-one years of calling on her twice a year—the safe by this time was outdoors—she couldn't open it now! I offered to furnish a safecracker and transport the damn safe anywhere she wanted it. Finally, she broke into it and there was a whole bunch of Leavitt maps of the White Mountains![51] That was an exciting day.

I've also completed the collection of Sweetser guides,[52] and I took a long time to get the last one. I discovered one day that there were different sizes to the books, and each book had different imprints. There was one that was primarily directed at Pinkham Notch, one primarily directed at Crawford Notch. It wasn't until after all these years, just three or four months ago, that I finally got the last of the fifteen books.

One day, I got a letter from an antique dealer in Michigan describing a Sweetser guide he had for sale. I immediately called this guy up on the telephone and asked him about the condition of it. It was a way of identifying my missing book. He said his copy had three little stars along the bottom, indicating that it was an edition directed at Pinkham Notch. That was my missing copy. Now, I've got them all! This is a collection that is absolutely coveted, and I believe I am the only one who has all fifteen.

[51] Leavitt maps were early representations and novel. They had caricatures of various mountain scenes on each map.
[52] These well-known early White Mountain tourist guidebooks by Moses Sweetser specialized in particular notches.

Doug Philbrook sits behind the wheel of the Mount Washington Auto Road's 1918 Pierce Arrow touring car in 1998. (Photo by Jonathan Kannair, jonathankannair.com)

Collecting is still fun for me. For example, there was the first guidebook that ever mentioned the White Mountains, and I had a copy. It was one of the things I lost in the Glen House fire, back in March of 1967. It was titled *The Northern Traveler,* and it dated back to the 1830s. It was in lovely condition, and I've never been able to find another copy of that.

I lost all kinds of things in the Glen House fire, including an early history of the auto road. Macomber was the guy who wrote it, and nobody's ever heard of another copy of that thing. And two unpublished Prang chromo-lithographs.[53] They were hanging in the lobby of the hotel. I also had a medal from the first race up the auto road, in 1904. Needless to say, that would be a damn scarce item. I used to put on display the unusual things I thought the public would enjoy seeing, the cream of the crop.

[53] Louis Prang was a famous lithographer, printer, and publisher.

But I'm still collecting. Mostly little things. I have a roomful of boxes, all full of stuff. All kinds of postcards. Magazines. Hotel brochures. I've got it all! The White Mountains are a unique area. Literature-wise, Bent's bibliography says there has been more written about the White Mountains than any other place in the world.[54] So, that is challenge enough right there—to find it all! And one thing leads to another, you know. I suppose it's like anything—like collecting matchboxes. Really, any collecting can be a challenge. It doesn't really make any sense. Even those old Burma Shave signs on the roadside are collectible!

Changes

So, I've seen a lot of changes. I am always amazed at the tourists coming in. The trains. The automobiles. And the decline of the big hotels and all their glitz. I'm old enough to have seen the tail end of that, and to have really gotten a feel for what it must have been like at its height. That lifestyle—people used to say it attracted all the rich people. Well, it wasn't just the rich people. I have stories about a gal who worked in Manchester. She saved all her money to come here and spend a week in the White Mountains. That was back when they earned twenty-five cents a day. The White Mountains have always attracted everybody, but I think culturally the caliber of the person they attracted was higher in those days. It is so much easier to get here now. And we advertise so damn much.

Of course I'd rather have the area all to myself. But you can't make a living that way!

When I look back on all I've done, you know what I'm most proud of? My wife. She is the best product the Mount Washington Auto Road ever turned out! And I'm also proud of having been caretaker of the auto road for so many years. It's a major part of the region. I've even been given a White Mountain Treasure Medal, and the auto road was also honored by a Newcomen Society award for its excellence as a business enterprise.

I also feel good about my contribution to the White Mountains Attractions Association. I'm honored to have received their Friend of the

---

[54] Allen H. Bent's noted bibliography of White Mountain literature, *A Bibliography of the White Mountains* (Houghton Mifflin Company, 1911).

White Mountains Award, in recognition of my contribution to recreation promotion. And, of course, I am proud of having picked up one of the major man-made tourist attractions in the White Mountains and improved it greatly from what it once was. That is my deep pride.

Doug Philbrook continued to stay interested in White Mountain history and the Mount Washington Auto Road, where he remained a director until his death on August 31, 2001, at the age of eighty-five. The Douglas A. Philbrook Red Barn Museum at the base of the auto road, home to a collection of historic vehicles that have traveled the auto road including an Abbot Downing mountain wagon, an 1899 Stanley Locomobile, and a 1918 Pierce Arrow touring car, was dedicated in his memory in May 2012.

Paul Doherty

The Woods Warden

Paul Doherty dons his uniform at the beginning of his career as a New Hampshire Fish and Game warden, circa 1947.
(Photo courtesy of Ginger Doherty)

TRAMPING THROUGH THE WILDERNESS of northern New Hampshire's Kilkenny mountains, Game Warden Paul Doherty once came across a deaf old man, deep in the woods. The stranger turned to Doherty and hollered, "What kinna man you?"

For Doherty, the answer was never in doubt. From an early age, he knew he wanted to spend his life outdoors. He started working in New Hampshire's North Country at the close of World War II, at a time when an entire way of life was fading away. A generation of old-time woodsmen who lived, worked, and died in the rugged backcountry was disappearing. Logging drives and trapping were giving way to cross-country skiers and snowmobiles.

Doherty knew he was watching something unique disappear, and he made every effort to get to know those woodsmen and to remember their tales and travails. Throughout his book, *Smoke from a Thousand Campfires,* and his North Country newspaper column "The Northwoodsman," which ran for more than forty years, he brought to life many of those characters and their times.

Though he introduced many new ideas to New Hampshire's Fish and Game Department, he also lived the life of the old-time game warden, spending four decades roaming the backcountry, rescuing hikers, nabbing poachers, and sharing his knowledge with generations of residents. From Gorham to Pittsburg, Doherty's exploits are legendary. The interview excerpted below was conducted in 1994 at his home in Gorham, New Hampshire.

In His Own Words

I was born in Wilton, New Hampshire, in the southern part of the state. I was the last of the litter, almost an afterthought, I guess. I'm one of these people that had a tremendous feeling for the outdoors as a kid. I never played baseball or basketball. I was in the woods, camping out all by myself when I was just a little shaver.

At the conclusion of the war, after spending two or three weeks hiking up here in the White Mountains by myself, I decided to apply for work with the U.S. Border Patrol, the Fish and Game Department, and the State Parks Division. Any one of the three jobs would keep me doing things outdoors. The Fish and Game job was the one I chose, and after about nine months of training on the job, I asked to be transferred to the northern part of the state. I got transferred in '47, and I've been up here ever since.

Blending the Old and the New

After the war, the Fish and Game Department doubled in size. I was the first new man to be transferred up here. Everybody else had been here for years. The nucleus of the Fish and Game officers in northern New Hampshire were old-timers. Christ, in those days they allowed you to work as long as you could walk.

I consider myself lucky that I came along at a time when there were a lot of the so-called old-timers still around, still doing their thing, whether they were lumberjacks, hunters, trappers, guides, or game wardens. I got a look at a past that was rapidly disappearing. I could see that World War II had started to change the country, change the way people lived. I knew that the way the old fellas were doing things was going by the boards. I was trying to blend the two together—to see if it was possible to carry some of the old ways along and incorporate them with the new.

I referred to myself like the old-timers referred to themselves—as a woods warden. I made up my mind I was gonna be that kind of guy, covering my territory on foot, patrolling and enforcing the game laws like they did in years past.

I also went into the schools. If I had an extra-large bobcat or anything interesting, I'd take it in. I had a standing agreement with the schoolteachers in all my towns that I could walk in anytime. They'd stop whatever they were doing. Well, some of the old-timers, they didn't like that. They called me a "goddamn schoolteacher." I was fighting that sort of thing all the time. But, not all of the old fellas looked at it that way. I guess they realized there were changes coming. They had seen some changes in their own lifetime. I could do a lot of the things they could do, and I had a reasonable knowledge of the outdoors; they realized that, but some of them sort of resented that I was breaking the mold in some ways. Yet I knew it had to be broken.

Many of the old wardens didn't like wearing the uniform. Curly Carroll never had it on unless he was gonna have his picture taken for the official photograph. He used to wear an old slouch hat. Skinny Norris, at the best, had a badge on his belt.

In northern New Hampshire, of course, many generations of people were outdoorsmen. They made their living working in the woods. Game laws were something they really didn't think were the greatest thing in the world. I remember at first I used to say to myself, "I must have two heads on today because everybody is looking at me." I was something new; they didn't know what to expect. They knew the old guys, and they knew what they could get away with, with them.

There was one warden who loved to drink. He'd patrol the Wild River. He had a place at the end of the trail where he would camp and wait for the fishermen to come out. Everybody had an over-limit of trout. Even though you could take twenty-five or thirty, they'd take fifty or sixty. This particular warden would sit at the end of the trail. They'd come out with a knapsack of fish, and he'd want to check 'em, and they'd say, "Well, would you have a little drink?" "Ah, I'd love one." Two or three of those, and it was, "OK, boys."

It was a job where you were responsible for a whole variety of things, not only law enforcement but public relations and landowner complaints. You had the latitude to do what you wanted. Having the interest I did and the territory I covered, there were some days when I'd simply decide, "Well, there's a brook valley that I haven't seen yet," and I'd spend the day on foot going from the headwaters. I spent time in lumber camps. I cultivated all the colorful old-timers around who could tell me what was over this or that ridge.

The present-day conservation officers are really tied down to the radio. At first we didn't have any two-way radio communication; but even after we got radios, I could sign off and say I was going to be in the woods for the next three days, and all they wanted to know was where I was.

Can't Catch a Deerjacker If You're in Bed

There was a lot of night hunting—a tremendous amount of jacking. I used to think I was back in the islands again [in the South Pacific during World War II] with the gunshots you could hear at night. I made a habit of getting to know all the farmers. I'd stop and talk with them on a regular basis. After a while they began to say, "You know, Saturday night you ought to be down in my back pasture. I hear shots." I got a lot of tips that way.

Sometimes I'd wake up at one o'clock in the morning and get my uniform on and go out. That was the way you caught somebody, because they never knew where you were or when you were gonna show up. I used to say, "You can't catch a deerjacker if you're in bed!"

One time, in the wee hours, I'd been chasing a deerjacker on foot in Shelburne. It was in the fall; it had rained and turned cold so the leaves on the ground had frozen. I got behind a big tree, figuring I'd catch him when he came out to his truck. I'd begun to hear footsteps, and in those frozen leaves you'd hear a few steps and then silence. I said, "What the hell is this?" He's smart now, he's taken a few steps and he's listening. A few more steps, then silence. He's coming right toward me. I thought, *Boy, I've got that son of a gun!* Of course, it's pitch dark. Finally, when the steps were right up close, I put the light on him. It was a great big bear. I didn't catch the deerjacker that night. But later I did.

Search and Rescue

For years, [AMC Huts Manager] Joe Dodge was *it* here in the White Mountains for search and rescue. Whenever Joe was looking for a crew, he'd always try and get in touch with me. When he was getting ready to retire—he swore worse than I do—he used to say, "That son of a bitch Doherty, everything he knows about search and rescue I taught him."

As far as the state was concerned, there were no guidelines. We had an incident in the early '50s: A plane went down on the northeast peak of Mount Success. They were flying into Berlin—five or six people in the plane. There was a lot of snow, extremely cold. Nobody knew where they were, but they knew the flight plan, and there was some reason to think they were somewhere in this area. I knew the plane was gonna be located on the ground somewhere and there was gonna be a need for a crew. So I had gone to the Brown [Paper] Company, and I'd gotten several of the woodsmen. A lot of rugged guys I knew could go anywhere that was necessary. We had a whole bunch of equipment ready. I was just figuring somebody had to organize, so I simply did it.

The weather broke, and Northeast Airlines sent four or five DC-3s. They wanted a pair of eyes for every window, and they began to fly the whole area between Laconia and Berlin. The plane that spotted the downed plane had a Brown Company woodsman on board. He knew exactly where it was, but everybody said we'd gotta be mistaken. There was this big discussion with people from Concord. Governor [Hugh] Gregg was there, and he said, "I think he knows what he's talking about."

Two people died and three survived. At the top of Mount Success the spruces are probably 15 to 18 feet tall. If they'd been another 10 to 12 feet.... You could see the airport. They were right on target for it.

Gregg went back to Concord and wrote an executive order that gave the Fish and Game Department the responsibility for search and rescue. It was later incorporated in a statute that spelled it out. I had a lot of criticism from some F&G people that I'd created something they were sorry about. I think my records show I was involved in some five hundred incidents over the years.

Snow Machines Arrive

I remember as a kid I used to follow the trappers around. Almost all of them would say basically the same thing: "When the hell is somebody gonna invent a machine to ride on?" I guess I'd long forgotten about that until I read in the paper the Polaris company out in Minnesota was making snow machines. I wrote to them in 1957, and it ended up that they came east with a trailer-load of machines. They left two or three in New York, two or three in New Hampshire, and some more in Maine. In those days, I envisioned a snowmobile as something pretty much limited to foresters, utility workers, trappers—people who had a reason to use a machine to go into the woods for work.

In 1960, through the contacts I had made, I was invited to go with Polaris up the Allagash in Maine. They wanted to test the machines in deep snow. One of the brothers that owned the company had taken two or three machines to Alaska and made a thousand-mile trip along the Yukon River. The Eskimos called it "the iron dog." That's where the term came from.[55]

After that, I crossed the Rockies with Polaris and made the first trip inside Yellowstone Park. By then, I had convinced Fish and Game that these machines could have some use, where there was a need to get around and cover a big area. The damn things began to appear on the scene, and they were suddenly appealing not just to hunters and trappers, but to all kinds of people. So I began to write articles about the dangers associated with them,

---

[55] Snow machines were called "the iron dog" when they were first on the market.

the possibility of going through thin ice, and the fact that you could go further in a day than you could walk back if a machine broke down.

Fish and Game officers, because we were out in the field all the time, were suddenly the ones getting the complaints from everybody about the snowmobiles running on the road, or too close to somebody's house, or on a golf course. I began to take a real interest in seeing if there wasn't a solution to some of the problems that were building up. Fish and Game finally gave me a free hand to do whatever I felt was necessary. I convinced the Fish and Game director that we had to have some rules and regulations. I wrote up a very simple bill for the legislature. I called it a license, not a registration. You'd only be required to have a license if you crossed a public way or went on public water. When I testified before the legislative committee, they laughed and said, "This is a fad; it's not going to last!"

On a trip with Polaris I got to know the president of the company very well. Around the campfire one night, I was telling him about my attempt at getting some regulations started. He said, "Would you send me what you've written?" Senator Fitzsimmons of Minnesota took my simple draft, rewrote it to fit Minnesota's needs, and they passed it. They became the first government entity in North America to start controls on snowmobiles. Two years later, one of the representatives who'd laughed in Concord sat right in my living room and said, "We gotta do something about this!" So the legislature began to make some regulations. Because of my interest and what I'd already done at that point, I was given the role of spokesman.

In the early days, the rules and regulations were very simple. You had a lot of people who loved [snow machines], and you had lot of people who hated them. The environmental people who had strong feelings about the outdoors were very vocal. There were some tremendous confrontations— some of them physical—between the snowmobiler and the cross-country skier and snowshoer. At one time we estimated there were some fifty thousand machines in use. There aren't as many today because they're more expensive. There are still people who hate them, but the tremendous problem areas are gone.

I felt strongly that there was a place in the outdoors for both pursuits, but you couldn't put them together. I agreed with the environmental people who said they wanted areas of solitude, and my role was trying to satisfy

Paul Doherty stands on a snowmobile, circa 1961.
(Photo courtesy of Ginger Doherty)

both, to give the snowmobiler a place to go where he wouldn't be in confrontation with the skier and the snowshoer.

One of the governors finally put together a study committee, and that was the beginning of real, in-depth changes. In 1973, the New Hampshire legislature created the Bureau of Off-Highway Vehicles. We were the first state in the U.S. to do that.

"A Hated SOB"

I had the opportunity then to head up that agency. It was a hard decision, because I had been a conservation officer for twenty-five years, and I thoroughly enjoyed what I was doing. But I also felt very strongly that there had to be some rhyme and reason to put into the snowmobile problem. It was a hell of a decision to make because I knew that some of my best friends thought I was crazy. They said, "You're gonna be a hated SOB." I did lose some friends in the AMC. The AMC was very outspoken. They wanted the snowmobiles out. There were moves at the congressional level to try to legislate the snowmobile out of existence. The AMC was very, very vocal.[56] It was an odd position.

Although the office was in Concord, for the five years I was with the Bureau of Off-Highway Vehicles, I was spending a lot of time outdoors. I walked miles with my little blazing ax, and laid out miles and miles of trails. I still was in the woods and I was still doing pretty much what I wanted to.

When George Hamilton,[57] who was State Parks director, resigned, I was offered the opportunity to become Parks manager. By then I had thirty years of state service. I wasn't getting younger, so I said, "Hell, I might as well give this a whirl."

The Parks job was different. There was more politics. I was more confined to the desk. I never really enjoyed being out of the North Country that much. But I ended up spending five years at Parks.

Changing Times

I'm seventy-five now, and I still run into people who'll say, "When I was growing up, my folks used to have a lot of bad things to say about the game warden, but I remember when you used to come into school and talk to us about the good things you should do in the woods or things you shouldn't be doing."

The same thing can apply to the snowmobiling thing. I remember when the AMC was very bitter about snow machines. There came a time when they were having a big meeting down at Plymouth College, and they invited me to come and present the snowmobilers' point of view. I said to myself, "The ice is broke."

Those are the kind of things that make you feel that maybe you were a success in what you were doing.

I grew up when you could go out in the woods, cut any goddamn tree you wanted, build a lean-to or a fire. We didn't think we were abusing the forest. Of course, even then you were conscious that you didn't make a mess of things.

---

[56] AMC's current policies promote responsible use and maintenance cooperation among all types of recreation while protecting existing trails and minimizing user conflicts and safety concerns. At its Maine Woods property, for example, AMC has worked with snowmobile clubs to create new trails and protect primary routes to ensure a high-quality outdoor experience for all forms of winter recreation.

[57] See page 81 for George Hamilton's story.

For a long time, I used to be very active with the AMC, especially teaching people about winter survival, showing them how to cut a big, thick spruce down and hollow the limbs out to make a cave. That's not the accepted thing anymore. I read about the new trend. They don't even want the Boy Scouts to build campfires anymore. I don't get up on a soapbox and say they're wrong, because I realize that there are more people using the mountain trails now. The kinds of things I did that were accepted are no longer accepted. I'm not arguing those points. I remember when you could climb Mount Washington on a busy day in July or August and you'd see a few people, but Holy Christ, when the weather's good now, they're tailgating one another. There have to be rules and regulations.

But I don't agree with some of the radical philosophies of some people who want to lock everything up and throw the key away. I don't agree with turning the whole northern part of the state into one great big national park.

"You Do the Best You Can"
I've been able to make a living doing the kinds of things I enjoy. I can hardly think of a day when I woke up and I wasn't happy to go to work. I've had problems, but everybody has problems. You do the best you can.

I've been retired now for eleven years. I have to chuckle when people say, "Well, what do you find to do?" Christ, there isn't time enough, and I'm doing anything that I want to. I'm hiking a lot. I'm going to places now that I haven't visited for five years. I'm on several boards and commissions in the state. I'll be going to the Northwest Territories in August for about three weeks.

I tried that trip once before. As a kid I was always fascinated with the North. One of the things I read about were the boats that were hauling supplies to the Eskimo villages on the Mackenzie River. Then, when I was hiking with Supreme Court Justice [William O.] Douglas,[58] he told about a trip he made down the Mackenzie with the Mounted Police on a patrol. That kind of sparked my old interest, so a few years ago I hired an outfitter up there, but the damn drive shaft of the boat blew up, and we drifted for three days. The Indians somehow passed the word to the Mounties and the Mounties came with a powerboat and towed us into Port Norman, where

---

[58] See page 89 for more about Justice Douglas's trip to the White Mountains.

Paul Doherty sits outside his Gorham, New Hampshire, home, with the Northern Presidentials in the background, 1994. (Photo by Jonathan Kannair, jonathankannair.com)

we hired a bush pilot to fly us out. I've made arrangements with a guy in Yellowknife who's got a bigger boat with two engines. I think we'll make the 1,200 miles this time.

The Art of Making Bean Hole Beans

Bean hole beans were traditional in the river-driving days, when they were moving the logs downstream. The cook put the beans in the ground at night and they'd be ready in the morning for breakfast.

A few years ago, I went up to the Woods Department at James River and was poking around. The log drives had long ended, and the barn was full of stuff. There was a cast-iron bean pot there. I asked the vice president in charge of the woods operation if I could buy it. I told him, "I want to use it to make bean hole beans before some woman gets it to plant flowers in." He called up the old guy in charge at the barn and said, "There's a fella comin' up. Will you give him that bean pot?"

It wasn't a week later, he called me and says, "One of my woods foremen just came into the office and said, 'That old bean pot up in the barn? I'd like it,'" and John Bark said to him, "What do you want it for?" He said, "My wife wants to plant flowers in it."

Here's how I make bean hole beans [for dinner]:

- To begin, I have a hole that's about three feet around and lined with rocks.
- I use Jacob's cattle beans and soak 'em overnight. I get up around 5 A.M. and build a rip-roaring fire (you've got to pick good, nice, dry wood, like rock maple or beech for good hot coals) and I keep adding wood 'til about 10 A.M.
- Meantime, I got the beans boiling in a big kettle on the stove in the house, or out here. You boil 'em until you blow on 'em and the skin's cracked. Put a lot of onions in there, add a great big chunk of salt pork, molasses, a lot of maple syrup, salt, and pepper.
- By then, I've let the fire burn down so there's nothing but hot ashes.
- I save the water that the beans soaked and boiled in. There's an inch or so of water across the top of the bean pot when you put the cover on. There'll be that same amount when you take them out eight hours later. The steam can't go anywhere.
- Drop the bean pot in the hole, and put all the hot ashes on top and on both sides. Cover it over with earth and leave it for eight hours.
- Take a long-handled shovel and dig all those hot ashes—and it is hot! You have to wear gloves. Dig all the ashes out and lift up the bean pot.

Out comes a hell of a pot.

Paul Doherty continued to sleep out under the stars for much of the rest of his life, often at one of his favorite spots: atop a steep drop-off with a view of the Moose River valley. He had a sharp mind to the end. Paul Doherty died on June 18, 2000, at the age of eighty.

AFTERWORD

CREATING THE "MOUNTAIN VOICES" SERIES has proven to be a remarkable experience. Though several people we'd heard of when we first came to work in the White Mountains had passed away before this project got under way—and two turned us down for personal reasons—we wondrously were able still to capture the voices of people whose collective contributions spanned a half-century or more.

As we concluded our work on this book, we both found ourselves wondering if a collection like this will come again and if so, when. It's a question worth reflecting upon, because the answer says a lot about our direction as a society.

Any future collection will, we think, be quite different from this one. While all of our interviewees have dedicated a significant portion of their lives to the White Mountains, in the twenty-first century we move around a lot more. One of the gifts our subjects gave to all of us was a commitment and dedication to place. Today, we are far less prone to settle in one area and make an impact to the region that spans a lifetime. We're not likely to find another U.S. Forest Service snow ranger like Brad Ray who works in Tuckerman Ravine for over forty years.

We feel both honored and fortunate to have been able to capture the stories of this last generation who "stayed put." Their commitment to place has been both deep and long. To document it, in this small way, has been a tremendously rewarding experience.

Of course, people are not done making enduring contributions to the White Mountains. The context for these contributions will change—and the nature of the contributions may differ—but there will still be those who have stories to share about their time in the mountains. A long time may pass before their legacy is known, but we hope that the day does come when someone feels as compelled to document their stories as we have, and carries on the spirit of *Mountain Voices.*

ABOUT THE AUTHORS

Born and raised in New York City, **REBECCA ORESKES** first came to the White Mountains to work in the AMC hut system. After six years working seasonally in the huts, she joined the White Mountain National Forest, where she held several different positions over twenty-five years, from wilderness ranger to member of the forest leadership team. A founding board member of the Waterman Fund, Rebecca currently serves on the editorial board for the *International Journal of Wilderness.* She lives with her husband, Brad Ray, in Milan, New Hampshire, where, when not exploring in the woods, they grow vegetables on Whiskey Jack Farm.

DOUG MAYER grew up in Sandwich, New Hampshire, where he enjoyed hiking, swimming, and breaking cross-country skis with his brothers and various family dogs. A summer internship with the Mount Washington Observatory led to caretaking for the Randolph Mountain Club (RMC). He has served as trails chair for RMC, was a founding member of the Waterman Fund, and is a longtime member of Androscoggin Valley Search and Rescue. He is a producer for the National Public Radio show, "Car Talk." He lives in Randolph, New Hampshire.

APPALACHIAN MOUNTAIN CLUB

Founded in 1876, AMC is the nation's oldest outdoor recreation and conservation organization. AMC promotes the protection, enjoyment, and understanding of the mountains, forests, waters, and trails of the Northeast outdoors.

People

We are more than 100,000 members, advocates, and supporters, including 12 local chapters, more than 16,000 volunteers, and over 450 full-time and seasonal staff. Our chapters reach from Maine to Washington, D.C.

Outdoor Adventure and Fun

We offer more than 8,000 trips each year, from local chapter activities to adventure travel worldwide, for every ability level and outdoor interest—from hiking and climbing to paddling, snowshoeing, and skiing.

Great Places to Stay

We host more than 150,000 guests each year at our AMC lodges, huts, camps, shelters, and campgrounds. Each AMC destination is a model for environmental education and stewardship.

Opportunities for Learning

We teach people skills to safely enjoy the outdoors and to care for the natural world around us through programs for children, teens, and adults, as well as outdoor leadership training.

Caring for Trails

We maintain more than 1,500 miles of trails throughout the Northeast, including nearly 350 miles of the Appalachian Trail in five states.

Protecting Wild Places

We advocate for land and riverway conservation, monitor air quality, research climate change, and work to protect alpine and forest ecosystems throughout the Northern Forest and Mid-Atlantic Highlands regions.

Engaging the Public

We seek to educate and inform our own members and an additional 2 million people annually through the media, AMC Books, our website, our White Mountain visitor centers, and AMC destinations.

Join Us!

Members meet other like-minded people and support our mission while enjoying great AMC programs, our award-winning *AMC Outdoors* magazine, and special discounts. Visit outdoors.org or call 800-372-1758 for more information.

Appalachian Mountain Club

Recreation • Education • Conservation

outdoors.org

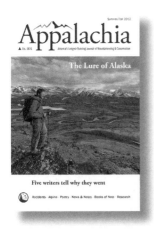
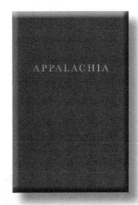

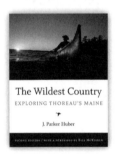